❧ TRESPASS ❧

⊰ TRESPASS ⊱

LIVING AT THE EDGE OF

THE PROMISED LAND

Amy Irvine

NORTH POINT PRESS
A division of Farrar, Straus and Giroux
New York

NORTH POINT PRESS
A division of Farrar, Straus and Giroux
18 West 18th Street, New York 10011

Printed in the United States of America
First edition, 2008

Library of Congress Cataloging-in-Publication Data
Irvine, Amy.
    Trespass : living at the edge of the promised land / by Amy Irvine.—
1st ed.
        p.   cm.
    Includes bibliographical references.
    ISBN: 978-0-86547-745-2
    ISBN: 0-86547-745-0
    1. San Juan County (Utah)—Description and travel.   2. Landscape—
Utah—San Juan County.   3. Deserts—Utah—San Juan County.
4. Wilderness areas—Utah—San Juan County.   5. Utah—Description and
travel.   6. Four Corners Region—Description and travel.   7. Irvine,
Amy—Travel—Four Corners Region.   8. Irvine, Amy—Philosophy.
9. Nature—Religious aspects.   10. Mormons—Utah—Biography.   I. Title.

F832.S4 I78 2008
979.2'590330922—dc22

                                                            2007025585

Designed by Cassandra J. Pappas

www.fsgbooks.com

For Ginger. My landmark.

And for John. Both cowboy and coyote.

Beware, traveler. You are approaching the land of horned gods . . .

—EDWARD ABBEY, *Desert Solitaire*

CONTENTS

AUTHOR'S NOTE

To respect the privacy and well-being of certain people and places, some names and other identifying characteristics have been changed or otherwise obscured. Also, throughout the text I have chosen to use two traditional terms: "Indian" and "Anasazi." Current etiquette has replaced the first term with "Native American," and the latter with "Ancestral Puebloans." I mean no offense here; I am only attempting to capture a mainstream, historical understanding of these cultures.

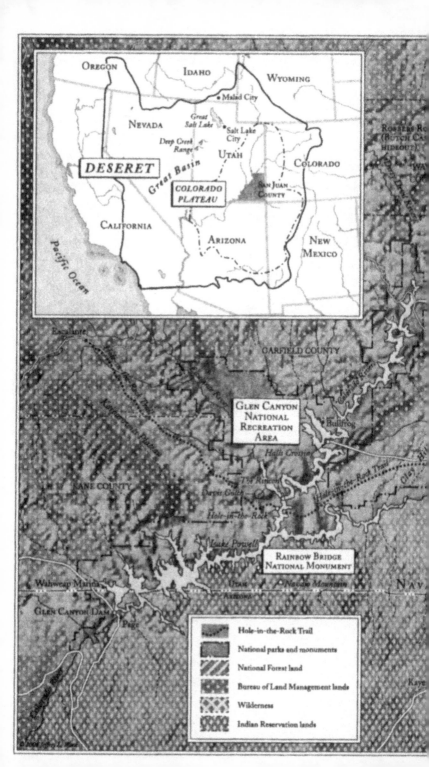

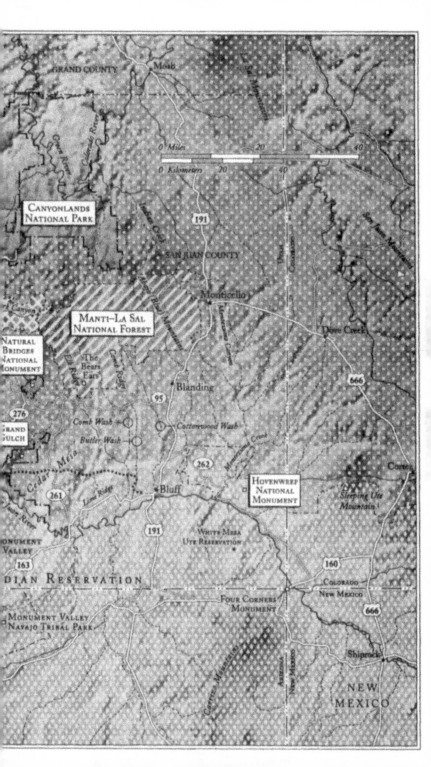

❧ TRESPASS ☙

Ruin

M Y HOME IS a red desert that trembles with spirits and bones.

There are two reasons I came here: my father's death, and the lion man who prowled my dreams. Perhaps it was coincidence, but a man—half wild, ravenous beyond words—slid from the dream world into the mud of the waking one the same year my father left this world for another.

Ghosts. Paw prints. I have tried to stay put.

The lion man is Herb. His name, his grandfather's. It doesn't quite suit him, but then, nothing about the civilized world does. Even my mother, who prefers all things tame, cannot accept it. Instead, she calls him Red for his long copper curls, for the heart pulsing on his sleeve. His eyes are a piercing topaz. And he purrs of dimensions other than this one—says he sees and hears things differently and that's why he makes up his own rules. Me, I am at a loss for words. After contending daily with the lion man's incorrigible ways, I still don't know what to call him.

If Herb is red, then my father was blue. Perpetually immersed in

water and nostalgia, to the point of inertia, he passed the days hunting—mostly in cattails on the edge of the Great Salt Lake, just outside Salt Lake City. There he sat motionless, as if he could halt time.
It was his attempt to deny the seductive sirens of civility—their incessant beckonings to behave, to belong. He acted as if all that mattered was the water, and the sound of wings flapping overhead. He
was a good shot.

But he lost his fluidity. The lake swelled, then retreated. Constrained by convention, dulled by bourbon, his primal reflexes failed.
When the banks of soft marsh mud imploded beneath his feet, he
simply could not respond. Finally, on the first night of the new millennium, as the rest of the world toasted a new era, my father put a
bullet through his own heart.

THE REDROCK DESERT where I made my home sits on a tall,
arid land mass called the Colorado Plateau. This physiographic
province sprawls across northern New Mexico and Arizona, western
Colorado, and nearly all of the southern half of Utah—my home
state. Perhaps the most isolated portion of the Plateau falls within
the boundaries of San Juan County, in Utah's southeastern corner.
After my thirty-four years in Salt Lake City—the state's urban capital, at the base of the Wasatch Mountains, in the northern region of
the state—this remote and rural portion of the desert was a welcome
change.

San Juan County is the size of three small New England states.
And of its 7,884 square miles, only 8 percent of the land is owned
privately. The rest is either Indian or federal land—managed by the
Bureau of Land Management, the National Park Service, and the
Forest Service. Included within these federal jurisdictions are
Canyonlands National Park, Glen Canyon National Recreation
Area, and Hovenweep and Natural Bridges National Monuments.
Also included are two million acres of BLM lands with hardly any

special designations—loosely managed for "multiple use," which means they can be utilized for grazing, mining, logging, and nearly any form of recreation.

So scenic are these lands that if any of them—any at all—could be acquired, they would be considered prime real estate. But San Juan County, by and large, is not for sale. The result: Less than two people per square mile. Not one shopping mall or gated community. Only two stoplights and a single liquor store.

But there are eleven Mormon churches—three of them built right on Indian lands.

IN THE LATE AUTUMN of our first year in San Juan County, Herb and I hiked into a deep canyon on Cedar Mesa—the connective tissue between the Abajo Mountains and the San Juan River. It was a cold and gray afternoon; the cottonwood trees in the canyon bottom had lost their gold medallions and stood wretched. The birds were gone. Everything was stripped, utterly silent. We tiptoed across stones made sleek and spherical by flash floods. Herb stopped and looked up at an ancient Indian ruin, high on the ledge above us. Perhaps a thousand years old, its earthen walls still stood. The two windows were dark and hollow, like the eyes of an unlit jack-o'-lantern.

The lion man turned to me, his eyes dilated in the fading light. He said, *I don't think I've ever felt so alone.*

I disagreed. The ghosts were everywhere, watching. And even their company would prove to be too much.

SOON AFTERWARD, Herb and I bought a cabin on ten acres. There were no phone lines, no power lines, no pipes to deliver water or gas. With no service to collect what we discarded, we were careful about what we used in the first place. And with scarcely an aquifer of groundwater in the bedrock beneath shallow soils, there was little point in drilling a well. Instead, we hauled water from town in an old pickup and stored it in a cistern.

In winter, the snow would come suddenly and pick dogfights with the sky. The wind would scream like a woman assaulted. On winter mornings, Herb and I wrestled beneath the covers, to see who must leave our bed to light the stove and scrape ice from the so-lar panels that stood in the yard like a broken-off piece of spaceship. Summers were just as trying. Mornings would heat up like a struck match, and by noon the sky was bruised with thunderheads. When we moved in, I had laughed at the three lightning rods on the tar-paper roof—now I know they weren't the least bit excessive. The rain comes and goes so fast, often it does no good. In this redrock desert, only one thing is constant: Evaporation duels saturation—a lesson on how easily matter can vaporize.

The cabin sat on the rim of a canyon, halfway between the towns of Blanding and Monticello. From the kitchen table was a stunning view—thousands of acres of scarcely interrupted public land and In-dian land, yawning south for over one hundred miles. In the middle of the view lies the Four Corners, where the Colorado Plateau states converge with rectilinear perfection. This ninety-degree meeting of state lines is arbitrary, and invisible to the eye. But each day, as the light shifted across the sky, I detected new canyons, new mesas. The bones of the earth illuminated.

IT WAS MY FATHER'S MOTHER, Ada, who first brought me to this desert, who taught me what to look for. I was six years old when I first sat in red sand, leaning over her shoulder to watch as she painted land and sky. She loved the capricious geography—how it rose and fell like the spikes and troughs on an erratic cardiogram. She pointed out the sagebrush plain that suddenly plunged one thousand feet into a canyon of bare pink stone, glistening with seeps and springs; the roiling river beneath a ragged, bloody spine of a steeply rising anticline; the expletive of a sandstone minaret, erupting from the desert floor like a bold stroke of red ink.

An artist of abstractions, Ada sometimes made the rock look like water. She taught me all that she learned from this place—to look past the obvious, to see what might emerge at the edges.

There is only wind, water, and stone, Amy. Because of them, the desert is constantly undone.

She understood erosion. How the fierce winds—Arctic air in winter, gulf streams in summer—could scour away the soil until there was only bedrock. How the Dirty Devil, the Colorado, and the San Juan rivers—opaque ribbons of chocolate and jade—could gnaw at the sandy banks, granule by granule, until there was nothing left to stand on. How even the smallest seismic shift beneath the earth's crust could calve pinnacles from canyon walls, or unearth the remnants of ancient peoples.

Early on, I remember sitting on a sandy beach at Lake Powell, in Glen Canyon Recreation Area. On a pad of paper, my grandmother sketched the cliffs that rose from the depths of the water. They were the color of raw salmon flesh. Sunlight leaped from the water and bedazzled the walls. Suddenly she dropped her pastel crayon, held her hands up against the sun. The rays burned through the pale webs of skin between her fingers.

And color. It shifts. Light changes everything.

She marveled at how, in one hour, a single rock formation could run the gauntlet of reds, oranges, even purples. Each shade was so exquisite, she said, that it defied description—or any other kind of human attempt at acquisition. This may have frustrated another observer, but in my grandmother's mind, that intangible, luminous fluidity was the key to liberation. An atheist, an aesthete, she never tried to reinvent. Instead, she unleashed her self on the canvas. In doing so, she managed to interpret the desert's sensuality, particle by particle. Back in Salt Lake, she presented her work in galleries. From desert to city. She glided effortlessly between two contradictory worlds, translating the liquid language of landscape—a place others have called barren and harsh.

MOVING TO southern Utah, I imagined myself as Ada. A visionary who could see, interpret, the desert's nuances. A woman free to go anywhere the senses led. A woman who could sustain herself on beauty alone.

The desert's people seemed only a minor obstacle. Mostly cowboy, mostly Mormon, they have their own way of seeing things. But I am used to this: My mother's side of the family possesses the same peculiar brand of faith—a rawhide religion unlike anything you see in places more verdant, more populated. On public lands, in the high desert of southern Idaho—in a place not at all unlike San Juan County—they too run cattle and submit themselves not so much to the government as to God. I have spent my life among them, loving them. It made me believe my desert fluency to be greater than Ada's. It made me believe that I could actually move to the heart of redrock country; that I could inhabit, even claim, its wild interior as only a native could. There, I would grind down preconceptions, abandon past notions, and finally see things reassemble themselves.

It was my only option. Places more crowded, more civilized, had become uninhabitable. To stay would have had me, eventually, duplicating my father's fate.

Ada tried to warn me. She knew how hard it was for me to stand my ground, to hold my own. She knew I was my father's daughter.

There are contradictions, you know. Stone becomes dust, then stone again. And the dead stand between the grains of sand.

PEOPLE LIVED HERE before the Anglos—long before even the Utes and Navajo. There were four eras of prehistoric culture: The first period of known human habitation, the Lithic, took place about ten thousand years ago, during the Pleistocene; the great game-hunters are understood only through a vague scattering of ancient campsites and spearheads. The second period, the Archaic, evolved as the region warmed, and was characterized by a highly mobile lifestyle of foraging. Then came the advent of agriculture and two phases of people that are collectively called the Anasazi: First, the Basketmaker period, named for the woven containers in which domesticated seeds were kept until sown—when the harvest's bounty could fill them again with edibles. The fourth period, the Pueblo, ended in mystery; it was marked by an increasingly religious and sedentary lifestyle that seemed like progress but was probably doomed from the beginning.

In San Juan County, the mark of the ancients is everywhere. High on the canyon walls. Strewn across mesa tops. Buried along the banks of rivers. So numerous are their relics and ruins that sometimes they are taken, literally, for granted. Of course, there are federal regulations to protect these cultural artifacts, to honor the lands on which the dead reside. But in San Juan County, people hang federal officials and environmentalists in effigy. They have enough rules to follow in building up the desert in anticipation of Christ's return to earth.

Sure, there are attempts at tribute. There is a museum in Blanding, and tour guides take tourists to some of the more spectacular ruins. When sites are vandalized, it makes the front page of the *San Juan Record*. But when the relics are removed, or even disturbed, they seem to lose their context, to be excised of their meaning. The loss of the past dislocates the present, makes it stagger and fall from what was once a stirring and sensual synchronicity between people and place.

I don't mean to romanticize, to promote the loincloth and life in a cave. But there is something in those primitive ways that deserves close examination—a way to measure the life that has evolved in its wake. To exhume those ways is to gain a glimpse at the architecture of our own rise, at the potential for our demise. To shed light on their remains, on their ancient animal affair with nature, is to disinter what is buried in ourselves.

The desert holds the past with the reverence of a pallbearer. I want to witness the procession.

I BEGAN to dig for what I needed to know. I thought that the people were something to work around—that my quarry could take place outside their peripheral vision. But the opposing forces were greater than anticipated, for they are fueled by something far more fundamental than a love of profit, or an ethic of progress—a belief so deeply inherent one could almost mistake it as primal.

My presence, my rooting around, would inspire resistance and uneasiness. Not that I blame anyone—even the most superficial existence in this country ravages the soul. There are deprivations. Depredations. And one is ultimately driven to commit passionate, irrevocable acts.

At some point, all desert dwellers are asked to submit. And eventually, the land sinks you to your knees. Then you have two choices: Pray, or crawl.

The desert's people most often opt for prayer. I was quite certain I would choose the contrary.

Salvation would come, I would learn, by a wearing away of the body, by a grinding of bones into slickrock until they mingled with sand and the howling dead. It would be how I found my way back to myself—to something more basic, more original, than all that has been prescribed to me. Only then would I understand my response to the lion man—the way the cinnamon hair on his wrists makes me tremble. Only then would I understand my father—how losing his ability to quiver with anticipation when the geese flew in slid him into the bottomless backwaters of grief.

It wasn't graceful. It was a messy business to walk on such disturbed ground. Still, an excavation was required. Even the deepest layers enlightened. Old relics brought new meaning.

Light changes everything.

There are questions that linger: Have I further intruded upon this desert by claiming it as my home? Has my father's memory, or the honor of my marriage, my family, my neighbors, been desecrated in the telling of these tales?

This unearthing of things, it threatens. The dead may be aroused. But how else does one dig without disruption? Without disturbing what is sacred?

From ruin to restoration. Already I beg forgiveness for the encroachments.

One must get to the bones of things.

PART I

⚜ LITHIC ⚜

⊰ 1 ⊱

Migration

FOUR MONTHS AFTER my father's death, I attach my pickup to the back of a U-Haul truck and drive it to the high desert hamlet of Monticello. A month earlier, I had rented a small blue house at the south end of town. It is twilight on a day in late April when I pull into the driveway with my belongings; before me the house stands crooked, paint peeled, its backyard bleeding into a row of trailers and portable satellite dishes at the Westerner RV Park just beyond. Five fence posts, connected by two parallel strands of sagging barbed wire, divide the two places. On my side of the fence there are ovals of matted grass—the imprints of deer that strayed into town and stayed for the night. Beyond the impressed lawn and shabby fence, the rough-edged silhouettes of men lean against the trailers and picnic tables. Others congregate around a barbecue. You can tell from their unkempt hair and beards, their stained and ragged clothing, and the beer in their hands that they are not Utah men. Soon it will be confirmed that they are indeed imports; they have been hired to clean up the town's Superfund site, a small mountain of uranium tailings still hot and blowing in the wind after the last mining boom. The next morning, and every morning for the rest of the summer, I will see these men wandering the sides of the highway, cloaked in white suits and masks. But for now, the air hisses as they pop the tops of their cans, as their dinner drips onto the coals. The aromas of charcoal and steak drift into my yard. Out on the highway that bisects town, two semis roll past, brakes grumbling as they head down the hill that links this small, forested plateau with the redrock country below.

Herb lives fifty-four miles away, in a tourist town called Moab, in Grand County. But he is with me now, helping me unload my life. I dare not point out the space I am making for his things—in the bedroom closet, in the bathroom cabinet. I only hope he will visit often—it's all I can hope for—given the complicated overlap between his former life and this new one with me. Little do I know how quickly he will relocate across the county line. Nor can I imagine that in just one year we will own a cabin overlooking a canyon, just a stone's throw from the Four Corners.

No one believes I will stay.

We give you six months down there. They'll cut your brake lines. Poison your dog. Burn your house down. Watch what you say, and, for God's sake, don't tell them who you work for.

BESIDES THE UTE and Navajo Reservations, San Juan County possesses three communities of note. The southernmost town is Bluff—on the north side of the San Juan River, across from the Navajo Reservation. Blanding lies twenty miles south of Monticello, the gateway to Cedar Mesa. Monticello is the northernmost town of significance—and cooler, more green than the others. The town sits at seven thousand feet above sea level, on a pedestal of land perched atop the larger Colorado Plateau—which also serves as base for the Abajo Mountains, an island range that presides over the lower canyon country.

I choose Monticello not only because it is the town closest to the man with whom I have fallen in love, but also because it reminds me of Malad, where my mother is from, where much of her side of the family still lives. Monticello and Malad are both cow towns, full of Mormon ranchers. They are places where you still hear the jingle of spurs, where racks of guns fill the rear window of nearly every pickup truck. Many of the homes, both inside and outside of town limits, are nothing more than trailers. Each yard, it seems, contains at least one old abandoned car or piece of machinery. But parked in juxtaposition is almost always a shiny new ORV, and of course, a good V8 pickup. Often, the truck has a window sticker displaying the cartoon character Calvin, pants down. He is urinating on the acronym of the Southern Utah Wilderness Alliance, my employer.

On the main streets of either town, many buildings are vacant, their *For Sale* and *For Rent* signs gathering dust in the windows until they are barely visible. These are poor communities, and even the fact that Highway 191 runs right through Monticello's Main Street, and I-15 nicks the edge of Malad's downtown, is not enough to keep most businesses afloat. Only the service stations get the passersby, most travelers don't stop for more than gas until they get somewhere they can order a salad with something less oxymoronic than iceberg greens.

Malad and Monticello both boast relatively few private pastures—most of the cattle graze the vast public lands at the towns' edges—places hemmed by piñon-juniper groves and laid open by plains of sagebrush and slender, intermittent waterways bordered by cottonwoods. Monticello differs from Malad in that it has less vegetation—thanks to its southern latitude. With so little water available for irrigation, you don't see the corn, wheat, and potato fields that you do in Idaho, or even northern Utah. Here you mostly see bean fields—grown with the ancient dry-farming methods of the Anasazi and a whole lot of prayer.

From Salt Lake City, it takes five hours to reach Monticello. You begin at the eastern edge of the Great Basin, the gray limestone desert that was once an enormous inland ocean. The Basin encompasses Salt Lake City and the body of water for which the city was named; it also spans the rest of northern and western Utah, almost all of Nevada, and southern Idaho. Along its former eastern shoreline, where Salt Lake City meets the Wasatch Mountains, runs I-15. Take it north, and in about one hundred minutes you end up in Malad. Take it south, and it takes that same amount of time just to escape the throbbing metropolis that my hometown has become. Finally, though, you cross the south end of the Wasatch Range and turn east until Price Canyon bends you south again and spits you out on the northern end of the Colorado Plateau. You know you have arrived in redrock country because the desert shifts suddenly from gray and gritty seabed to soft, uplifted sandstone in a dizzying array of reds, oranges, pinks, and creams. Highway 191 continues in a straight stretch before the town of Green River, where crusty badlands lash together two magnificent mounds of geology—the Book Cliffs and the San Rafael Swell. At Green River, you barely notice when you cross over the placid waters that thrilled Major John Wesley Powell, the one-armed Civil War hero who in 1869 took four boats nearly one thousand miles through this and other uncharted Colorado River tributaries—to emerge out of the Grand Canyon with only half his men. You are more apt to notice how the speed limit picks up as you head east again for a brief stint on I-70 before meeting 191 at Crescent Junction. From there you head south through Moab, paralleling the entire length of the Canyonlands Basin until the road climbs steeply up toward the Abajos, to Monticello and my new blue house.

DRIVING INTO Monticello this time, I see it with new eyes—eyes that are not looking for a quick fill-up on my way to hike a canyon or run a river, but that seek out the grocery store, the Laundromat, and the post office. And there is sudden apprehension, as if I hadn't really thought about what it meant to live deep in redrock country. Indeed, the move was sort of impulsive—fueled by my desire to be near Herb, and by my nostalgia for childhood summers on my grandparents' ranch in Malad.

But as I drive into town, I realize how much more the outside world has penetrated Malad—if only by its proximity to Salt Lake. San Juan County, on the other hand, is hours from anything remotely urban, more insulated than nearly any other county in the lower forty-eight. The thought strikes like a viper as the bright white of the Mormon temple comes into view, glittering starkly against the green wooded foothills. The ink-blue peaks of the Abajos. The red desert beyond. At the temple's apex stands the Angel Moroni, sheathed in gold. He stands looming over the land, a golden trumpet pressed to his lips, ready to sound the call that will gather Mormons to Zion during the last days on earth.

I GREW UP in the shadow of the main Mormon temple, in downtown Salt Lake. It is the temple of all temples, the template for all the other Mormon temples across the globe—which total 124 in operation, six under construction, and five announced.[1] The one in Salt Lake is the most grand, made from great blocks of severe white granite, quarried from the Wasatch Mountains' Little Cottonwood Canyon by early Mormon pioneers. I was born just blocks from it, at LDS Hospital, an acronym for the Church of Jesus Christ of Latter-day Saints, the Church's official name.

The Church. In Utah, we say it and spell it with a capital "C."

My father's side of the family has been in the Salt Lake Valley for six generations. They were originally Mormons, but more recent generations have become Gentiles, or non-Mormons. And although there is a general, ongoing tension between the two groups, the Irvines get along beautifully with the Saints—largely because my father's family is an exceptionally considerate and well-mannered bunch—conservative in dress as well as deed. These are the trademarks of a good Mormon, and they'll tolerate you if you model the same. My father was especially well liked among them; when he wasn't drinking, his conduct and appearance were exemplary. Since his boozing took place outside of Mormon circles, they had a hard time seeing him as anything but one of their own—in fact, in a lineup, one would have been hard-pressed to separate him from the state's majority. It was a good thing. In Utah, fitting in—not standing out—is paramount to all other qualities. In both a social and professional sense, it is how one survives.

The Irvines' forefather, my great-great-great-grandfather, was Major Howard Egan. Egan was a leader in the Mormon militia and one of the first pioneers to set foot in the Salt Lake Valley. He served as personal protectorate—first to the founding prophet, Joseph Smith, who said "he felt safe when Howard Egan was on guard,"[2] then to Smith's successor, Brigham Young, who led the Saints to Utah in 1847. My ancestor moved easily within the Church's most inner circle of power and privilege—an exclusive group of men sanctioned by the First Presidency. The Church's leadership was and still is composed of the president, a man who rises in the Church and receives prophetic qualities along the way, and two other men who act as private counsel to the president. Together this powerful group of men divine from God the revelations that direct the Twelve Apostles, a group of men who oversee Church business and teachings. It was through his proximity and service to this hierarchy that Egan became one of the first to be told in hushed tones that God willed Mormon men to take multiple wives. Over the course of his life, Egan took three.

But Egan was a man on the move, and maintaining wives and progeny hardly slowed him. Before coming to Utah, he had helped build up the Church—first in Ohio, then Missouri, and then Illinois. Each new settlement resulted from a flight from the last, for in each location the Saints had courted trouble. The prophet's odd ways offended many of his neighbors: it didn't sit well with them that he saw visions in stones. That, for a fee, he hunted for treasures that he swore were buried beneath the crops of poor farmers. That he married up—and impregnated—young girls as fast as he laid eyes on them. That the Saints voted en masse—which most often resulted in the election of candidates with the same religious affiliation. That they were successful entrepreneurs who managed to acquire (some say not honestly) the most lucrative businesses, the most desirable lands and resources. These didn't do much to help their reputation either. Finally, in 1844, the prophet was jailed in Carthage, Illinois, after the state and federal governments put their collective foot down and tried to rein in the Saints. A group of exasperated, riotous Gentiles stormed the jail and shot Joseph Smith. He fell from the window into a mob who desecrated his body with a merciless glee.

For the third time, the Saints were on the run, and Egan was with them. It was then that Brigham Young assumed the helm, moving the brethren across the Missouri River, temporarily out of harm's way. But the Gentiles were too close for comfort, and still feeling vengeful toward the Saints. So Young chose Egan and 143 others to accompany him out west, in search of the new Zion, leaving the others at Winter Quarters, in Nebraska. They would be sent for after God had revealed to him the promised land.

Egan, a rugged Irishman, proved to be a worthy choice for such long and difficult travel—part of a small group quipped by Wallace Stegner as the "general strong-arm men of Brother Brigham."[3] These were Mormonism's fiercest and fittest, men who were ruthless with their guns not for self-preservation or self-gain, but because their religion asked it of them. They moved confidently through Indian territory. They could bring down a buffalo without fail. They could even cook it over a fire made from nothing but the animal's own dung. When food was scarce, Egan and his ilk could give up their share to the others—for they had the wherewithal to eat their own saddlebags if necessary. There was Hosea Stout; "to the extent that Zion was a police state," he was its "enforcement arm."[4] There was Porter Rockwell, "that long-haired, cold-nerved instrument that Joseph had created," who was "surely as dangerous a man as existed on the whole frontier."[5] Some say that in the course of his life he avenged the blood of the prophet nearly one hundred times—his alleged actions justified by a scripture in the Book of Mormon that explained how some sins were only forgiven if the sinner's blood was shed in retribution. And there was John Doyle Lee, the man who would later be made the Church's scapegoat for his gruesomely enthusiastic participation in the Mountain Meadows Massacre—an event that Mormons would just as soon forget about—in which a wagon train of Gentile men, women, and children were slaughtered not only by Paiutes, but also by Mormons dressed as Indians.

Egan and these men—known collectively by some accounts as the Avenging Angels, although the Church balks at confirming the existence of such a group—helped to guide that first cross-continental expedition of Saints with militaristic flair. Brother Brigham had divided the pioneers into wagon companies of ten; Egan served as captain of the Ninth, the wagon company of Heber C. Kimball, one of two men in the First Presidency alongside Brigham Young. Kimball was also the man who adopted Egan as his spiritual son, another Mormon tradition. So competent were these wagon companies against the forces of nature, and against wild savages, that the first Mormon exodus across the continent was, by frontier standards, totally benign. Nobody died, and only one man bowed out of the expedition to return to the East. He had claimed illness as his reason, but Egan, a devout man who would have crawled to the ends of the earth for his God and prophet, swiftly dismissed the man as being "weak in the faith."[6] The first group arrived in the Salt Lake Valley on July 24, 1847, and, looking out at the glittering lake, the pioneers sang three hosannas. Finally, they had found a home, a place where they were free from the Gentiles and their big, bossy governments. They didn't care that the lake was more salt-laden, more lifeless, than the Dead Sea. That the deserts beyond looked barren, desolate, and foreboding. They would never be bullied again.

Their backs were turned on the East, on the United States of America. Everywhere else, in every direction, there was vast desert: to the north and west, the Great Basin; and to the south, the Colorado Plateau. Brigham Young quickly claimed all of it—two physiographic provinces and then some. By today's standards, we would define those lands as portions of California, Oregon, Idaho, Wyoming, Colorado, New Mexico, and Arizona—and virtually all of Nevada and Utah. Irrelevant to Young, or to Kimball and the rest, was the fact that Mexico still owned it. Irrelevant was the fact that it already possessed native peoples who claimed it as their indigenous territory. To Brigham, it was the Kingdom of Deseret—the place to "get out from this evil nation."[7] Heber C. Kimball simply called it "the promised land."[8]

The promised land. When recording Kimball's words in his personal diary, Egan highlights them.

I WAS BORN and raised within the promised land. But for a homegrown Utahn, I had an unusual relationship to its faith. My mother was born a Latter-day Saint—and in my formative years she had evolved to a loosely practicing one known as a "Jack Mormon." My father was a Gentile who, despite his Egan pedigree, was devout in his lack of religious affiliation. As Utahns, my sister and I had a unique half-breed status, for it is rare for Mormons to marry outside their religion. In some families, it would be grounds for the severing of family ties.

Some Sundays, my mother urged us to go to church. Other weeks, she and my father took my sister and me fishing, skiing, or camping. And in an almost teetotaling state, where Mormon doctrine frowns mightily upon drinking, our home was stocked with alcohol—and plenty of it. Often the arrangement produced great awkwardness. One day in Sunday school, when asked what we would do if Jesus came to our house, my sister, barely five years old, raised her hand. "I'd fix him a cocktail," she said.

Such situations branded us. My father took a perverse but private pleasure in this—although he was careful to maintain a genteel manner in public. So, although our neighbors were as gracious as Christ would have wanted them to be, we weren't frequently invited into their homes. For me, the social exclusions were unbearable. Still, my father refused to let us be baptized. He said the whole religion was witchcraft—but he said it only within the confines of our home, and then it was usually after a few drinks. It was a waste of a good day, he said, to sit on a church pew when the pheasants were thick enough to flush from the brush by the dozens. Eventually, I think his objections came down to this: the state of Utah so tightly controlled liquor distribution that on the Sabbath, after being outdoors all day, if our cupboards were empty, my father couldn't get a drink to save his life.

EN ROUTE TO Monticello in my rented U-Haul truck, I had crossed the lower Canyonlands Basin and seen in the distance the white flash of several dozen antelope rumps. An entire herd, shifting across the landscape en masse. I had been reminded of my own kinetic impulses, how they have been shaped by pursuing such movement, for I had grown up watching my father's irresistible desire to follow wild animals. For him, as compelling as the winged migration of birds was the hooved travel of ungulates—how they rolled back and forth like a tide between high mountain country in summer and low valleys and plains in winter. In autumn, he would pace as the light shifted and the days shortened. He would forget to set the clocks back from daylight savings, but he'd be up before dawn, knowing exactly where to go to make good on his game tags. He moved through time by seasons—pronghorn season, mule deer season, then elk and moose, punctuated by time spent shooting fowl and fishing trout. He wasn't a macho kind of man—he was slight and fair and clean-cut. He didn't have all the latest hunting gear or a fancy four-wheel drive. Indeed, a grubby army-issued duffel waited in the back of the station wagon—and in that family car, guns and fishing rods were far more common than a road map and tire jack. Stashed in the duffel were ratty long-johns, moth-nipped wool socks, ancient hip-waders, a camouflaged slicker left from his brief stint with the National Guard, and a mildewed down-filled vest. That car logged more time in the backcountry of the intermountain states than it did to malls and supermarkets. Armed for weather and adventure, my father seemed helpless to do anything but move with the animals. He never mowed the lawn.

His name was Donald Karr Irvine. He was handsome and charismatic—even when he was blackout, reeling drunk. At his memorial service, the word used most to describe him was "gentleman." But he was not cut out for the world prescribed to him: the three-generations-old family lumber business, a marriage, a mortgage, and two daughters. As sweetly civilized as his appearance and demeanor were, when the alarm rang on weekdays he turned savage at the thought of going to work, of seeing his children off to school. Half the time, he stayed in bed, then slunk out in the afternoons to cast his rod in the nearby stream of Millcreek Canyon.

When I was nearly two years old, my mother was about to give birth to my sister. "What about the baby?" she called to my father from the porch, holding together a bathrobe that barely reached around her middle. My father was in the driveway, loading the car with his fishing gear.

"Call the highway patrol," he said over his shoulder. "They can find me if it's time."

He made it back just before my mother went into labor. And when they brought my sister home from the hospital, it became apparent just how much I was my father's daughter—hopelessly nomadic, roaming the outdoors to escape the entanglement of human relations. When my parents weren't looking, I slid a chair to the front door and undid the deadbolt. And then, without so much as a look at my newborn sister, I galloped off into the woods behind our house.

Peripatetic ways run in the family. In 1846, en route to Utah for the first time, Howard Egan detoured to Santa Fe, New Mexico, to retrieve the paychecks of the Mormon Battalion, the Saints' army which had been offered to the U.S. government in its war with Mexico. They had not gone as loyalists—the Battalion was employed to give the Saints leverage. After they helped win the war, after the West was secured as part of the American Manifest Destiny, they were banking on the fact that the United States would be grateful—grateful enough to leave the Saints alone, especially if they settled in some remote and undesirable part of the acquisition, so they could live and worship as they pleased. It was a trip on horseback, through formidable country that crawled with outlaws, Indians, and wolves. But Egan returned unscathed. And he handed over the soldiers' paychecks to Brigham Young, who would use them to fund the massive Mormon relocation that had just begun.

The following year, after entering the Salt Lake Valley for the first time, Egan spun around and went right back to Winter Quarters, where he helped mobilize the rest of the Mormons toward their new home in Deseret. At that point, nearly any other man would have been happy to settle in with his family and friends, but Egan set off immediately to blaze the Overland Mail Route and portions of the Pony Express line. He also made countless trips to California, to work the gold mines that had been discovered, and to sell livestock on behalf of the Church. Once, he even set the record for making the trip by mule.[9]

It is no wonder, then, that two of his three wives eventually left him. And no wonder my mother eventually left my father—for he too was impossible to pin down. And, like Egan, my father believed he had a higher calling in life, which justified his missing piano recitals and birthday parties. For years we accepted his stories, with their divine intimations and thrilling details, which filled and soothed his absences. With reverence I told his tales at school, for Show and Tell; I can't remember if the kids were impressed with my recountings, or if it was simply my own rapturous state that seemed to magnify those moments when I stood before the class—telling of the opening day of an unseasonably wet deer hunt, a day when my father got the station wagon stuck in rain-soaked knee-deep ruts. The tracks filled with so much water, he said, that toads came out of their burrows in full chorus. Suddenly a county bulldozer appeared—a near miracle so far in the backcountry—and my father rode its front shovel all the way back to civilization. When I got older, I realized that, at that time of year, toads would have been in hibernation, and that, in Utah, county bulldozers are always in the backcountry, maintaining an endless labyrinth of dirt roads and sometimes making new ones. Still, I could give him this: the next day, sizzling in the oven, there would be some succulent meat he had shot, dressed, and rubbed with sage—then stuffed with fine ghost-blue berries of juniper.

Itinerant legs. Good shots. Good cooks. There is also a pattern of Irvine men marrying undevout women—my father and mother were not the first. Howard Egan's grandson, my great-grandfather Robert Lee Irvine, married a coal-haired nonbeliever named Sue Ulmer. She was as small-boned as a hummingbird, and somewhat of a Freemason. She added her own traits to the family gene-stew: For her all-purpose firearm she toted a Winchester 94 .30-30—a classic Western model often found in the saddle holsters of cowboys. Almost daily she roamed the salt-crusted flatlands surrounding the Great Salt Lake, where she and R.L. had built a haciendalike homestead. Without fail, Sue brought down some kind of small game, then dragged it home where she coaxed a fire beneath a cast-iron pot and concocted a hearty and delicious meal for her brood. She must have had brilliant aim, for the rifle, although small and light, was really meant for large game and medum-sized predators like coyotes. In order to knock off a large bird—a goose or swan—or any medium-sized creature (I wonder, what did she kill that she could dress and drag home? Fox? Badger? Antelope?), she would have needed a clean shot at close range. And in order to avoid blowing the meat to inedible smithereens, she would have had to hit the animal square in the skull.

Sue's hunting rifle was passed down to my grandpa Lee, her eldest child, who married Ada Chamberlain, another Utah Gentile. Ada had already begun her artist's career on the sidewalk of South Temple, in front of Snelgrove's Ice Cream, where she sketched children's portraits for a nickel apiece. When Ada and Lee's children were grown, Sue's rifle passed on to the eldest of their sons—my father. Of all his firearms, it was my father's favorite. It was the weapon he used to end his life.

THIS IS my heritage. This is what comes with me in the U-Haul, part of the baggage I convey to San Juan County. I am ambivalent about this legacy, my place in it, and it is through this lens of uncertainty that I now look upon the Mormon temple. Since birth, I have lived in the shadow of such a building, but this one stands in what is true outback country—an icon that exemplifies not only how saturated the West is with Mormon history and tradition, but just how deftly the religion appeals to a variety of worlds. The temple of my childhood stood amid an urban epicenter, and though that center was predominantly Mormon, it was a relatively sophisticated and worldly brand of faith—if only by necessity. But San Juan County has changed little since the first Mormon pioneers settled the area.

It is a relic of the oldest kind; its people and culture seem to outsiders not only oppressive but nearly prehistoric in their ways. The temple before me represents a different kind of Mormonism, less diluted, more insulated—almost oblivious to the machinations of the outside world.

Yes, this move is impulsive. Not something I can explain in rational terms. One year earlier, the idea had risen from the ashes of a failed marriage—but after my father died, the idea of actually inhabiting the desert outback engulfed me with a certain inevitability. My belongings were boxed weeks before I actually left.

I am going on a leap of faith. There is the obvious: watching the pavement and subdivisions of Salt Lake creep outward, into the desert, up into the mountains, has become unbearable. There is the grief I hold for my father, the belief that if I stay in a place where the pace is so rapid, I too will lose my already precarious hold on life. And there is the affair for which I have forsaken nearly everything—a complicated sum of southern-Utah sandstone and the man who lives there.

This is not the first time I have felt the urge to escape the city. The day after we scattered my father's ashes, I fled west, to the Great Basin. The desert of my mother's family, in Malad. The desert of my father's pheasants. The desert of Howard Egan's trailblazing.

"Where are you going?" my mother asked. She had come from England, where she lived with her second husband. She had been divorced from my father for twenty-four years—since I was ten years old. She posed the question as I frantically rammed my clothes into a backpack, mud-caked lug-sole boots on top of clean underwear. It was the dead of winter.

"I'm going somewhere where I can grieve," I said.

"Grieve?" she asked. "You have seemed at such peace, so strong."

I was neither—not about my father's death and for that matter, not about anything in the realm of human relations. I have always lived at the tip of a frail, slender branch that threatens to break whenever I am forced into close quarters with others. Even at my father's death, I put on a good show that even my mother cannot question—a show that has been good enough to draw many friends and lovers. But then they would get too close, and I sent them running for cover. It had been the thing that kept the lion man at bay for nearly a year—and it would be the thing that would push him away again. It was also the thing about me that aligned me with my father. It was, above all reasons, why I have always turned tail and run to remote places. Which is why it was only a matter of time before I ducked into a place like San Juan County.

AFTER THAT first trip to the Salt Lake Valley, Howard Egan returned almost immediately to Winter Quarters, to help guide the brethren to the new home that awaited them. The first wave of the exodus was called the Big Company, roughly two thousand veteran Saints who in their efforts to settle in three different locales had already honed the skills needed for frontier life. Like the first group, they made the trek without much mishap. Death and hunger infrequently visited their ranks. And the Indians gave them little trouble. That's not to say that the going wasn't the endurance test of a lifetime, but they had already lost so much in Ohio and Missouri—and then there was Joseph Smith's martyrdom in Illinois. From there they had fled for their lives, some with little more than the clothes on their backs. They had looked back over their shoulders to see their prophet's mutilated body hanged in public display, to see their beloved Nauvoo Temple in flames. Later, they would hear that the mob of Gentiles had vomited and urinated in that original temple's baptismal font. All because God had given them the political and economic acumen to dominate the communities in which they settled. All because they were virtuous and obedient to the Heavenly Father, multiplying and replenishing the earth more rapidly than anyone had ever imagined was possible. But the Gentiles had been jealous, had resented the Saints' access to the true and the right—and made them pay dearly. By comparison, their travel through the wilderness seemed both a blessing and a reprieve.

The Mormon emigrants who crossed the continent after the Big Company didn't fare so well. Between November 1855 and June 1856, three years after the Stateside Saints had completed their exodus to the Salt Lake Valley, 4,395 converts were brought from overseas. Fresh off the ships from England, these foreigners were mostly down-and-out millworkers from England, Scotland, Wales, Ireland, and Scandinavia. Most of them had been loaned travel funds by the Church's Perpetual Emigration Fund—money they would pay back once they prospered in Deseret. They didn't share the American Saints' history of violent persecution and frontier know-how. They were simple village folk, armed only with the promise of a less impoverished life and, when it was all over with, an especially seductive version of heaven that would welcome them with open arms: there, in the celestial kingdom, there would be infinite wealth—even streets paved with gold.[10] There, each man was guaranteed eternity with his family. What's more, he would transcend to godhood and receive a planet to rule as his own. The rewards were tantalizing enough to send thousands across the Atlantic.

In New York, after the last of the emigrant companies had arrived, they were outfitted in haste, in an effort to arrive in Salt Lake before winter. They were sent off with handcarts made of green wood and loaded with the absolute minimum in supplies—the rule was seventeen pounds per adult. They were "propertyless, ill-equipped, untried and untrained,"[11] emboldened only by the Church's overseas mouthpiece, the *Millennial Star*, which assured them, "The gathering poor, if they are faithful, have a right to feel that the favor of God, angels, and holy men is enlisted in their behalf."[12]

Some would later say that the emigrants weren't devout enough. But most of them suffered simply because they were civilized people from the civilized world. Never before, in their wildest dreams, had they hunted big animals or confronted hostile natives or slept under an empty prairie sky. Ultimately, it was a mass migration of the most pitiful kind. Those who survived would pull those cracked and splintering wagons nearly fourteen hundred miles. Those who did not would be buried along the way—unless the wolves got to the bodies first. With so many wagons crossing the plains that year, game had waned. The last handcart company to cross, the Willie Company, saw hardly any animals and was reduced to eating personal daily rations consisting of ten ounces of flour. By October of 1856, when the weather turned, they were still nowhere near the Salt Lake Valley. They had little warm clothing or shelter, and finally their meager food stores ran out. Disease from lack of sanitation settled in with a vengeance.

It was nothing like the crossings that Egan had known. Before the Willie Company reached Deseret, more than two hundred members of its party perished. One night, a young girl awoke in screams; a boy from another family was eating her fingers. He died after they carried him off, but not before he tried to eat his own hands. On their knees, the newly converted emigrants turned their faces toward the heavens. They asked for patience and the will to endure this dirty, destitute land. Soon the Saints possessed more than an underlying sense of maltreatment in their group identity; as the crossings became less successful, there developed a cultural conviction that the wilderness was an adversary of the worst kind. Pioneer journals are littered with comments like one made by John Chislett, written after his train crossed the Sweetwater in Wyoming. He wrote that the river was "beautiful to the eye . . . but when we waded it time after time at each ford to get the carts, the women and the children over, the beautiful stream, with its romantic surroundings . . . lost to us its beauty."[13]

I MAKE IT to Monticello under far less dire circumstances than my forebears, but the sight of the town's temple instills a sense of perilousness. I remember when my grandma and grandpa Blaisdell took me on a tour of a newly built Mormon temple; it was open to the public for a short time before they closed the door and "dedicated" it exclusively to baptized Mormons who had been good enough to receive a temple recommend from their bishop. It was before my parents were divorced, so I hadn't yet been baptized. I guess at that point my grandparents figured that a public tour might be the only way I'd ever see the inside of a temple.

For the tour, we were given little white booties to wear. My grandmother explained that they wanted to keep the temple's new carpets clean, but also that they didn't want the place contaminated with the filth of the unworthy. On the latter point, I didn't know if she was telling the truth or was just trying to scare me into being a Mormon, but when we entered, everything else was white too. White floors, white walls, white lamps. The temple tour solidified my image of the celestial kingdom—the Mormon version of heaven—as a place that would be a sterile-looking white room. I had imagined entering it in a white robe, and now I imagined I would be wearing those dreadful booties too. A very large man with a long white beard would hand down the judgment of my life. He would tell me that I hadn't been good enough, that I would have to go to a lower level of the kingdom, but my family—at least those good Mormons on my mother's side and my father's illustrious ancestors—would be free to visit me down there. As God spoke, I would look down at the spotless ivory tile. There would be not one speck of dirt. I would hear no wind, or birds. And through the robe, hanging heavy and opaque, I wouldn't feel my own body. It was there on the temple tour that the idea of heaven began to terrify me—not enough to keep me from getting baptized, but enough so that I would quit attending church by the time I was twelve.

My father was delighted. One might think we would have grown closer then, with this obstacle between us finally removed. But it was as I stood on the threshold of adolescence that my father began to recede from my life. That he quit taking me camping and skiing and duck-hunting. By the time I was twenty-six years old, we had no re-lationship at all. When he died, I hadn't practiced Mormonism in twenty-two years, and my father and I hadn't spoken in eight.

IT WAS the day after we scattered my father's ashes, the day I fled to the Great Basin, that my inherited sense of persecution caught up with me. I followed my father's antelope across the Thule Valley. Scared up his pheasants near Fish Springs. Tracked his mule deer among the gothic granite crags of the Deep Creek Range. In the Deep Creeks I found the place where my great-great-great-grandfather Egan had homesteaded during his mail-courier days. In a narrow ravine nearby, amid aspens with bright-white bark that glittered like the spires of a thousand granite temples, I found an enormous spearhead. It appeared to be a Clovis point—a remnant from the earliest-known humans to move across the deserts of Des-eret. With the exception of this tool, this ancient culture of Paleo-Indians is almost completely obscured from us. As they followed the migrations of beasts larger than anything that we can imagine, they toted no possessions, traveled without laying claim or name to the landscape that carried them.

Pleistocene. A time when mud mattered. A way of life lain for-gotten in the coils of our DNA.

In his wanderings across the land, Egan had thrived. But my fa-ther lost his momentum. On a south-facing slope where snow had melted to reveal talus, I squatted and traced the spear point where it lay. Then I thrust it at the sky, like a middle finger. A perfect projec-tile of geese flew overhead, headed straight for the Great Salt Lake. I was surprised. I thought the geese had gone south by then.

There in the Great Basin, stroking that hard and ancient tool across my palm, I resolved my own migration. To the Colorado Plateau. From one desert to another. Life there would demand skills that I hoped were inherent in me. It didn't occur to me then, just as it has never occurred to me, to leave Deseret entirely. I would simply creep farther to the edge, away from its society. The instinct was as natural as anything I have ever known.

SITTING IN my U-Haul that first night, I realize that this journey to the heart of the desert is a permanent move, not some brief respite from which I will return. I take inventory: I have what my grandmother had—a ravenous appetite for beauty. And I have what my father did not—the love of a lifetime, the kind for which you would crawl across the most formidable of lands. These are enough, I tell myself. They will sustain me. It is a pioneering kind of faith that fuels these beliefs.

But Utah is a modest place. There was a time, long ago, when the physical aspects of life were seen not as adversities but as miracles. Now, in the shadow of Moroni, expressions of the sensual offend—whether committed by man or nature, it does not matter. One's passions are forced to stagnate. Movement is no longer admired.

I formulate my plan: if I am to remain here, to survive here, all must be hidden. My animal appetites for the land, for the lion man. And everything else born of these yearnings: my politics, my writing, my work as a public-lands advocate.

But I will learn. In redrock country, everything is eventually revealed.

⇥ 2 ⇤

Origins

ONE WOULD HAVE *heard them first—the desperate, rumbling thunder of hooves. Shards of light tumbled from the sky and shattered on the desert floor, made the sagebrush and relic seashells glitter a silver-green. Across the Western states, the Great Basin bled its ancient seabed: Nevada. Idaho. Utah.*

It was across this desiccated ocean they ran, the ocean that spanned much of the former Kingdom of Deseret. Their dust gathered and moved across the hardpan, a swirling vortex of sweat and breath. To the men on their heels, it didn't matter that, after the U.S. annexed this portion of the Basin from Mexico, the government had not left them alone, that instead its shadow loomed over their settlements and tried to police their practices. It didn't matter that eventually Washington had portioned off the land to surrounding states. It didn't even matter that the seriously truncated version of their homeland, their Zion, had been renamed Utah—a tribute not to God but to one of the region's established tribes. In their minds, no map, no proclamation—unless divinely ordained—could ever alter Deseret.

From the cloud the band of wild horses broke, running for their lives. Three cowboys were on the band's left flank, with two on the right and one off the back. Their heels dug hard into their mounts as they bore down on the herd, the tame forced to terrorize their wild cousins.

Hollering harsh single syllables, the cowboys drove the band toward an outcrop of limestone cliffs. There the animals were bottlenecked into a dry wash, carved out of a flat grassy bluff that stood above them. Two by two the horses stumbled over stones as they ascended.

They broke out on top of the bluff. The cowboys circled them once, folding the herd into itself. There was a quick turn of hand from the man at the back; then they pushed the confused cluster of animals across the meadow. The herd became a galactic nebula, indistinguishable except for whines of panic, a blur of muscled bodies and thrashing tails.

At the edge of the bluff, the cowboys reined in their mounts at the last moment. The herd's momentum launched them into the silver-green light. There was a gorgeous brief moment when the horses looked winged, as if buoyed by currents of wind. And then the thud of bodies, the clock of hooves and bone striking rock below.

The cowboys grinned at each other, held their gloved thumbs up in the air. They'd given it to the federal government, and to the congressional act just passed to protect wild horses on federally owned lands. The buzzard-pecked carcasses would be found the next week by a Bureau of Land Management employee, who had received an anonymous tip. By the end of the week, the news would be broadcast across the nation, the feds furious at the Sagebrush Rebels who had demonstrated that no one would tell them what to do with their deserts or with any critter who competed with their cows for food.

It was 1971—over a century after the first wagon train of Mormon pioneers arrived. That year, a federal study allocated forage for animals on Western public lands. Of those lands, tens of millions of acres lay within the original boundaries of Deseret.

Seven percent of the forage was designated for indigenous wildlife:

deer, elk, antelope, bighorn sheep. Thirteen percent went to wild horses
and burros—not even native to the land.

Eighty percent was dedicated to domestic livestock.[1]

THAT FIRST NIGHT in Monticello, when Herb unlocks the door
and I enter my newly rented house, I am surprised by its interior.
The dark veneer paneling I had seen the month before and resolved
to endure is now a bright white. Herb proudly explains how he had
driven from Moab a week earlier and jimmied a window, how he
had painted until sunrise because he knew such a dark space would
quickly depress me. The house needs airing, so we spread out sleeping bags on the porch. My Australian shepherd, Pablo, curls around
our heads like a comma. I dream of hanging my grandmother's
paintings, vivid bursts of color, on the blank walls of my new home.

The next morning, I awake to the rattle and hum of RV genera-
tors and idling pickups—the stirrings of the uranium-tailings clean-
up crew in the trailer park behind my house. While Herb sleeps, I
make a cup of tea and give a low whistle to Pablo, who follows me
out into the neighborhood. We cross the street to the edge of the
municipal golf course—its green and manicured acres a bizarre sight
in such arid country. Along its edge is an old dirt two-track, a road
only in the sense that the passage of vehicles has worn away two parallel strips of vegetation. It cuts a swath through thick clusters of
Gambel's oak, and piñon and juniper—the high desert's quintessential evergreens. These foothills are the transition zone between the
redrock desert below and the more alpine environment of the Abajos, where tall, yellow-bellied ponderosa pine and quaking aspens
dominate. This zone is very much like the woodlands at the base of
the Wasatch Mountains, which surrounded my home on the Great
Basin's ancient ocean shoreline above Salt Lake City. It's also much
like the landscape that surrounds my grandparents' ranch in Idaho.

It is much like anywhere in Deseret, that in-between land that anchors islands of high country within desert.

And, as anywhere else in Deseret, there are cows. Pablo and I skirt the golf course and push through trees to enter a clearing full of them—a small herd that has gathered for the sun's first light. The entire meadow—which should have been thick with fresh spring grasses and flowers—is bare to the soil. The entire setting is polka-dotted by enormous dollops of cow pies.

It is unclear if these cows belong here, for I have crossed no fences. If they so chose, they could easily stray into the neighborhood—onto the golf course, or into my yard. That they are not sectioned off means nothing: in San Juan County—as is the case in many of Utah's rural counties—ranchers have no obligation to fence in their livestock. If you don't want them grazing on your property, it is your job to fence them out. And if you are driving across open range and suffer the misfortune of hitting one of these enormous beasts with your car, you will be legally obligated, if you survive, to compensate the rancher for his loss. But the privileges of bovines do not pertain to other creatures. In fact, I am nervous walking through this herd, on the lookout for a nearby cowboy. Only the year before, a friend was hiking with her dog, near Blanding, through public lands permitted for grazing. The rancher was there, moving his herd. The land was open to other uses as well, but that seemed irrelevant to the man on the horse. From the saddle, he took aim and shot the dog on sight, its master only yards behind, screaming in protest. She complained to the BLM, but the agency did nothing.

Not that I completely blame the rancher—dogs can be a grave threat to livestock. Nor do I blame the BLM. There are instances when it has tried to reprimand such a man and found itself face-to-face with the local sheriff—guns, posse, and all.

IT COMES DOWN to this: in the more urban parts of former Deseret—places like Salt Lake City—life has become more civilized. You don't become a major metropolis without interfacing with the outside world, without learning the skills of tolerance and compromise, even if only for the sake of getting along. But in the more rural corners of Deseret, things are very much as they were 150 years ago, when the first pioneers arrived. Even now, when you enter a rural community in Utah, or in one of the surrounding states that were once part of Brigham's vision for a massive Mormon territory, you must understand just how many degrees of separation there are between the locals and the nation's capital—or any other form of outside regulation or influence. You must understand how unyielding the people can be to your overtures, the lengths to which they will go to protect their way of life and all that they see as theirs.

You must recognize that the term "democracy" really doesn't apply, that only God's laws and cattle rule the land. Everything is described, measured, and comprehended in terms of divine will and forage. With the exception of the missionary work—aimed at bringing the rest of the world into the fold—and government subsidies for ranching and farming, the world outside Zion remains largely irrelevant.

I believe myself to be familiar with this insular way of life. I had learned it as a child, experienced the contrast between my home in Salt Lake and my grandparents' cattle ranch in Idaho. And I knew how difficult straddling the two worlds could be, how I lived mostly in a no-man's-land in between. Sometimes there was outright rejection. As a teenager, I had tried to describe to my grandma Blaisdell the foreign-exchange-student program to which I had been accepted. I rattled on about meeting the Portuguese family to whom I had been assigned, about my worries of learning to speak such a difficult language, about the thrill of experiencing such a different place and people.

My grandmother was leaning over the stove. Her hair was in a hairnet, her housecoat splattered with the tenacious purple of beet juice. She had gotten up before dawn, to feed the men before they went out to turn the water. Now she worked furiously to get her beets canned before the day got too hot. As I spoke, her brow sank deeply into her sweat-beaded forehead. Finally, she turned to me, her mouth a grim gray line of disapproval.

"What's the matter," she said, "ain't it good enough for you here?"

Months later, when I returned from the exchange program, she and my grandfather joined my parents and my father's parents at the airport. I came off the plane in a flood of Mormon missionaries, young men returning from two years in the field. They were set apart from other travelers by their polyester suits—cheap and nondescript, but totally identical to one another. Even after two years abroad, they were amazingly provincial—as if they had never left their hometowns. Other folks welcomed people off the plane with small bouquets of flowers, but, for each young man there were handmade banners, stuffed teddy bears, balloons, and masses of people. As I wrestled my way through the suits, I caught a glimpse of my grandma Blaisdell's face. She was looking wistfully at the missionaries. I knew what she was thinking: the only good reason to leave our homeland was to teach the Book of Mormon and beckon the rest of the world, if only figuratively, into the new Zion.

LATER THAT FIRST MORNING, while Herb and I are carrying my desk down the U-Haul's ramp, a young couple emerges from the house across the street. They approach us with wide, eager smiles. Trent, who looks to be in his mid-twenties, introduces himself as a law-enforcement officer for the state's wildlife division. His wife's name is Charity. Fair-skinned and fair-haired, she appears even younger than her husband—but already she has the soft, full figure of a woman who has borne several children, a figure that is barely visible beneath her long, full sundress and a white embroidered sweater with a lace collar. The couple's accent matches my own—a distinct regional cadence that ascends the scale toward the end of each word before dropping off in sudden staccato.

"We're so glad to have another young couple in the neighborhood," Trent says. "There's hardly any folks our age here, seems they all have to move away to find jobs." I nod my head in understanding. Many of my relatives had taken second jobs—driving semi trucks, for instance—to support their ranching lifestyle. But I am also taken aback. We don't look like Mormons, and so this eager overture is a bit unusual. Then I realize Herb's long hair is tucked up in a ball cap, and I am wearing baggy, nondescript sweats. We have not yet been identified as the Gentile and Jack Mormon that we are.

Then Trent asks what we do for a living, and if we have kids. I talk over Herb, so he won't blurt out his occupation as a public-lands attorney. No kids yet, I say. For now, I'm a writer and Herb commutes to Moab to earn a living.

"Maybe we can go for walks in the afternoons." I look directly at Charity when I say this, hoping that the tangent will get us off the subject of work. I point to the long swath of oak and juniper that runs from the Abajos down to our street, alongside the golf course. "I'd be delighted for you to show me the woods."

"Oh, I just really stick to the street," she replies.

There is a pause. And then Trent asks Herb if he is a Cougars fan. I wince when he is forced to explain that they are the wildly popular football team that plays for Brigham Young University.

Another pause.

"Will you be attending church?" Charity asks.

I wince again. No chance for distraction this time.

"Herb here is Catholic, and I . . . uh, I'm no longer active in the Church."

The Church. I wonder if Herb, the only nonnative Utahn among us, can hear the capitalization.

Again, a pause.

"Well . . . I guess call if you need anything . . ."

My new neighbors are gracious, even as they struggle to mask their disappointment. Even as their voices and smiles recede onto the pavement, back into their home.

THE END OF my first month in southern Utah, and still I have hardly left the house, except to walk along the golf course. There are the tasks of unpacking, and working under deadline. I do find time to hang Ada's paintings, and to order off the Internet some curtains I cannot afford. My grandmother's art begs for natural light, but I keep the draperies closed. My first encounter with the neighbors has left me realizing that maintaining a low profile in a small Mormon town is going to be more difficult than I had imagined.

One morning, the landlord stops by for the rent check. He smells the pot of coffee Herb brewed before he left for Moab and asks for a cup. This small request eases the intense self-consciousness that plagues me, for it means the man doesn't abide by the Word of Wisdom—the Saints' prescription for proper living—which requires abstinence from caffeine, along with alcohol, tobacco, swearing, gambling, and sexual relations outside of marriage.

We sit on the porch, sipping from steaming mugs, talking about the weather. Finally, I ask about his life in Monticello. He was born here, in a building just across the street from my newly rented home—a building that was once the hospital before it became the clubhouse for the golf course. His parents were born there too.

"So you're a real local," I say.

He shakes his head. "Nah. Around here, you don't count as a local unless you descended from Hole-in-the-Rockers."

He's referring to an especially notorious group of Mormons who, in 1879, were called upon to settle the San Juan country—some thirty years after the Saints had first set foot in Utah. Surrounded by deep, labyrinthine canyon systems, occupied by outlaws and "depre-dating Indians,"[2] it was known as the most impenetrable region in Deseret—if not the nation. Even the Old Spanish Trail had de-toured far north, just to escape the impossible topography and the confounding gash of the Colorado River, where it sliced through the San Juan portion of the Colorado Plateau. The Saints had at-tempted to claim the country before, but it was the unlikely Hole-in-the-Rock expedition, which arrived by squeezing through a narrow chasm high above the Colorado River, in the southwestern corner of today's county, that succeeded where all others had failed. Indeed, there were far less arduous ways to have entered the region, but the expedition sought a shorter, more direct route. It was not long after Brigham Young's death that his presidential successor, John Taylor, chose a group of faithful to gather in the rugged settle-ment of Escalante, named for a Colorado tributary on the opposite side of the river. From there, a wagon train assembled and then headed out onto a canyon-carved bench beneath the purple shadow of the sixty-mile-long Kaiparowits Plateau.

It was tough country to begin with, and, as in the last of the em-igrant exodus from New York, the Saints got off to a late start. When winter seized them by the throats, they had reached the point of no return, for their precious horses and cattle had grazed every-thing behind them. Besides, a Mormon may have turned his or her back on the government, but one never turned his back on the Lord's will. So they persevered through gnashing storms. Huddled beneath cotton quilts and animal skins, the women gave birth in the backs of the wagons. Game was scarce on that long stretch of bad-lands, so when the flour ran out they foraged from the wild grasses, whose tips barely stuck out of the snow cover. This they ground in their coffee mills (somehow coffee was acceptable back then—perhaps because the boost was needed for settling such tough lands as Deseret). They lived on this fine dust, for they dared not cull the herds that would sustain them in their new home.

It never occurred to them that they might not make it. What they lacked in nourishment they made up for in prayer. And despite their diminished strength and cold, rattling bones, they danced by firelight to fiddle music within a grand amphitheater of sandstone. Through the dead of winter, they plowed forward across the rough and ragged country, only to be stymied at the end of the Kaiparowits Plateau. There the party was to cross the Colorado, but the bench on which they traveled was like an enormous step—part of what is now called the Grand Staircase—and it loomed nearly a mile above the water. One way off the bench was through the canyons that led to the Escalante River, but they were found to be too narrow and tortuous. Eventually, the scouts concluded there was only one way to descend the great stone terrace, and that was through a notch barely wide enough for a wagon. Beyond that notch, the cliff dropped away; a dugway of the steepest kind would have to be constructed from its face.

That they even considered such an improbable route was astonishing. And there they were, through the dead of winter, dangling their best men from the escarpment above the Colorado. Spooning rationed gunpowder into the rock, they blasted a steep and narrow ramp to create a downward-sloping trough just wide enough to hold the inside wheel of a wagon. Five feet below the ramp, they drilled by hand an inclining succession of holes that paralleled the ramp's slope. The narrowly spaced holes were plugged with oak staves, carved from trees growing below the bench. From the wall, the staves stuck out in a perpendicular row; they were covered with a broad mat of brush, branches, and broken chunks of stone—which stuck out far enough to support the wagons' outer wheels. The result was a road, suspended in space.

The settlers pushed eighty-two wagons and eighteen hundred head of livestock through the Hole-in-the-Rock, a thousand feet above the water. Then they loaded each wagon onto the dugway and worked it down the face, with ten men braking the rear wheels, and several more up front, holding back on the tongue. Down the matted staves the wagons creaked—followed by herds of animals, women, and children. Raining red stone into the sky, pieces of the road gave away with each load, each footstep.

With gaunt bellies and worn-out boots, their horses' and mules' hooves ground to the quick, the San Juan settlers then ferried their cargo across the Rio Colorado, over the Clay Hills, across Cedar Mesa, and down Comb Wash, to the banks of the San Juan River—where they would found the town of Bluff. When it was said and done, the expedition had traveled 260 of the most circuitous and laborious miles known to humanity. Not a single life was lost, save the cattle they finally relented to slaughter to prevent starvation. After all, they had planned for a six-week trip, not the six-month journey it became.

As they neared Bluff, the Saints had met a local Ute man, to whom they described their route. The man threw up his hands in disbelief and rode off disgusted—dismissing the Saints as liars. But the Hole-in-the-Rockers were unfazed. They were the chosen people, destined to command the promised land. Their journey had been the result of fusion—of bottomless faith welded to tenacity. They would settle Bluff, then Monticello and Blanding, with that same amalgamation. Indeed, the Hole-in-the-Rock expedition would remain a source of *hauteur* for the residents of San Juan County—the springboard for a culture of cowpunching, road-building, and wilderness-conquering.

YOU DON'T LIVE in Utah all your life without hearing the Hole-in-the-Rock story with some frequency. But now, as my landlord tells it, he points to the houses in the neighborhood where Hole-in-the-Rock descendants live. Their family names I have heard forever—in history books, in newspaper quotes, attached to Church officials and county commissioners. I am still captivated as he rises from my plastic lawn chair and tosses his coffee dregs into the grass.

"Nah, if you got here any other way," he says, staring into the bottom of the empty cup, "it just don't count."

As he climbs into his car, he points out an old rusted mower and plastic sprinkler head, stashed beside the shed. In this landscape of strawlike bunchgrasses, cactus, and rock lichens—drought-tolerant natives that evolved to withstand the extremes of the desert—these yard implements seem as out of place as my lawn and the golf course across the street. And though my landlord may not be Mormon, he knows what matters around here.

"Folks in these parts really care about their lawns, you know."

THE ENGINE IS CHOKED and won't start. I refrain from asking Herb to fix it, because he is exhausting himself with almost daily drives from one county to another, to keep up his work. A month goes by before I resort to taking up the offer of our neighbors, and finally I knock on their door to beg use of their lawn mower. Charity answers, with two small children peeking out from the folds of another long and full dress. Then Trent appears and shows me out to the garage.

"So you work at home," he says, squatting to check the fuel tank. "Now, what is it exactly that you do?"

"Well, I write a bit . . . freelance . . . and, well, I work for a wilderness-advocacy group."

He looks up at me. "Really, which one?"

"The Southern Utah Wilderness Alliance."

Something in his face shifts and sets, like the pin of a deadbolt sliding into place. He stands up, hands me the gas can. Then he smiles and takes a step back, the polite and perfect neighbor at a distance.

"It's full. Use all you need."

————

I RETURN the lawn mower early the next morning, and then stop at the post office to rent a mailbox. Before noon, I am headed south to Blanding, where I will turn west and climb onto Cedar Mesa. Its sinuous canyons, home to the densest concentration of archaeological sites in the nation, weave their way from the southern end of the Abajo Mountains down to the San Juan River. I am going with an archaeologist friend from Colorado, and I look forward to the lesson—as well as to getting out for some desert sun and socializing. It is a hot day in late June—not the best time of year for desert hiking—but I am inspired by visions of Hole-in-the-Rockers, parched and starved, trudging across the same terrain.

This is my first journey into the desert as an official resident of San Juan County. When I turn west onto a sunbaked Highway 95, the mesa's dark, dry forests of piñon and juniper reel for miles in every direction. Periodically, the forest opens up and I glimpse the engraving of a canyon, or a dune of delicate yellow tendrils called prince's plume. Soon the highway drops into Comb Wash, not far from where the Hole-in-the-Rock party camped before slogging their way up and over the San Juan Hill to reach their new home in Bluff.

I have made this journey many times in my life, but Cedar Mesa feels very different now that I live on its perimeter. My new residential status seduces me into thinking that I have been granted a new authority here. It is a foolish notion, because these lands are managed by the United States Department of the Interior's Bureau of Land Management—on behalf of the collective American people. I have as much entitlement to them as the ranchers who run their cattle, or the oil companies who have plunked down gas wells. I would have as much to say about their fate no matter whether I lived in Monticello or Salt Lake—or Florida or New York, for that matter.

My friend waits for me where Highway 95 heads west out of Blanding. He hops in my truck, and we head down 95 until we hit a remote road called 211, which bisects the southern end of Cedar Mesa. Together we drive 211 and turn off onto a stretch where harsh weather and an overzealous road-grader have scoured sand from bedrock—a stretch claimed and maintained by the county as an official road. Finally, we pull onto the shoulder and park; from there we walk for a mile down an old two-track. Before us, the high desert forest suddenly divulges a deep, flesh-hued canyon. Creeping right to the canyon's edge, the two-track does a loop, creating a makeshift viewing area—a kind of crude cul-de-sac. The BLM has legitimized the casual pullout by placing a kiosk, which tells the public to respect their public lands and the cultural resources on them. The lands before us are part of a twenty-three-million-acre statewide system, managed as part of a nationwide network of lands under the same mandate; unlike national-park or monument lands, these lands are open for "multiple use." Many consider BLM lands to be the trailer trash of all the public lands under federal jurisdiction—and, indeed, many of the Utah lands were offered to the state at the end of the nineteenth century, but the state declined ownership because the lands seemed fairly worthless. Such devaluation doesn't stop the local rural counties from continuing to fight for authority over them. To this day, it remains a matter of almost spiritual principle.

We walk to the canyon's edge. Below, the vivid spring green of coyote willows envelops several potholes of water—water pockets so deep and shadowy they look like large deposits of obsidian. The leaves and pools are a sublime contrast to the burnished rock walls. On the opposite side of the canyon, my friend points to a well-preserved cliff dwelling tucked into a shelf.

Descending a series of ledges, we cross the canyon bottom and scramble up to it. The structure is made of mud and stone—precisely the color of the cliffs that shelter it. There are several chambers, each with a portal the size of a human face. The windows look as if they might have served as lookout posts, for each one is angled directly at an obvious point of approach.

There is not a single relic left in the ruin. The place has been scoured by archaeologists and looters, and even the last potsherds and flint knappings have been picked up as souvenirs. The place feels barren and sterile—more like a museum than someone's former home.

Taking care not to lean on or touch any portion of the dwelling, we peer into it. The red walls of one room are charred by fire. Each surface is painted with what looks like a separate lunar phase—white on black. The moons leap out of the darkness at us. My friend says most archaeologists think they were painted by the last of the prehistoric people—in the years after the ancients abandoned a nomadic life of hunting and gathering—sometime between A.D. 700 and 1300. Such symbols most likely conveyed fertility, he says—drawing them was perhaps an act of faith that beckoned the cycles of new human life, or new crops, for when these people discarded their former ways—moving about for meat, roots, and seeds—they began to farm corn, squash, and eventually beans.

But it is anyone's guess what the moons really mean. All the prehistory of the area is open to interpretation—the clues ferreted out and assembled from possessions and abodes left behind. For example, some people have concluded that the local Indians descended directly from the Anasazi; others believe that they inherited the region by some other means. There is a discrepancy between the Navajo stories of origin and the origin/migration models generated by researchers; the Navajo often claim to be related to the prehistoric residents, and often their stories and symbols match those of the prehistoric Cliff Dwellers, who evolved from the Basketmakers. Conversely, much of the linguistic evidence—a popular method for determining the origins and migrations of cultures—yields the conclusion that the two groups had little or no contact with one another, that the Navajo most likely moved in at a later date.

The Mormon interpretation of Utah's Native American heritage takes quite a different perspective: as one of the lost tribes of Israel, the Saints believe that contemporary Indians have been here since Biblical times, that they are the direct descendants of Hebrews—an unruly bunch that were cast off by boat to North America, as punishment for their sins. In the early days of settling Deseret, to fulfill the prophecies in the Book of Mormon, Brigham Young urged the Saints to take the Indians and "dress them up[,] teach them our language & learn them to labor & learn them the gospel of their forefathers." He encouraged the brethren to "raise up children by them," and, so they would be received by God, make them "a white and delightsome people."[3] Even now, despite DNA testing that proves Native Americans are not of Hebrew descent, the Mormons anticipate that their long-lost dark-skinned cousins will play a significant role in the Second Coming of Jesus Christ and the end of the earth as we know it.

Ancients. Indians. Mormons. The notion of genesis is precarious.

WE CLIMB OUT of the canyon and follow the two-track back to the main road, where our car is parked. Along the way, my friend points out an old circle of stones—scuffed and blackened by the passage of tires. He explains it is an ancient campsite, most likely built by the nomadic hunters that predated the Anasazi who resided in the canyon below. An obscure site of this nature is called lithic scatter; the term refers to the vague and spare signs left by Paleo-Indians—pieces of the San Juan country's most original human history that are usually undetectable, that are usually buried beneath many other, more modern eras of habitation. Even in its most obvious, well-preserved form, such antediluvian history is difficult to decipher, but my friend says that there is almost no chance of learning anything from a site like this one. An endless stream of modern-day boots, hooves, and tires has rendered it impossible to interpret.

We are staring at the stones when a large brown Ford truck appears, coming straight toward us. We step to the side, and the driver slows, rolling down his window.

"How you doin' today?" The man is smiling. There is a woman on the passenger side, and a herding dog in back. The woman nods pleasantly. The dog yips once; then the man quiets him.

Fine, we say, and smile back. My friend asks where they are headed.

"Down to the ruin," he says. "The wife's never seen it, even after all these years." The woman beams and nods in agreement.

"It's a nice hike," I offer, but the man waves the words away.

"Aw, we're just driving to the edge to have a look down in," he replies.

"You know," my friend says, "there's a good pullout back on the main road. If you parked there, you'd have a real nice walk through the trees and avoid driving over some of these old cultural sites." He smiles again, then points at the stones just beyond the truck's front bumper.

The man's eyes follow his finger, but then his face darkens like a thunder cloud. Spittle forms on his lips.

"Son, my family has been coming out here, running cattle, scraping out a living, since long before you were born." His mouth casts off the spit, like sparks off flint. "And that there is nothin' but a pile of rocks."

The words are barely out, but already he is rolling up the windows, then floors the gas and peels out over the lithic site. As they speed away, the woman looks back over her shoulder, out the back of the pickup truck, her face pale through the red dust.

———

THE WORD "Deseret" was derived from the Book of Mormon and means "honeybee," a tribute to industriousness and the notion that the individual's wants are subsumed by the collective's needs and goals. For the Saints, there was no more perfect mascot: within hours of arriving in the valley, the first settlers had pastured their livestock, plowed and planted five acres of land, and diverted City Creek for irrigation. In those same hours, land was measured and divided into plots for each family. As the lots were doled out, Young told the brethren that the land had been promised by the Lord, who "has given it to us without price."[4] Thomas Bullock, Brigham's clerk, in a letter to his former British home, declared to his fellow Englishmen that if they came they would "have no land to buy or sell; no lawyers waiting to make out titles, conveyances, stamps or parchment." He boasted, "We have found a place where the land is acknowledged to belong to the Lord, and the Saints, being His people, are entitled to as much as they can plant, take care of, and will sustain their families with food."[5]

IT WAS ALONG the shores of the Great Salt Lake, beneath the majestic Wasatch Mountains, that Brigham Young was finally able to draw around his people a shining, bright line. That line distinguished Zion from the United States, and with its demarcation came the warning from Brigham that no Gentile was to "blaspheme the God of Israel or damn old Jo[seph] Smith or his religion, for we will salt him down in the lake."[6] As for the federal government, Brigham blamed its officials for the death of the founding prophet and told his followers that if the feds "ever sent any men to interfere with us here they shall have there [*sic*] throats cut and [be] sent to hell."[7]

All this history reaffirms what I experienced growing up in Mormon surroundings. So deeply territorial, so internally loyal is its nature that the Mormon identity is almost tribal. To be Mormon is to belong—to a place, to a people—and in a way that one is hard-pressed to find in the modern world. Perhaps for this reason alone, the religion lured me despite the wishes of my father. By the time I was six years old, a sure ticket into heaven and the smug knowledge that I would be so interconnected, so entitled, and so hailed in God's eyes above all other people, was enough to make me betray my father's beliefs. Besides, I saw the religion as an alternative to his alcoholic world, and I did my best to show him what that life might afford him. On later weekend mornings when he was too hungover to have made it to the duck marsh, as he stumbled into the kitchen for his coffee and eggs, I would sing the song I had learned that week in Primary—the children's after-school Church gathering:

> *I'm a Mormon, yes I am,*
> *So if you want to study a Mormon I'm a living specimen*
> *Maybe you think I'm just like anybody else you see*
> *But trust in my word, you'll quickly observe*
> *I'm different as can be.*
> *I'm a Mormon, through and through*
> *So if you think that I am peculiar in the things I say and do*
> *Remember I know the rules, the do's and don'ts for happy,*
>   *happy living,*
> *I know to say I will, I won't*
> *I try to be forgiving*
> *Maybe you'd like me to tell you about the things that I*
>   *know are true*
> *Then you can be a Mormon too.*"[8]

But my father would have none of it. There were nights when my mother was away at a bridge game and he would load my sister, Paige, and me in the car—sometimes in our pajamas—when we should have been in bed. We'd go to visit his Gentile friends, and on their couches, my sister and I would fall asleep to the clink of ice cubes against highball glasses, the stench of cigars.

The drive home was a zigzag race to beat our mother's return. Through the neighborhood, the car careened across lawns, garbage cans, a mailbox. Bird shot and fishing lures rolled like ball bearings across the back of the station wagon. Paige and I would roll too, and, with hands entwined, four tiny sister hands, we prayed. Then we'd stand barefoot on the cold concrete, the night nipping at our legs, while our father extricated himself from the car. From the driveway I could see the neighbors' dark silhouettes pressed against many kitchen windows on the block.

It's not that he didn't believe in God. My proof was when I asked to pierce my ears and he replied, "If God wanted you to have more holes in your skin, He would have sent you down with them." But each time I asked to be baptized, something all the other kids were doing, he said, "Over my dead body."

Finally, when I was ten, my mother packed my father's booze and belongings. After he was gone, she drove us straight to Castleton's, where the clerk at the jewelry counter shot hypoallergenic studs through my ears. When we got home, my mother crossed the yard to our next-door neighbors—an especially kind and caring Mormon family who often took my sister and me in for dinner and other occasions. When Mr. Roberts agreed to my mother's request to baptize us, I was so relieved. I think my mother was too; she may not have been a Mormon in good standing, but she wanted her girls to have entrée into both heaven and the neighborhood.

The anticipation left me breathless. Joseph Smith had said that only by baptism could one "purge out the old blood," that by doing so one actually became "the seed of Abraham."[9] After the ceremony, I would be a true child of Israel.

We were taken to the Stake House, a Mormon building that accommodated certain rituals and gatherings for a number of neighborhoods. In a locker room, Paige and I changed into little white jumpsuits, then were led out to a small pool. My mother and her parents, who had driven down from Malad, were sitting in the seats facing us, smiling and moist-eyed. Instructions and incantations buzzed like locusts over our heads.

But I really only remember one concrete phrase:

You must be completely submerged.

The water terrified me. It shouldn't have—it was so warm and clear, with white tile and mirrors all around. But I couldn't stop thinking of my father. As I went under, I considered keeping my big toe above the surface, so not all of me would violate his beliefs. In the end, though, I fully submitted—I was betting on the fact that my father might forgive me, but the neighborhood and God would not.

It was shortly after he found out about the baptism that my father began to recede from my life. And, despite the ritual, the neighborhood reacted badly to my parents' divorce—another taboo among Saints. In their minds, it would have been better for my mother to stay married—even to a nonbeliever. This was not so much because they hoped to win my father over. Single women were just not a part of Deseret's cultural fabric. You were either actively seeking a husband, or you were married with children. End of story.

After my father's departure, invitations to birthday parties and sleepovers became increasingly rare, and our Mormon friends were no longer allowed to play at our house after school. Things really got lonely when my mother went back to work, and then downright solitary when she began to date again. We were still encouraged to attend church, but, overall, our half-breed status became a glaring obstacle to friendship.

After the baptisms, my mother and my grandma and grandpa Blaisdell took us to Fernwood's for starlight mint sundaes. There was a red glass giraffe standing in my whipped cream—the parlor's signature for children's desserts. I pulled the animal out and walked it to the end of the table, then popped it in my mouth to suck the chocolate sauce from its legs. My grandmother scolded me. Just as she would scold me a year later, when I began asking why, if the Latter-day Saints believed that Christ's Coming was imminent, there had been so many generations of Mormons awaiting his return.

My mother's mother was a hard-edged woman. I have seen her kill a litter of sick kittens with a shovel, then singlehandedly put out a runaway ditch fire with that same tool. Once I drove with her to Preston, following a trailer of cattle to be butchered. We stood outside as the men pushed the animals down the ramp and into the slaughterhouse; I could hear some kind of hard object cracking down on each skull. All the animals were bawling—it sounded as if some were still alive when the blade hit them. I remember looking to my grandmother in horror, but she was expressionless. Running a ranch in Deseret had worn down any soft perimeters she may have inherently possessed, and those hard edges shaped her response to my question—made me see how narrow and concrete her view of the world was. For her, it came down to this: the earth was a mere stopover on the way to the celestial kingdom—a place one was meant simply to endure.

And so my question about Christ's return was met with a swift, decisive answer—not open to debate.

"God put us in this forsaken place for a reason, and I don't have time to waste second-guessing Him. Now, there are cows to feed and crops to bring in, and that's all I got time for. If you got time to be wonderin', missy, then you ain't living right."

On another occasion, I might have stopped to ponder why she thought that the earth was so forsaken, but on the day she rebuked me in Fernwood's, I was utterly preoccupied, scanning my small body for sign of Abraham's blood. After the baptism, I had expected to feel different, to be awash with the purity and serenity of my soul's salvation. Instead, there was a single thought, too precise and calculated for the child that I was.

I've got cover now, I'm in.

IT'S NOT ONLY that I wanted to be a Mormon, I wanted to be the oldest kind of Mormon—a pioneer. In fifth grade, I wrote a report on Howard Egan. Ada and my grandpa Lee had suggested it, and had taken me to the Salt Lake City Public Library to read his diary, which was housed in the Special Collections. I was instantly in awe of his travels, his adventures—the same way I revered my father's. But Egan's life was lived in service to God, and that put his pursuits head and shoulders above my dad. It was that kind of purpose I wanted in my own existence, that kind of justification for the time I spent wandering in the woods.

But I also wanted to be a cowboy—so Egan's stints as a Pony Express rider and cattleman both impressed me. Then there was Grandpa Blaisdell, the handsomest man I had ever seen in a saddle. I remember when he took me to my first rodeo, how we first visited a Western shop in nearby Logan, where he bought me caramel-colored cowboy boots and a red-plaid shirt with pearly snaps down the front. I couldn't have been more than five years old, and I felt so proud in my new garb as we hiked up the bleachers, my small hand in his. High in the stands, we watched my uncle Scott ride broncos and rope calves, my cousin Julie race barrels. I brushed away the feeling of being an impostor, of being the half-breed city girl who couldn't even straddle a horse because she was so allergic to them. Instead, I lost myself in the fantasy of riding out on a cattle drive with my grandfather and my uncles—for no life seemed better. To be swallowed whole by the landscape. To swim in your senses—the scent of sagebrush, the sound of coyotes, the sight of the sun hovering on a horizon that was larger than life itself. To be on the move, riding the edge where life unfolded. I may have romanticized it a bit, but I knew that, no matter what the cowboy life's downside, it beat the hell out of anything I could ever do in suburbia.

JUST WEEKS AFTER my baptism, I visited Ada, who lived not too far from our house in the Salt Lake Valley foothills. She was painting in her underground studio while I sat on the basement steps, which I often did while she worked. Although I hadn't yet gotten up the courage to tell my father, I announced to my grandmother that I had been baptized. She set down her brush, removed her glasses, and rubbed her eyes. Then she looked at me—hard. It was as if the image of her own granddaughter had blurred into something she hardly recognized.

"Why on earth did you do that?" she asked.

She truly didn't understand. Ada had married into the Egan family line, the third generation of Gentile wives to marry its Mormon stock. Not once had she felt pressured to conform to the state's or the family's predominant way of life. Admittedly, the Irvine contemporaries were hardly Mormon by the time she came along, but she didn't view the world through that Deseret lens in any case. She inhabited her native status with a certain grace that exempted her from feeling conflicted. Next to her artistic talents, that grace was the quality I most wished I had inherited.

She turned back to her work, a passionate, flaming smear of pink-and-orange canyon walls. Later, she would name the piece *Escalante*, for the canyons that had denied the Hole-in-the-Rockers an easy descent. Canyons that had just been inundated by the backwaters of the Colorado River, thanks to an engineering feat called Glen Canyon Dam. And without ever taking her eyes off the canvas, she told me that this world was lovely, and that this life was long, and for her, that was good enough.

———

IN MIDSUMMER, just two months after I borrowed the lawn mower, I see Charity one last time. She is in the checkout line at Blue Mountain Foods. In between handing items to the clerk and telling her children to put various sweets back on the candy shelf, she tells me that they are leaving Monticello, that Trent has found a better job in St. George, a much larger town, in the southwest corner of the state—a town that has a temple but is less than two hours from Las Vegas.

I follow her out to the parking lot to hear more.

"That's where we grew up, so we'll be back among family," she says with her head down, digging for keys in her purse. When her hand resurfaces with them, she looks up at me.

"And, to be honest, we're excited to go." She looks around to see if anyone is within earshot, then allows herself a long sigh.

"Trent's had trouble with the locals' taking the law into their own hands. They shoot anything and everything—in or out of season, permit or no. He's not an environmentalist or anything, but these guys here just hate any government officer—state, federal, it doesn't matter. Makes it kind of hard to do his job."

She sighs again. "So, you see, we just never really got to feeling a part of things."

I consider this, and ask her how long she thinks it might have taken them to assimilate. After all, they are largely of the same stock—native-born, rural Utahns in good standing with the Church.

"Oh, I don't think anyone who didn't evolve from this place ever really does," she replies.

Her response carries weight, for she is a faithful, compliant daughter of Deseret. If Charity couldn't fit in, then how would I? My bloodline may be one of the most original among Utahns, my accent homegrown, but this is not enough.

I look carefully at my neighbor. I want to ask her if she feels claim or entitlement to this promised land, if she finds it lovely or forsaken. I want to ask her if, in her desert upbringing, she has come to hold things only in terms of her faith, or if she has found that there are also things that prowl more deeply in her bones. I want to tell her how my personal copy of the Book of Mormon, along with my little-girl cowboy boots, gathered dust just as soon as my father bought me a pair of buckskin moccasins, soft and beaded. I want to ask if there is some part of her that, after living in a place so raw and uncultivated, would choose those shoes too.

But there are limits to what you can ask a devout Mormon woman. I know that from dealing with my grandma Blaisdell.

"Did you ever have a chance to get out into the woodlands behind your house?" In our parting moment, it is the only question I dare utter.

Her answer is predictable. Her tame words chase into midair any semblance of animal nature.

"No time," she says, neatly folding her receipt and tucking it into her purse. "Between keeping house, taking care of my children, and getting to church, I've got all I can manage."

⇥ 3 ⇤

Mire

MY FIRST YEAR in San Juan County, the rains begin to recede. This isn't a new phenomenon for southeastern Utah—every group of people that has ever lived on the Colorado Plateau has been tested by some prolonged lack of water. It is most likely why the ancients abandoned their magnificent canyon cliff dwellings in A.D. 1300. It is the reason some Hole-in-the-Rockers packed up within the first year or two of settling Bluff and returned to greener, more northern settlements. It is the reason so many written accounts of this desert, both early and contemporary, call it "unforgiving."

At the post office, the topic among the locals is the imminent drought—their concerns muttered in low, grim tones. I catch the words "fifty-year cycle," and the phrase "worst one in my lifetime." And I hear that if things get worse it will be the environmentalists who are to blame.

"Better get the BLM to drill you some stock wells now, Lamont. If them tree-huggers lock up the public lands and close our roads, we'll never be able to truck water in to our cows."

Such talk—about the lack of water as well as who is to blame—is common in the outposts of former Deseret—even as far as Idaho, where it's cooler and there's more precipitation. It's not an easy life, trying to make a living off such dry and futile land. I have a memory of my grandpa Blaisdell, elbows on the kitchen table, grazing regulations, bank statements, and a calculator spread out before him. His cornflower-blue eyes were glazed from scrutinizing documents and numbers. Over and over he jabbed at the machine's buttons as if they were culpable. Then he cradled his silver-haired head in gnarled, spotted hands—hands that forever smelled like hay and engine grease, no matter how many times he washed them.

"We're not going to make it." His voice would crack when he said it. I held my breath as my grandfather rose from his chair, his face pinched with the complaints of his overworked back. Then he shuffled across the kitchen, took his John Deere cap from the coat rack, and stepped outside. Next thing, the Blaisdell brothers and sons were gathered under the shelter of the carport, airing their woes. A few leaned against the carport's support posts; others occupied the porch glider and the back steps. They would clean lunch from their gums with toothpicks while I crouched behind my grandparents' Oldsmobile, my body leaned into the back fender, my cheek pressed against its weather-beaten bumper sticker:

FARMING IS EVERYONE'S BREAD AND BUTTER.

From my inconspicuous spot, I listened. For a good hour, the brothers berated the banks and the BLM, and ranted about the Sierra Club. Many of their endeavors were collective, and they talked about how to manage them: Should they invest in the latest baler? Or make do with the old one? And even in the wettest years, they talked endlessly about not having enough water.

I wanted so much to be a part of those conversations. For starters, I wanted to help console my grandfather, who was a sensitive soul and took the tough times harder than most. Even at six years of age, I worried that he and my grandmother might lose the ranch and have nothing to eat. I knew they couldn't live with us in Salt Lake City. My grandfather would have died living away from the land he had known his entire life; besides, there was nowhere to put their horses and cows—our backyard was just too small.

But I also wanted to be a part of those conversations because I wanted to be more intimate with that world—a world where putting up hay and moving cattle were group efforts. I envisioned myself in Wranglers, a toothpick between my teeth, my feet in leather work boots—one propped up on the front bumper of the car—as I talked with the men. We'd stand there together and raise our fists in the air—against something, anything, I didn't care what. I was so impressed by the Blaisdells' solidarity, how bound they were not just by blood, but by a way of life that, in turn, bound them to the landscape that surrounded them. And the bonds between them were all the more powerful because they were positioned in opposition to the rest of the world: indeed, their relationship to God and to cows made their stance adversarial by definition.

But I was a girl. I was from the city. And I was a half-Gentile to boot. Their domain was completely inaccessible—as inaccessible as God Himself.

AT SUMMER'S PEAK, it is hard for me to take the threat of a drought seriously—in southeastern Utah, July and August get an intense summer jet stream from the Gulf of Mexico that never reaches the northern portion of the state. This monsoon season is deceptive. Every afternoon, the sky turns murky, like the bottom of a staid pond. Then a dark mass of weather swells around the Abajos, disgorging a storm as substantial as sheet metal. What I haven't yet realized is that the clouds disperse as fast as they congregate, that the desert sun burns off the moisture before it can soak in.

The weather takes me by surprise. The idea of a drought had been perversely appealing, for I am tired of water. The way it shifts things so suddenly, the way it happens so fast I cannot respond. But the monsoons are not the only thing to catch me off guard. Herb and I receive an invitation to our first Monticello social event—the wedding reception of the postmaster's daughter, who also works at the post office. She knows us only from stamping our mail and handing us packages, so I am both surprised and flattered to have been included. I fret for hours over what to wear, tearing my closet apart. I find a long floral skirt, not too form-fitting, and a pale-lavender top with sleeves that don't reveal too much arm or chest. On the other hand, Herb chooses a bright floral Hawaiian shirt and a bolo for a tie. His long red hair tumbles freely from beneath his grandfather's cowboy hat. I try to convince him to change the shirt to something more subdued, and to pull his hair back—so we don't draw unnecessary attention. He looks at me as if I have just walked off a spaceship.

What he doesn't understand is that wedding receptions are one of Deseret's most important social events—and in a way that is entirely different from the rest of the nation. Everyone in town will be there, even though there will be no champagne fountain, no crostini passed on a platter. Instead, there will be fruit punch, and small paper cups filled with nuts and mints. Still, I am eager to attend: despite my commitment to lying low, I am starved for some social interaction. So desperate am I that I'm willing to walk into a group of locals on Herb's arm, even though he's the man they blame for many of their woes. Whether it's cows, off-road vehicle trails, or jobs pulling fossil fuels from the earth, they know him as the young, half-cocked lawyer who tries to stop their every economic or recreational venture in the desert.

My environmental work is behind-the-scenes stuff—I'm not someone they would have seen in a BLM or county meeting. And, these first months in Monticello, I have made it my goal to slip by unnoticed, not to raise any red flags. On the way to the reception, I beg Herb to remember my general agenda.

He waves me off. "I am who I am," he declares. "Either they'll love me or they won't."

The reception is in the bride's father's backyard—and it is fortunate the rains have ceased for the occasion. When we enter, the postmaster is gracious, and even ignores the turning of heads, the stalls in conversations. He is of a rare southern-Utah breed, a man who doesn't attend church and has nevertheless risen to a position of great acceptance and respect. Still, it amazes me how unconcerned he is by the effect our entrance has had on his guests. With great aplomb, he escorts us over to the bride and groom. I hug his daughter, say how honored I am to have been invited. She is unaware of what we do, the way it sets us apart from the community. She smiles. The long white taffeta of her gown crinkles when she hugs me in return.

"Oh," she says, "I just think you guys are real nice."

I've got cover now, I'm in. The response is so deep it feels more like instinct than emotion.

We make our way to the punch bowl, Herb grinning and nodding at folks with whom he has gone toe-to-toe. This is like the parting of the Red Sea, and it's all I can do not to run home.

Herb fills his punch cup, downs its contents, and fills it again. Then he turns and dives into a conversation with a man who used to prepare oil and gas leases for companies that had applied to the BLM for the right to drill on public lands. Bob is a handsome man, and well spoken. And although he is officially retired, he remains one of our group's greatest adversaries. He greets Herb warmly—he's not one to make business personal. I am surprised by this, for in Deseret everything is personal.

An older woman elbows her way through the small crowd that has drifted over to play voyeur on these two enemies. She is short, but the fierce look in her gray eyes makes her seem ten feet tall. Bob barely has time to introduce her as his wife, Racine, before she puts a finger right up into Herb's face. "Young man, if I ever see you out there standing in front of a county bulldozer when it's tryin' to keep my public lands open, then I'll climb up in the driver's seat and run you over myself."

Everyone is quiet. Even Herb is uncharacteristically taken aback. This overt kind of confrontation is not the norm in my home state. Not in a social setting, where strict civility applies.

And then, with one impulsive response, my cover is blown.

"That's not a very Christian thing to say . . ."

The air in the garden cools. I stand horrified. But Racine's face bursts into a wide grin. Later, when she invites me to her house for a visit, I will learn that she and Bob are Catholic, that their front door bears a sign saying that all who enter will be treated as Christ would have treated them—no matter who they are. Of all the people I meet at the reception—people I will mingle with, if only at arm's length, again and again—they are the only ones who ever open their home to me.

I return to the blue house that evening in low spirits. The reception had been nerve-racking; more keenly than ever, I had felt the impenetrable wall of Deseret. That night, as Herb sleeps easily, I wonder why it is that my landlord, the postmaster, and Bob and Racine can move so freely within its confines. All I can guess is that they are lifelong southern Utahns, which gives you more credibility than if you come from northern Utah. Briefly, I wonder if I should return to Salt Lake City. But life was just as awkward there.

THAT NIGHT, I dream of the desert. Of blooming cliffrose and the pranks of ravens. A place where I can touch the slow, steady pulse of geology: Wingate. Kayenta. Navajo. The layers run a sensational gauntlet of reds and creams—sedimentary strata composed from tiny particles of sand deposited by water and compressed over time. Each particle is one-sixteenth of a millimeter to two millimeters in diameter—each one distinguishable, tangible, without magnification.

There's a supple sureness to sandstone. Cousin to water, it shifts shape with relative ease. But there's always substance, something you can see and feel at face value. And among those particles of sand, from natural cements—like lime and iron oxide—there's intense cohesion and bonding. But with stone, the bond is purely physical.

I HAD BELIEVED Herb to be a part of this move to the desert. We have been lovers for only a year and a half, and yet his devotion has been the most concrete thing I have ever known. But we have lived at opposite ends of the state. Now, within just months of living in proximity, I see that his life is a flash flood—a torrent of deadlines, obligations, acquisitions, and ambitions. He doesn't see that there is a certain debris he leaves behind, an overwhelming flotsam that inundates my life.

One day, I return home to find several young men unloading a white bathtub, a basic American Standard, into my front yard.

"Herb told us to put it here," they explain. "We're remodeling that building down the street and had to tear it out. He thought you could use it as a planter box."

Later, I hear his van backing into the driveway. When he doesn't come in right away, I step out onto the porch. He is pulling things out of the van, piling them in my backyard: A horse trough. A hinged steel gate. A plastic doghouse. Behind the van he is towing two motorcycles and an ancient pull-along trailer.

In this moment I feel how much Herb is like my father. The chaos they cause—and the way they slip through your fingers. And as they slide away, what each of them takes is the solid ground beneath my feet.

The difference is this: my father was always in disguise, always hard to decipher. Even his suicide note was cryptic; the police found it unfinished and crumpled in the garbage, a stream of thoughts that meandered and ended before we could make much of them. He was liquid, lithic scatter: difficult to detect, impossible to grasp.

But Herb is transparent, and like a great, hulking desert formation on the horizon—he is almost painfully obvious—and totally detracts attention from the rest of the landscape. And standing on my porch, towering over me, his shadow flung far and wide, he is oblivious to his effect. He chatters excitedly about all the things he is going to do with these objects: Build a corral. A dog run. A place to change the oil in his cars and work on his bikes. There is a manic edge to all his announcements, as if filling up the space with acquisitions and creations will somehow make his own existence more substantial. And when I say no, that I want the backyard left empty—a safe haven where wayward deer can continue to bed down at night—he is stunned. And because he lacks opacity, I see him chalk up this veto as my first attempt to topple his tower of life; I see him file it away in his memory.

I should have recognized then what I was up against.

SOON I AM MIRED in grief. I am slipping and sliding with every human I encounter. It is not a new feeling, but it has intensified with the new surroundings, the new relationship, the resurgent realization that my father is dead.

I return with even greater conviction to my strategy of concealment. I turn away from people, turn toward objects. Things I can grasp. Things I can understand. Obtaining knowledge about things becomes a cheap substitute for intimacy.

I become obsessed with a mammoth bone.

The bone is a remnant from the Pleistocene—a time when long fingers of ice held the earth in their grasp. Although the frozen masses did not directly clench the San Juan country and other deserts of the Southwest, their effect on the region was lavish. It was nothing like the hot, thin, unadorned crust that dominates today—or that dominated when the Hole-in-the-Rockers arrived. Or even when the Anasazi dwelled here. In that ancient era of organic opulence, the San Juan River corridor that borders the southern edge of the country was a verdant and fertile basin. There was water everywhere, and it sustained a complexly rich tapestry of soil and life forms—which in turn sustained the region's first known inhabitants, the Paleo-Indians.

Preferred pastime: hunting. Prey of choice: woolly mammoth. With long, bowed tusks, the great shaggy beast weighed in at between seven and nine tons. It thundered across the land, wading in and out of bogs, feeding on tall, thick grasses. This animal could hold its own against a geography of such scale—but it needed water, and the succulence of plants that grew in wet places. When the ice that kept the Colorado Plateau in a mild, temperate state melted away, when the earth warmed, the skin of the San Juan country dried up and cracked open. Across its surface, everything was scorched but a skeleton crew of hardy shrubs and trees.

The Paleo-Indians who depended upon mammoth meat would not have survived had they not adapted to smaller game. The mammoth, however, did not adapt—and therefore failed to survive the renovation.

There was doubt that the mammoth roamed this far south. But not too long ago, an old cowboy drove his cattle through Butler Wash—one of Cedar Mesa's most prominent rain gutters. The wash is dry except when storms spill off the mesa and gather in its wide, cobbled bed; then the wash runs the water hard and fast to the San Juan River. Each torrential flood scours away sand, stone, and brush. Sometimes when the waters die down, objects are revealed. In the cowboy's case, the object that surfaced was the fossilized femur of *Mammuthus primigenius*. Its discovery verified that the animal, as well as the nomads who hunted it, actually were residents. So novel, so telling was this bone that, for a time, the rancher had allowed it to be featured at the local museum, in Blanding's Edge of the Cedars State Park.

Seeing the bone seems essential. One afternoon, I drive south for twenty miles hoping to get a glimpse. Blanding is a totally austere place—within city limits, you cannot buy a six-pack of beer, and the video store, Clean Cuts, rents only movies from which all sex and swearing have been excised. It is also a vindictive place. Its people competed strenuously with their Monticello counterparts—first for the title of county seat, and then, later, for the hospital and the only Mormon temple within several hundred miles. In each instance, Monticello won out. In my few months of living in San Juan County, I can see that Blanding took its defeats personally, and has yet to forgive.

I have trouble finding the museum—for it is not like the coveted temple to the north, a structure that boldly announces its location in a dazzling skyward spectacle. When I finally locate the plain brown building, it is on the outskirts of town, tucked into the side of a knoll. Wandering the halls, I see clay pots, sandals woven from yucca leaves, atlatls and darts—the weaponry used to kill big game before the bow and arrow came into fashion. There are the tips of arrows and spears, and dozens of baskets. There are grinding stones, and necklaces of shells traded from coastal people. The relics were all collected locally—from Basketmakers and ancient Puebloans—post-Pleistocene cultures collectively known as the Anasazi. People known for their possessions and, later, their architecture.

But there is no mammoth bone. I even steal into a dark hallway in back and peer through a window, where I see shelves stacked with endless items—each one tagged, some in bags—gathering dust.

Finally, I return to the front desk and ask the staff person if she knows if the bone was returned to its owner—and, if the owner is still alive, has he remained in the area? She has no idea what I am talking about. She detects my frustration.

"We have some very nice man-made artifacts—much more contemporary and interesting, don't you think? Wouldn't those appeal to you just as well?"

THAT NIGHT, I dream of mammoth-hunters, an entire clan of them, hovered over a fire from which they have pulled great hunks of smoking meat. I see them tear the roasted flesh from the bone, hear their grunts and slurps of satisfaction. In the firelight, grease glistens on their chins. I awake thinking of how my father once plunged my hands into the warm chest cavity of a deer he had gutted, so I would connect with what was on the dinner table. I remember staring at my warm, bloody hands until my mother admonished him, telling me to wash up quickly.

After that, night after night, I dream of my great-grandmother Sue's gun. Each time, a flash of gunpowder ruptures the darkness, and I wake to tangy wisps of smoke above my bed. My ears ring from its report—the reverberation of four generations of Irvines who have pulled the trigger. In the flesh of my palms are impressions of the wooden butt; on my fingertips, the greased cool of a well-maintained metal barrel.

These images, the sensations they provoke are what remain from my father's life. Each night, I beckon them to me—for they are easier to grasp than the memory of a life watered down so slowly that no one saw what was coming: New Year's Day 2000. It seems significant that he chose to commit this final act in the apartment complex's poolside club house—a quintessential symbol of engaging with society at close range. It was overlooked by my father's apartment, a mere cubicle surrounded by the concrete labyrinth of city. Blood splattered on its walls like a Pollock masterpiece. A black Labrador named Sam, my father's faithful hunting companion, whimpering and padding circles around his master's sprawled body.

ONE MORNING in late summer, I call the SLPD and ask for the detective who investigated my father's death. She sounds more like an elementary-school teacher than a police officer; her response is gentle and explanatory when I ask if I can reclaim the gun. I have imagined it wrapped in plastic, tagged with an identification number, and stored away—not unlike the relics in the back room of the museum. The detective explains that department policy is to destroy all firearms used in suicides.

"Besides, honey," she says, "I don't think it would have been a good idea for you to have kept it around the house. When someone takes their own life, their children's chances of killing themselves increase by sixty-five percent."

LATE SUMMER, and I am in the mood to hunt again. It seems the closest I can come to reconnecting with my father—as if I might make up for the eight years we didn't speak. The forested Abajos and large rivers make it possible for the region to sustain game—although nothing like the megafauna of earlier times. I imagine starting out small, with rabbits, maybe wild turkeys. Eventually, I would work my way up to deer, even elk, for I especially loved its rich, dark meat. But when I imagine myself out tracking an animal in the woods, or sitting quietly in wait at the edge of a clearing, it is my great-grandmother's gun that is in my hands.

The destruction of the gun disrupts everything, makes it impossible to reach conclusion and resolution. It also seems a desecration—the irreverent obliteration of an object that glimmers with significance. An object that fed my family. An object that transported my father to another realm.

I stand there listening to the dial tone long after the detective has hung up.

———

IT IS ONLY in the last few years, before moving to Monticello, that I have remembered how I thrived on meat—especially wild, savory game. Our freezer was full of every kind that inhabited Utah—mule deer, moose, elk, antelope. There were birds too, ducks, and geese, and fish—along with half a cow from the Blaisdell ranch. And if my father ever asked me to run down to the basement and pull something out to thaw for dinner, I always chose the wild over the domestic—that fresh, uncultivated taste that could almost be described like a fine wine, with hints of cedar sap, wild mushrooms, and sagebrush after a hard rain. And, as with good wine, I had acquired a taste, for my father put game on my plate just as soon as I had enough teeth to chew it.

After my parents divorced, there had been a ten-year respite from animal protein. This was not so much a political move or a healthy-lifestyle kind of statement as an unconscious response to my father's retreat from our life. After all, I no longer came home to find two pheasants on the counter, a note calling me by his nickname for me: *Pluck and clean these, Amos. Tonight we'll baste them in apricot chutney and lace them with bacon.*

When I was thirty, several years after I ended my relationship with my father, I married a vegetarian. Then I fell sick with a terrible flu, one that kept me in bed for weeks. When I finally emerged, the recovery could hardly be called that; what remained was a fatigue so crippling that I couldn't brush my hair, or walk out to the mailbox. No Western doctor could help me, so I turned to a doctor of Chinese medicine, who told me I wasn't living in accordance with my physical needs. He said that such self-denial allows bad energies to inhabit the body. He said too that I needed meat—that many people like me had lost touch with their original appetites. Some had adapted, he said, but I had not. In order to survive, I needed foods with a central nervous system.

In desperation, I heeded the doctor's advice. I brought home a thick T-bone steak and set it under the broiler's blue flame. As the aroma of meat saturated the kitchen, my husband shuddered and left the house.

I didn't leave the steak in the oven for long. I laid it on a plate, next to a roll and a mound of green salad. Red juice seeped from its sides and pooled. I took a bite. Then I gorged. When the meat was gone, I mopped up the juice with the bread. Finally, I gnawed at the bone, abandoning the salad entirely.

That night, I brushed my hair—a thousand strokes. The next morning, I walked around the block. A year later, I was out the door, hunting for sustenance.

My skills were crude and primitive. It was not a graceful exit.

IN HINDSIGHT, my return to meat paralleled the departure from my marriage. I had tried to be a good wife. After the wedding, for our small brick bungalow in Salt Lake's Sugarhouse district, I bought white sheets, white towels, white dishes. I started a garden, obsessed over the eradication of weeds and snails. I threw dinner parties, and cleaned incessantly. I tried to plan for the future.

But the present crept in. At night, it washed over me in the form of poems—gritty, sexy strings of words that left me gasping for breath. I tried to share them with my husband, but he was tired after a day at the office. He and our friends enjoyed their budding wine collections, and talked about building mutual funds. They worked out at a fitness center. Some slept with trays of bleach in their mouths, to whiten their teeth.

I tried to fit in. And I was hopeful—after all, these people weren't Mormon; they were registered Democrats in the most Republican state in the Union. They recycled, and paid dues to the Sierra Club.

And they spent a lot of time outdoors. But they wore Lycra. Some hired personal trainers. Others thought that time spent in nature meant speed-climbing the face of El Capitan in a day, or riding the White Rim—the hundred-mile bike trail that follows the curve of the Colorado River through Canyonlands National Park—in less than twenty-four hours. They took with them little more than stop-watches and PowerBars.

I don't mean to find fault—and on the surface, I wasn't all that different. It's just that no one mentioned poetry. Or the way the light in the desert moved down the red cliffs like a woman slipping out of a dress. They grew bored with me because I couldn't keep up. And so, while they went to the climbing gym, or sampled the latest Shiraz, I applied to graduate school in creative writing. I bought binoculars and wandered slowly, aimlessly, across the deserts of Deseret. I took a week to walk a single trail—and I took beef jerky. My teeth turned brown from sipping too much tea when I wrote. My belly grew soft from a lack of cross-training and too much time with paper and pen. I bounced checks, and didn't shower for days.

When going back to school didn't parallel my husband's career track, I looked for a job. But by corporate standards I was unemployable. Finally, the Southern Utah Wilderness Alliance, a nonprofit public-interest group for whom I had volunteered, took me in. They entrusted to me the task of writing proposals to foundations, to raise funds for the group's work. It involved saving the desert, and it demanded putting passionate words on a page. It was the perfect, perhaps only, job for me.

The group's mission was to defend against development of the most fragile and lovely portions of the Great Basin and Colorado Plateau. At the heart of the effort was a congressional bill that would permanently protect the endangered lands under the 1964 Wilderness Act. In the meantime, while the group built grassroots momentum to push the bill through Congress, my co-workers fought off oil rigs and coal mines and off-roading events. Herb was one of them, a nascent attorney who came to work for the organization not long after I did. I was awed by him and the others, who kept the faith burning bright, kept the desert eligible for wilderness designation. The disciples of the desert fueled my own fervor, and I was quickly converted into the fold.

For once, there was no question which side of things I stood on. In my convictions, among these people, I had found cohesion.

I MAY HAVE IDENTIFIED my calling and my clan, but life in the city was still all wrong. And after my father died, I could feel its walls, its hustling masses of population bearing down on me. All I could think of was how my father came to life when he was out seeking food for our table. How he withered when he was forced to bring home shrink-wrapped, USDA-inspected, skin-and-bone-less breasts of chicken. Or, worse yet, pasta.

I knew how he felt. Even when I was a child, the idea of so many people compressed into one place and hardly knowing one another seemed unnatural. I read books like *The Call of the Wild* and *Little House on the Prairie*. I yearned to inhabit those stories, where landscape was part of life, where the food you procured required that you dirty, even bloody, your own hands, where the people were few enough so they really mattered to one another. Indeed, across the globe, throughout time, traditional hunting societies have tended to live in two small and basic groups: The tribe is the larger of the two, one that is spread out over a broad geographic area to assure enough resources for each member. The tribe ranges from two hundred to fifteen hundred individuals—about the number of people you find in each of San Juan County's communities today. Tribes are typically broken into bands—smaller groups, more intimate and familial. Evidence from the Paleo-Indians of the Pleistocene shows that these smaller bands averaged a living unit of about twenty-five people.[1] Today's hunting societies, in the few places where game remains abundant and outside pressures are absent, still naturally tend toward these group sizes. Referred to as the "twelve-adult group," it is considered biologically ideal—for it is small enough to curb population overgrowth and stave off epidemics of contagious disease, but is able to interact with a larger tribe to prevent inbreeding. Anthropologists theorize that the twelve-adult group probably evolved from Pleistocene living, for the group is the right size to make a meal from the Paleo-Indian food of choice. In such a group, there would be enough mature males to stalk and kill the mammoth, and a few other hardy individuals would be ready to defend the carcass from scavengers, butcher the meat, and transport the food and skin back to camp. Throughout the process, a few adults would remain free to watch after and care for the band's young.[2]

So ancient and universal are these band sizes that deep ecologist Paul Shepard asserts that they also satisfy optimal human psychological requirements. Within such a group, the individual is able to bond with every other member in some meaningful way. Larger groups, he surmises, tend to fragment, or develop cliques that ostracize others.[3]

Shepard also points out that modern-day hunting cultures who adhere to the twelve-adult group size and have access to adequate food supplies display a distinct lack of anxiety—especially when compared with the cultures in industrialized, urbanized areas. Where meat is abundant, this relaxed state is believed to stem from having no reason to worry about the future—and the extreme rarity of famine, malnutrition, and stress-related disease in these groups seems to support this theory.[4] In other words, the hunting life is a healthy one, gratifying both psychically and physically, and has inherent in it an in-the-moment quality that is lacking in farming, ranching, and corporate desk jobs—jobs that depend upon the unknowns of the future for their production of sustenance.

Movement. Meat. Tribe. It all made sense to me. And then there is my primal pull toward the lion man—the fact that he too satisfies my optimal biological and psychological requirements. This is why I eventually concede to the bathtub in my yard.

MY FATHER WAS a lonely man. After my mother, he never found himself a real companion—not the kind that shared his love of the outdoors, anyway—just a few temporaries who were willing to sit next to him at the bar. There were possibilities, but his sober self would not allow for the kind of abandon that love demands. In this sense, he fit in with the rest of Utah: even though his repressions may not have been rooted in religion, something in him rejected such passion as an impropriety.

What he lacked in an intimate partnership, he made up for with his hunting buddies. They were men he had known all his life—other Gentiles with whom he went out into the field, with whom he returned to feast. This tightly knit group filled the rows at my father's memorial service; in tribute, one especially old and dear friend even wore camouflage. Never have I seen men so heartbroken, so sorrowful. For all the empty places in my father's life, at least he had this brotherhood—a group with whom he had shared the most basic parts of himself.

For the service, we had ordered fifty chairs. But when the day arrived, the arboretum at Red Butte Garden was standing room only. It seemed that half of Salt Lake City—Mormon and Gentile alike—had turned out to pay tribute.

The day spilled shapeless and gray into the Salt Lake Valley. The lake and the Great Basin beyond were veiled in dense, low clouds. I remember one man who stood apart from his other friends—the orthodontist who had straightened my teeth in adolescence. When he greeted me, I called him by the wrong name. He stood there in a rather over-the-top full-length overcoat, camel or cashmere, and took offense. I didn't care. He had been merciless in his efforts, and still my teeth ended up as crooked as an old picket fence. And he was a man who had mounted big African animals all over his office—garish displays that had nothing to do with nourishment. While he hammered the metal bands down into my gums, he would brag about his conquests to my father, who sat beside me, unimpressed. He was not a trophy hunter, and, other than a pair of moose antlers over the fireplace in the family room, he didn't show off his kills.

I remember looking at him from the patient's reclining chair. When he took me to those appointments, it was about the only time I saw my father anymore.

MY AUNT MARIE, who is married to my father's younger brother Bob, began the service by reading the obituary she had written for the *Salt Lake Tribune*. As family historian, such tasks fall to her. In the details she mentioned about my father's daughters, my job as a wilderness advocate wasn't mentioned; it wouldn't have been right to highlight work that my father so vigorously opposed. On more than one occasion, he had said that the "outfit" I worked for was *nothing but a bunch of long-haired, wild-eyed critters*. It didn't matter that he loved the wild places we were seeking to protect; it was more that tree-huggers were too passionate. Their displays of ardor and defiance offended his genteel sensibilities.

Two guitarists played a Sons of the Pioneers song—one of my father's favorites.

> *All day I face the barren waste*
> *Without the taste of water, cool water . . .*
> *Old Dan and I with throats burned dry*
> *And souls that cry for water, cool, clear water . . .*[5]

I COULDN'T HELP him. There were almost daily rescue attempts as a child, even after he was out of the house. Later, between classes at the University of Utah and two jobs, I spent every day for a month in Bountiful, north of Salt Lake City, where my father was in rehab for the first time.

He was there not because he finally saw his problem, but because the Irvines had threatened financial retribution. His parents, Ada and Lee, were tired of paying his way, especially after he let the family lumber company sink into Chapter Eleven. At the rehab center, I sat next to him through the family sessions that took place every other afternoon. After the third meeting, we stood alone at a window in the center's great room, watching the sun set over the marshes of the Great Salt Lake. I knew it was killing him to be behind that glass, away from the wetlands across the valley.

I had to turn away from him—the hard bulb of his nose, its sprawl of blown-out veins exaggerated in the amber light that streamed through the pane. That morning, he had received a physical. His gastrointestinal tract was corroded beyond repair. The doctor had given him only a few years to live—even if he stopped drinking.

My father waved away the prognosis like it was a mosquito.

"Did you hear all those poor folks in those meetings today, Amos? Boy, talk about a lack of class, gushing in front of everyone like that. So sad it's almost funny."

As he said it, he held his chin up high. Then he snorted, lightly, a subtle expression of his social snobbery and denial. But then he laughed. It was a deep belly laugh, a sound with plenty of life in it. It had given me hope. If he can just get out there and hunt, I thought, he'll be all right.

> *The nights are cool and I'm a fool*
> *Each star's a pool of water, cool water . . .* [6]

After he was released from rehab, I took time off from my job and lived on savings so I could be with him. It was summer, and I was out of school. There were dinners to cook, an apartment to clean, and nights to fill with Woody Allen movies. Anything to help him stay sober. But he wouldn't attend the AA meetings, which the rehab center had insisted were critical. He said that he thought the Twelve Steps were hocus-pocus, that he couldn't relate to all those Jesus freaks, putting their fate in the hands of God.

He began to drink again. At two o'clock in the afternoon, I'd stand beneath his apartment window and throw pebbles, trying to rouse him from bed. The tiny stones would peck at the glass like sparrows' beaks. I'd finally resort to lobbing fist-size rocks that nearly shattered the window. Not once did he even part the curtains.

> *The shadows sway and seem to say*
> *Tonight we pray for water, cool water . . .*[7]

After the service, there was a gathering at the home of my father's second-youngest brother, Bruce. All of my father's friends were there—some still drunks, some finally sober. They knew that he and I had not spoken for eight years, and I could see that they wondered about that. But we had all abandoned him in one way or another, for these devoted friends—men who in the brush had watched each other's backs, who in late-season hunts had nearly frozen to death but had instead managed to keep each other warm— had let my father drive home sideways from their parties.

A few days later, my sister and I walked out onto a frozen Great Salt Lake, my father's remains in a gray cardboard box between us. The marsh around us was dormant, its muddy mires solid for a time. Dead cattails rattled in the wind like skeletons. Ice crystals straddled beams of winter sun, hip-slung low in the January sky.

Paige opened the box, and we peered in. Black-and-blue ashes specked with white bits of bone.

It was all we had left of him. Together our hands plunged into the dry cinders, and for once he didn't slip between our fingers. Instead, this desiccated version of our father clung to our skin. A bald eagle circled overhead, just out of arm's reach, as we flung our father into the salt-kissed wind.

> *And way up there He'll hear our prayer*
> *And show us where there's water, cool, clear water . . .*[8]

The wind was blowing from the north, headed directly toward the Colorado Plateau. As the ash was carried away on its current, something in me broke loose and followed.

4

Ambush

HEY ARE THERE when I emerge from the woods. Parked up the street from my house, they sit in a faded brown sedan. Waiting. Watching.

It is a Saturday in early September, the most pleasant month yet on Monticello's high desert plateau. The Superfund site has been cleaned up, although one of the men in the trailer park told me, from across the fence as he loaded his belongings, that the soil around town was still hotter than hell. About the only other local news is the golf-course expansion. Nine holes will soon become eighteen, with funds received from the federal Environmental Protection Agency for cleaning up the uranium tailings.

I have made it through the rest of the summer by keeping mostly to myself—my only discomfort caused by an article in the *San Juan Record* announcing that Herb McHarg had moved to town and opened a field office for SUWA. The article in no way had a welcoming tone, and it made me feel like a bull's-eye had been painted on my front door. It didn't help that Herb would spend his lunch hour in the front yard, wearing nothing but a blue sarong he had brought back from Mexico, waving at the ranchers as they drove past.

Days that aren't spent writing are spent down in the canyons; Herb's and my appetite for exploring them has become insatiable. And there are walks in the woodlands beyond the golf course—a midmorning ritual on which both my dog and I have come to depend. We have found a favorite route—it circumvents the cows and takes us through a tangle of the oak brush to a small creek flanked by curmudgeonly cottonwoods. From there we scale a rocky, south-facing hillside sparsely speckled with yucca and prickly-pear cactus; higher still, we finally enter towering groves of ponderosa pine and aspen.

The route is a bit contrived, but the reward is in not crossing a single dirt road or dirt-bike track. The grasses and flowers are thick. There are more birds. On a variety of occasions we have observed elk, coyote, kit fox, rattlesnake. And we have spied the tracks of black bears and mountain lions. On those mornings, Pablo's ears perk and his nose quivers. On those mornings, we tend to walk with our wits about us.

But nothing we have seen in these foothills alarms me like the sight of the car.

I RE-ENTER the neighborhood through an empty lot next to Trent and Charity's former home. Its curtains are drawn and the garage is padlocked—not a lawn chair or toy anywhere. It is not the empty look of the house that is unnerving, but the fact that nearly every house on the block appears just as lifeless. Sure, there are a few other vacant residences—unable to be sold or rented because of the flaccid local economy—but most houses in Monticello are occupied by large Mormon families. That should mean children playing in the yards, chasing balls into the streets. That should mean mothers pushing their infants in strollers. But I only really ever see the men of the neighborhood. They cut the grass or change the oil in their pickups, and then disappear back inside their homes.

There is a park in the middle of the circle drive that forms our street. It has an enticing playground, covered picnic tables, and lots of tall trees. And there is an enormous lawn, which the city waters at midday—no matter how hot or windy it is. The playground is a stone's toss from my house, and in a two- or three-week period, I see one, maybe two families out there. Usually they are Navajo or Ute Indians. Maybe they live in town, but I'm betting they have driven up from the reservations, which are the most dusty and barren lands in all the county.

Today, though, the place is empty. There is only the sedan, and the two young men that sit in it. As I cross the road, the car begins to creep toward me. My heart quickens. If I can avoid eye contact, if I can make it to my house before they get out of the car, perhaps they'll go away. My knee nearly brushes their chrome bumper as they pull up in front of me, but I am already up on the curb, crossing my yard, dog on my heels. The car doors open as I round the corner to the side porch. I propel myself through the door into the kitchen, breathless and sweating.

There had been a brief glimpse of white shirts. The dark, plain neckties. In Salt Lake, the missionaries appeared on the doorstep of every house I ever lived in—from the crowded cabin of ski bums at the mouth of Little Cottonwood Canyon to the brick bungalow I had owned with my former husband. In fact, the missionaries found me everywhere—even during a brief stint in New York, even during a winter working in the French Alps.

It's always been like clockwork. They show up before I even have my belongings unpacked. So I am not surprised at their appearance, only that it took them so long to find me. Not that they are always looking for me specifically; sometimes it's a random visit because they notice there's someone new in town. It will turn out that this visit is a chance one—but the one after this will be intentional. It will come after I read some of my writing on public radio. The very next day, the Church will call my grandpa Blaisdell and ask for my new address.

The car surprises me. It is tempting to chalk up the missionaries' use of it to the vast and remote nature of San Juan County—a place where people are few and far between, where both weather and topography are often extreme. But in every other state or country I have ever visited, the missionaries were always seen on foot or bicycle—crossing other rugged landscapes, in every kind of weather imaginable. I had always assumed that these two muscle-powered forms of transportation were the only ones approved by the Church, but one day I overheard a man in the Monticello BLM office telling the staff that there was no need for more trails in the county, it was more roads that were needed.

"Only tree-huggers hike and ride bicycles," he said.

Later, a glowering rancher will make precisely this same assumption about me, and mockingly swerve his pickup at my bike—just on principle. Then I will figure that if Church policy hasn't changed perhaps the boys—with permission from their mission president, of course—decided they needed a special course of action for San Juan County. In other words, they figured out pretty fast that in Hole-in-the-Rock territory you're more warmly received if you stick to some method of movement that devours fossil fuels.

SERVING ON a two-year mission is part of how young Mormon men come to obtain the full power of the priesthood, which gives them an almost literal authority to act in God's name. The priesthood sanctions them to preach the Book of Mormon and to convert Gentiles to Mormonism. It also gives them the gift of revelation and the ability to bless and heal by the laying on of hands.

More than anything, this priesthood authority is what Mormon men seek. The more stature one gains in executing God's will, the better chance one has of making it to the highest level of heaven, the celestial kingdom. It is at this highest level that men themselves are exalted to godhood. They believe that God too started out as a human—blemished with imperfections and weaknesses, which were overcome through faith and perseverance. As one former Church president said, "As God once was, man is. As God is, man may become."[1]

Going on a mission helps to prepare you for deification. You get in good with God by bringing others into the fold, so young men aspire their whole lives. They sing "I Hope They Call Me on a Mission." They save their money to pay for their suits, and for two years' worth of travel and living expenses. And so, with the ink barely dry on their high-school diplomas, young Mormon men who have been ordained into the lower level of the priesthood are sent to one of sixteen Missionary Training Centers around the world. At the MTC, those who will be sent to non–English-speaking nations receive eight weeks of what is mostly language training. Those going to English-speaking destinations receive only two to three weeks of basic orientation. Then they are sent out into the world as laymen preachers. They may be gods-in-training, but they are by no means professional clergymen.

In 2002, there were some sixty-five thousand Mormon missionaries out in the world—the overwhelming majority of them male.[2] They leave the MTC in assigned pairs, to participate for twenty-four months at one of the 330 missions around the globe. During that time, each pair of missionaries—*companions*, they are called—must be together at all times. Apparently this constant companionship acts as a buffer for temptations—especially those of a sexual nature. The problem with the arrangement, according to many of my male friends and acquaintances who served missions, is that boys at that age are just coursing with hormones. And though this is only anecdotal evidence—indeed, there's a good chance that perhaps I tend toward the more unruly of the returned-missionary pool—I am surprised how many of them resorted to sexual contact, if only the swapping of hand jobs, with their companion.

Physically intimate or not, the companions go door to door in search of receptive ears. Whenever a pair is detected, they are filled with LDS doctrine, which is based on a set of golden plates given by the Angel Moroni to Joseph Smith in 1823. Smith translated their hieroglyphics with a pair of stones that he swore explained to him what the strange symbols meant. He then preached that their teachings surpassed even the Holy Bible as "the most correct of any book on earth." He swore that man "would get nearer to God by abiding by its precepts than by any other book."[3] He began to preach that Gentiles—including any and all Christians other than Mormons— "belongeth to that great church . . . which is the mother of abominations, whose founder is the devil . . . and [that church] is the whore of all the earth."[4] The prophet's vitriolic message and the method by which it is delivered were obviously persuasive: in 1830, Joseph Smith established his church with only fifty members; just a few years into the twenty-first century, the Church boasts almost twelve million members worldwide.[5]

For Mormons, aside from seeking godhood and converting others to Mormonism, producing a family and ensuring that family's solidarity throughout eternity are paramount to all other goals in life. What this means in practical terms is that Mormon girls aren't pressured to serve on a mission. Their main concern, even now, is preparing themselves for marriage, homemaking, and motherhood; their main goal is to make earth suits for the souls who are waiting to inhabit the planet. This means that for LDS women college is also quite optional. Brigham Young University in Provo, south of Salt Lake City, is where most Mormons hope to be accepted, and for young Mormon women, time spent on campus is largely about finding and securing their future husbands. The men they meet there are those who have already served their mission and are seeking an education largely as a means to enhance their ability to provide for their future family. Other higher-learning ideals—such as liberal thought and free speech—aren't so important. To give just one example: when the famous bronze sculptures of Rodin visited the campus, the administration excised the artist's magnificent nudes from the exhibit without any real campus protest.

AS A CHILD, I dreamed of going on a mission, despite the fact that in the 1970s even fewer women went on them. I really had no concept then of what a mission would involve; I simply liked the idea of traveling to some exotic and foreign place and mingling with people unlike those who surrounded me in Utah, one of the most homogeneous states in the nation. My vision did not entail the drab garb of missionaries, nor did it require the tedious work of proselytizing. Instead, I envisioned a journey to the South Pacific, where I would don a grass skirt and fragrant tropical flowers. I would sleep in a thatched hut at night, and during the day the small tribe of island people would include me in their social interludes as well as their chores. Also in my vision were mangoes and fresh fish, and dancing in firelight to drums, wearing nothing but painted symbols on my face.

The part about serving a mission in the South Pacific wouldn't have been a stretch. Mormons thoroughly infiltrated there long ago—converting islanders by the hundreds of thousands, especially in Tonga and Samoa. The part that was problematic was something I clearly couldn't grasp: that the idea was not to convert oneself into a native but, rather, to convert the natives to Mormonism. Still, they did just fine without me. As early as 1845, the Church presidency sent out a proclamation to the "rulers of the world" announcing its intent to "reduce all nations and creeds to one political and religious standard."[6] It wasn't just talk. Today, of the twelve million members the Church claims, almost half live in 164 countries outside the United States.[7]

Long before the Saints shipped off their men to convert the indigenous peoples of the world, the Mormon Church was busy at home, baptizing the Native Americans. These people, regardless of distinct differences between tribes, were "about to be gathered, civilized, and made one nation in this glorious land."[8] For they had a role to play in Christ's second appearance, and a rather bloody role at that. According to the Book of Mormon, during the last days on earth the Indians will "act as a young lion among the flocks of sheep." The herds were to be culled of unrepentant Gentiles, "who, if [the lion] go through and through, both treadeth down and teareth in pieces."[9] Apparently the already established Saints didn't want their own white hands sullied in the process of reckoning.

But in 1849, many of the Indians of Deseret had demonstrated that they had no desire to cooperate with Brother Brigham's plan, and continued to raid settlers and rustle cattle. Finally, the Church leader was forced to announce that the Indians of the present were too savage to be civilized, let alone converted. His backup plan called for the Saints to take Indian children—many of whom were orphaned during the extermination campaigns that frustrated Mormon settlements resorted to—and raise them in their homes as Mormons. Later, Young counseled, the young Mormon men would marry Indian women of the new era, who, over the generations, would produce increasingly light-skinned, better-behaved children. The plan brought the Church one enormous step closer to their goal of creating the "white and delightsome people" that had been prophesied.

As late as 1990, the Church also operated the LDS Placement Program, which relocated Indian children into Mormon foster families under the pretense of offering them accessibility to a better education—for the best schools and social services were in white communities, not on reservations. Though the program was touted as being strictly voluntary, there was a catch: in exchange for their participation, the children were to become members of the LDS faith.[10] Although the program is now defunct, there remains an informal tradition among Mormons of providing foster homes to Native American children.

I learned just how alive and well this tradition was from a Ute woman named Nora, whom I met at the Laundromat not long before the missionaries showed up. She was round-faced and wide-hipped, with shiny black hair that reached the sway of her back.

She was quiet but noticeable, thanks to a persistent cough and dishpan hands as cracked as an old sidewalk. She lived on the White Mesa Reservation, just south of Blanding, but commuted to Monticello, where she worked as a housekeeper at a motel. On the short break between her double shifts, she often came to the Laundromat to do her family's wash. We got to talking because she abruptly pointed to my stacks of folded laundry and said, "You must have a lot of kids to be washing so many clothes."

I confessed that the clothes belonged only to my boyfriend and me. Shaking her head in disbelief, she pointed to her own piles—one-fourth the size of mine.

"These belong to seven kids, plus me an' my husband," she said.

"Wow," I replied. "You have seven children?"

The woman shook her head. "I have ten. Three are in foster care, 'cause I couldn't manage them. Church was nice enough to help me get them situated with families up in Green River."

I asked how often she got to see them, and if they maintained Ute traditions or language. She said that she saw them every few months, but that no one from the Rez did anything that traditional anymore. "Everyone goes to the Mormon Church now. If you don't, you're kind of looked down upon."

She seemed to scoff a bit as she said this, so I pried further. "Do you believe in the writings of the Church?"

"Oh, you know," she sighed, tossing her waterfall of hair back off her shoulders, "it's nice, because they give us lots of assistance and they plan lots of social events—which keeps the kids out of trouble. And they have helped some of my people stop drinking. But do I believe the teachings? Hmmm."

She looked out the window, at Highway 666. The more righteous locals have petitioned to renumber the highway; they say the road is cursed by its diabolical name.

I don't know why I felt so bold, but then I asked her if she prayed to the Heavenly Father—the Mormon name for God.

"Oh no. For the serious stuff, like when one of my children is sick or my ol' man is beatin' on me, I go to the medicine man. Problem is, there is only one left. No young person working as an apprentice, learning the old ways or the words. Huh, I can barely remember them myself."

She continued to stare out the window. Trucks thundered by and rattled the building's cheap windows. She stayed like that, transfixed by the world outside. She looked exhausted as she finally turned and pulled her last load from the dryer.

"When our medicine men are gone, we will no longer be Ute."

She picked up her baskets of clothes and headed for the door. My mouth hung open like a half-moon. I wanted to say more, to maintain some thread of connection, but everything I could think of sounded either contrived or patronizing.

She spared me by turning around and pointing to my piles of clothes.

"If someday you find you don't need all that, my older girls are 'bout your size."

Nodding, I scribbled my number on a piece of paper and handed it to her. "Please. Call me."

It was the first time I had given my number to a local.

THE MISSIONARIES ARE NOT yet to the front step when I launch through the side door and into the kitchen. Herb is standing at the counter, brewing a stiff pot of coffee. He has just pulled an all-nighter, writing until dawn in legalese. He is trying to stop a coal mine up near Price, where some of Nora's kids live—one that would drain the groundwater from an area we have proposed for wilderness. With one hand he pours a cup; in the other, he holds a red pen. The document he has spent hours writing is spread out in front of him, the red ink superimposed on the black type. He is so busy editing that he doesn't notice my staccato breath, my tense stance. He doesn't even notice that he has overfilled the mug, and that a dark, shapeless mass of coffee is creeping across the counter toward his papers.

Document. Coffee. Pen. Still, he looks nothing like a lawyer. He wears only his sarong. Long wayward curls spring every which way from his head. His eyeglasses are held together with frayed strands of duct tape. When the doorbell rings, he yanks his paper from the counter just in time, then jumps up and down like a schoolboy. He has a good feeling about this, he says. Whoever they are on the other side of that door, he is certain they will be our new friends. And before I can explain to him that I already know who is calling, before I can ask him not to answer, Herb has thrown the door wide open. He grins, almost madly. Then, above my protests, he bellows a warm welcome and gestures for the missionaries to come inside.

I race to the door, to block their entry. But they haven't moved. They are frozen in place, gawking at Herb. In all of their preaching to San Juan County, they haven't encountered anyone else quite like him. Sure, there are a few long-haired river-runners down in Bluff—men who guide commercial float trips down the San Juan—but they are never home to answer the calls of missionaries. And there are the Indians, but, other than a few of the Navajo's "velvet grandmothers," these days they dress like everyone else.

I push Herb aside and puff myself up, trying to fill the doorway with my body. It is a ridiculously defensive stance, especially for such a small woman. It is a stance not unlike the one my father had me practice as a young girl—just in case I came face-to-face with a mountain lion.

Stand your ground, Amos. Try to look as large as possible. Never turn and run, or you'll look like prey.

Now it is Herb's turn to gawk—first at my bizarre body language, then at the missionaries. They are dressed in pressed black polyester pants that gleam in the sun like magpie tails. Sweat pools on the seams of their white oxford shirts, and their short hair reveals the last traces of teen acne on their necks and foreheads. They introduce themselves as Elder Stevens and Elder Sorensen.

Elders. A title that conveys a stature far beyond their postpubescence.

I REMEMBER the day I learned just how much clout the priesthood carried—and how little access I had to it. I was only ten years old—my parents barely divorced, and me newly baptized. The older girls in the neighborhood were gathered at the Robertses' house, talking about the future. Whom they would marry. What their wedding gowns would look like, and how they would decorate their homes. And, of course, how many children they would bear. Holly Roberts, who was my age and the little sister of one of the older girls, had invited me to eavesdrop on their conversation.

That day, I learned more about the celestial kingdom. I discovered that one earned entry in degrees, and that at its highest level there were roads, and they were paved and glittering with gold. But in order to get to that highest level of heaven, I learned, not only must I be married, but the marriage must have taken place in a Mormon temple, to a man who had been ordained into the priesthood. I remember how the girls described the temple ceremony in hushed tones, how I leaned in and strained to hear every word. I knew enough to know that Mormon temple rites are not a subject for discussion—in fact, those who participate in the rituals are sworn to a certain secrecy that was reinforced, until 1990, by having them perform the gesture of slitting their own throat.

That day, I learned that during the temple marriage the husband and wife were each given a secret name. The man's name—the woman would never know it. But the woman's name would be told to her husband. As far as I could tell, when you got to the celestial kingdom, you uttered your name like a password, for identification. God alone would recognize and determine the man's heavenly eligibility. The woman would receive confirmation and judgment not only from God but from her spouse too.

I felt ever so confused. In order for me to get into heaven, must my husband die before me? What if I died first—did I just float around in the atmosphere until he passed on? And what if I never married? Or got divorced or widowed?

The neighborhood girls talked about being pulled through a veil. I guess, once I uttered my secret name and my husband accepted it, God would allow the hard wall that separated this world from the next to turn ephemeral. I would extend my hand through the billowing gauze, and my husband would have the power to pull me to the other side. During the course of this conversation, I also realized that, upon my arrival—no matter how good I had been on earth—I would not be receiving my own planet to rule. My role for all time and eternity would be as—and I winced when the girls said the word—a *helpmeet*. Apparently my husband would need someone to act as a personal assistant while he attended to the lofty business of exercising dominion over an entire world.

These details came as quite a shock. I had thought it was enough to get baptized—and that event had already caused me enough distress. But I was a child of God, and I figured that the prescribed scenario was still better than burning in hell. At that time, I hadn't learned that Mormons don't really believe in an underworld; I only knew that my grandma Blaisdell was always clucking her tongue at me and saying that, given all my bad behavior, I'd "go straight to hell in a handbasket." Only later would I learn that, in Mormon doctrine, there isn't really a hell. Only a few really bad seeds will ever be condemned to a Mormon version of Outer Darkness, where they would be known as Sons of Perdition. The rest of us are divided up among three levels of heaven: The ultimate level, the celestial kingdom, is the ultimate glory and is reserved for the devout, temple-certified Saints. The middle level, the terrestrial kingdom, is for Mormons and Gentiles alike—those who lead decent lives but aren't valiant in their churchgoing. The telestial kingdom is for those who haven't lived too well. It involves a period of suffering as penalty for sins committed, but then apparently allows for a quality of life beyond what we can imagine. At the time, I didn't know anything about the levels and all their requirements, but if I had, things might have been easier. For the terrestrial kingdom—given its name—sounded a whole lot like living on earth. And if it had trees and birds and rivers, that was good enough for me.

But I didn't yet possess this important knowledge. So, then and there, in the Robertses' family room, I resigned myself to my fate. In seconds, my dreams of the South Pacific dissolved. What's more, I would no longer play in the field behind our home. From then on, I resolved to stay indoors. And in our basement, where no sunlight fell, I would play House. I would dutifully wash and feed and dress my baby dolls. I would put them in their cradles, and cook supper for the imaginary husband, the provider and holder of the priesthood who held the key to my salvation.

I began losing sleep. I had always believed that God was listening to my prayers, but I began to fear that He was ignoring me until I found a husband with direct access. From beneath my pink gingham quilt, I whispered into the night and waited for a divine response. None ever came that I could hear.

I was afraid to confide in another Mormon, for fear that I'd be pegged as a fraud. After all, I had worked so hard to fit in; besides, a real Mormon understood almost inherently how things work with God, and so would never question these things. In fact, a real Mormon would never really question anything at all.

In desperation, I turned to my father. I hadn't yet told him I'd been baptized. He and the other Irvine men had returned from the opening day of duck season, and in Ada and Lee's garage, they sat huddled over buckets of liquefied wax, bubbling hot on Coleman stoves. I dunked the birds for my father; then, together, we stripped the feathers. Next he gutted them, setting aside the giblets for gravy. The dogs, wet and tired from romping in the mud and the retrieval of birds, halfheartedly begged for scraps from their repose on the concrete floor.

After one or two drinks, my father was easy to talk to, easier than when he was sober, when social proprieties kept him tight-lipped and emotionally disengaged. And easier than later, when he'd imbibed so much that he made no sense at all and his affections got too desperate. So I timed his cocktails, and halfway through the second one, I whispered to him what I had learned about my fate.

He chuckled gently, shaking his head in disbelief.

"Amos, you can talk to God any old time you want," he said.

He pointed a waxy finger toward the lake, where he had spent the day. Then he pointed east, to the Wasatch Mountains. And then south, to the desert.

"Out there, you and God can talk just fine. And without any silly password. And, besides, who cares about golden streets? Because, my dear . . ."

He leaned over and winked at me, again pointing toward the marsh on the lake.

". . . that out there is heaven."

ELDER SORENSEN IS tall, and he knows his height has a powerful effect. He wastes no time asking if I'd like to hear about the Book of Mormon. I tell him that I know enough about it, that I had been raised a Mormon of sorts.

"So you'll be attending the ward?" It was more a statement of expectation than a question. His tone riles me.

"No, I will not," I reply—emphatically. Behind me I hear Herb's sigh as he retreats to the kitchen for more coffee. He had hoped this visit would be more fun—a diversion from our rather solitary life. *Our.* By now, Herb's things have filled up my closets, my drawers, my garage. His phone in Moab is disconnected. Apparently he has decided to move in.

Elder Sorensen steps right up to the threshold. We are standing toe to toe, with only a piece of wood between our feet. He looks down at me, smiles. I think of a fox who is about to enter the henhouse. This encroachment would not be happening, I am sure, if Herb were still standing there.

"Have you had a falling out with the Church?" He asks this a bit too knowingly.

I make the fatal error of shaking my head with vigor. This betrays my intense emotions, and the boy, emboldened, presses further. Was I angry with the Church? With God? Did I not realize that this was the *one, true Church?*

I should be laughing at his presumptuousness. Instead, I am trembling. So many men for whom I have deep love and admiration—my grandpa Blaisdell, his sons and brothers, the neighbor who baptized me—they all held the priesthood. They were men who at one time or another laid their hands on my head and administered comfort, or cure. And here is this pimple-faced young man. He could place his hands on me too. He would one day pull his wife through the veil, and rule a planet as a god. And he is half my age.

I am trapped. About to be waylaid by all the fears that keep me acting more tame and well behaved than I really am. That keep me acting like the good Mormon girl I am not.

Elder Stevens, who is my height, detects my instability and opens his mouth to smooth things over, but Elder Sorensen raises his hand to indicate that he has the situation under control.

"You seem to have quite of bit of anger, ma'am. Perhaps we could help you with that. You know the Holy Spirit is here for all of us . . ."

ONE SATURDAY, my father talked my mother into letting me skip a church event. And, given her own "Jack" status and ambivalence, it didn't take much to persuade her. He took me to the Museum of Natural History, on the University of Utah campus. There we both fell for a certain exhibit, a diorama that depicted Utah during the Pleistocene era.

I went to see it the week after my father died. The diorama was still there—faded but intact. It portrayed my father's favorite kind of place: A wet marshland cups a muddy pool of water. Migratory birds of every color decorate the grasses like ornaments on a Christmas tree, and ducks scoot in and out of the reeds. Swollen storm clouds hang precariously from the painted backdrop, above a horizon of mountains that adumbrate like somber priests in dark robes.

Peering into the diorama was no static matter. The scene freeze-frames a herd of woolly mammoths drinking at the water's edge, but hunters have sprung from the bog—their bare, lean muscles flexed and rippling. Spears are poised, and aimed.

Vital organs: Heart. Lung. Kidney. The targeted beast rears back, the whites of its eyes rolling in surprise. The other mammoths scramble to escape the ambush. Each spearhead, a long fluted Clovis point—the earliest handmade tool known to exist in the Great Basin or on the Colorado Plateau—pierces the immense, shaggy coat.

Blood streams from the creature's neck and sides, swirls vibrantly red in the mud and water.

The diorama scene could have taken place in San Juan County. On a long red prow of land above the San Juan River, west of Bluff, Paleo-Indians left behind the faint remains of a campsite used exclusively for mammoth-hunts. The site is perhaps ten thousand years old—from a time before Anasazi cultures, which we compare with the mammoth-hunters and say were "more advanced," or "less primitive." We say this because of the elaborate goods they left behind, the agriculture and architecture they achieved. But to me, when I stare into the diorama, the Clovis point—a weapon of such slight proportion and simplicity relative to the creature it killed— seems highly sophisticated. After all, I knew what it took for my father to bring down a bull elk.

Terrestrial kingdom: Tribe. Meat. Movement. I am my father's daughter, and such things sounded like heaven.

THE MISSIONARIES STAND before me, poised to pierce the most vulnerable parts of my psyche. But I am back in front of the diorama, my father standing behind me. In the reflection of the exhibit's glass, I hunt for the details of his face.

His expression is intense. Peering into prehistory, he confronts the origins of his own nature. I can almost hear his lips smacking in anticipation as he imagines the group stalking its prey—then the kill, the butchery, the carcass roasting over open flames. And then the meat sizzles on his tongue, and I can see how he grins, feral and barely restrained.

I stand up straighter still, look the tall missionary squarely in the eye. Thoughts of what I'd like to say rush through my veins.

Oh yeah, Missionary Man? Have you ever loved someone so ravenously that every social contract by which you have lived is broken? Have you ever been required to touch the dead—to reach into the gaping hole where a heart once resided and contemplate your own complicity? Have you ever cared about anything on this earth, other than getting the hell out of here and cashing in on your own sweet salvation?

Who knows how long I stood like that, muscles clenched, nearly panting with adrenaline. But Elder Sorensen waits me out. When my breathing slows, he smiles. It's almost a smirk—like he's got me where he wants me.

"Do you mind if we come in?" He steps forward before the words are even out of his mouth.

The elders want in. The power of the priesthood is most effective inside—between the walls—where domesticity tames even the most wild of beasts.

But I want out. Into the woods. Into the desert.

Into heaven.

I am my father's daughter. I still possess a few instincts. And, despite everything I have been taught, despite the way the shadow of the Church can still cow me, I ultimately know how to save my hide. When they are gone, I will get on my bicycle and pedal out of town, by way of some obscure old county road that will drop me down into redrock country. When I get there, I will stash the bike in the sagebrush and walk out across the slickrock, that sleek scarlet stone that sparkles like rubies beneath my feet.

I know that the missionaries will report back to the mission president, or perhaps the local stake president. They will tell him how difficult I was. Soon the whole town will know, and my reputation as an outsider will be sealed. Not my ancestry, not the proximity of my post-office box, not my intimate knowledge of the landscape—nothing will lend legitimacy to my residency.

It comes down to this: I didn't come to town through a certain slot above the river. I can't be brought back into the fold. And my role is that of a desert defender, not a Saint bent on beckoning the

Last Days. These things, I can feel already, will ensure that my claims to this land are seen as conditional, and forever suspect.

I am marked by the sign of the beast. And for this, I don't know if I should blame God or thank my father.

"Come back and preach at me," I bellow, "when you've made love—to someone other than each other. When you've seen death. When you've walked—not driven—across the desert."

I close the door on their pink and earnest faces.

PART II

❧ ARCHAIC ❧

5

Extinction

O CTOBER. The plateau holds up the town like an offering to the deep-blue autumn sky. The sun comes at an angle now, casting light in gold coins. From my front yard, I can see the stands of oak beyond the neighborhood, their leaves blushing like the skins of pumpkin and pomegranate. The colors of flesh. The colors of the warm stone desert below town.

My former husband pays a brief visit. He is passing through, on his way to a professional engagement. He steps into my crooked blue house, takes scrutinous inventory: A thrift-store couch matted with dog hair. Red dirt tracked across vintage shag carpet. Piles of books and dirty dishes around a perpetually glowing computer screen. His house, a glass-and-cement loft in downtown Denver, I knew would be spotless and full of designer furniture. The car he pulls up next to my old truck is a shiny new Audi. He asks where the nearest sushi bar is. My reply is, Over three hours away, in Colorado. He cocks his head and grins. It is a warm, forgiving grin—the expression of a good man who doesn't hold grudges.

"I guess it's a good thing we're not married anymore," he replies.

Then he asks if I'm happy—now that I live a life free of convention, a life devoted to my passions. I say that I don't know, that I am not sure I've succeeded in doing so. And if I have, I say, I'm not certain whether or not I will survive them. What I don't say is that, even though Herb and I have lived together only a few months, already we are wondering if such an ardent life is compatible with everyday living. And there is a creeping sense of disillusionment. With my new lover, I had envisioned a steady rhythm of quiet romantic nights on the porch, and adventurous weekends out in the desert, but I am learning that these experiences are the exception—rare events crammed in when Herb is not needed elsewhere. I didn't realize how often his commitments would take him away: To Washington to lobby on behalf of the desert. Or to Moab for visits with a boy for whom he remains a father figure. I take his absences personally, and then grow so used to my time alone that I find it hard to welcome his returns. In response, he interprets my distance as a rejection of his big, generous self—for he is certain there is plenty to go around. A fine but distinct fissure has appeared in the ground between us, and all I can think of is my grandmother's observation: how even the smallest bit of seismic action, coupled with erosion, can annihilate the shape of things as we know them—no matter how solid they once seemed.

THE MORNING AFTER Brian's visit, Pablo and I walk up to Main Street to pick up the mail. My dog spooks easily around strangers, so I tie him to the railing outside the post office. I tell him to behave, then turn to find the door already open for me. The man standing inside the foyer can't be less than seventy years old; his face is carved and burnished by decades of desert sun and wind. Hard labor has hunched his shoulders, and he wears greasy Wranglers and a straw hat ringed with perspiration. As I pass through the door, he solemnly bows, then sweeps the air before him—ushering me inside with an air of grand chivalry. I nod thanks, and as I step into the post-office foyer, his face cracks into a wide, warm smile of yellowed teeth. Tipping his hat and hitching his thumbs into the belt loops of his jeans, the old man turns back to a conversation with two other old-timers.

I can smell them. Hay. Gasoline. Manure and leather. The scent of my grandpa Blaisdell and my uncles. An intimate scent of family and place. A scent I want to lean into and make my own.

I retrieve my mail from the box and stand at the counter to sift through the stack of envelopes. Behind me, the old man and his cronies are deep in discussion.

"Early summer, me 'n my boy got ourselves twenty-five, maybe thirty," my doorman is saying. "Lots of dens this year—even with the drought. Hooks worked best underground. Could get maybe two, even three little itty-bitty ones in one pass." He says "itty-bitty" with something that sounds like tenderness. "As for them bigger ones, the snares are workin' pretty well 'bove ground."

"That right?" The deepest of the three voices responds. "I ain't gettin' so many. Just some smaller females. And I'll be darned if some of the mothers weren't still pups themselves—the damned things reproduce faster than you can blink. Let my dogs have some fun with a few of 'em. Pulled 'em off before they ruined the ears, though."

The other two chuckle. I hear their boots prodding at the linoleum floor.

"Where you settin' most of your traps?" the third voice asks.

My doorman names a few places. They are public lands that I know well, where he has a permit to graze his cattle. They are lands where I often walk, where my dog runs ahead in search of birds.

THE BOUNTY HUNT for coyotes had been announced in the *San Juan Record* just after I moved to town. The paper explained that funding had come through from both the state and the federal government. It also quoted County Commissioner Bill Redd, who was encouraging everyone to participate: "I assume it's one of those things we ought to pay people to have fun."[1] Any private citizen could kill as many coyotes as he wanted, wherever he wanted, with nearly any means he preferred. Then, if he brought the fresh scalps, ears and all, down to the county building, he'd get a crisp twenty-dollar bill for each one.

Canis latrans. The Latin name means "barking dog," which refers to the complex vocalizations that coyote packs use to communicate among themselves and with other groups. Researchers have identified at least eleven different coyote sounds—one identifies location; another, a fresh meal. There are also calls to join a game, and to define territory. And there are yips and howls that seem to be nothing more than an expression of sheer joy—sounds so rapt and full of pleasure that biologists have failed to explain them in any objective terms. It seems that Coyote is a most playful and sensual creature, a fact Native American folklore has always appreciated. The Navajo tell stories of how Coyote takes great pleasure in the body—even its emissions. Indeed, Coyote will belch or fart with glee; he has even been known to reach around and sniff his own anus in childlike wonder. Coyote is also known for his sexual appetites, which are characterized by a distinct lack of discretion and inhibition. He has been seen parading his erection in full public view, just looking for a place to use it. So, if a man isn't paying attention, Coyote will devise a way to sleep with his wife. And once he has her on all fours, howling and panting with abandon, no man will ever again satisfy her. In one particular tale, Coyote seduces a fair Indian maiden, and in their union she becomes a powerful bear, losing all her respectable human traits in the process. She methodically tracks down her brothers and kills all but the youngest. When he realizes he cannot contain her newfound wildness, he kills and dismembers her. Her body parts are scattered across Cedar Mesa—two prominent landmarks called the

Bears Ears are part of her remains.[2] What's more, Coyote is virile—he creates offspring with many of his conquests. This is why men loathe Coyote—they fear his carnal appetites, his prolificness, the way he makes beasts out of their women.

There was a time when coyotes were tolerated by Western ranchers, back when the focus was on getting rid of bigger threats—wolves and grizzlies. The coyotes actually did the cattlemen a favor—by controlling rodents that consumed a surprising amount of forage range. But soon hundreds of thousands of cattle were being grazed, and in such a barren and arid climate, even with coyotes doing their part on the food chain, the grass wasn't rejuvenating fast enough for so many competing mouths. Ranchers grew unwilling to share precious stalks of vegetation with a single prairie dog or cottontail, and by the 1930s, a series of intensive rodent campaigns were under way. When the natural diet of coyotes all but vanished, the wild dogs grew desperate. They turned to livestock with increasing regularity. Guns that had once been trained on larger predators now had their sights set on coyotes. Across the open range, they were shot by the dozens.

The coyotes responded to this persecution with the most natural of instincts—by having more sex. Under normal circumstances, it was only the lead female in a coyote pack, the mate of the alpha male, who would reproduce. But suddenly beta females were bearing young as well. Usually coyotes bear offspring at two years of age, but in a situation as dire as this, they began to have pups much earlier. And, despite a diminishing food supply, the litters were often more than twice their normal size, and with more pups than average surviving into adulthood.[3]

Typically, Western ranchers felt nothing but antagonism for the heavy hand of government, but they heartily welcomed the new agency provided by the feds to fix their problem. After classifying the coyotes as vermin—which meant anyone could kill any coyote at any time, by virtually any method—the government allocated a disproportionately high number of tax dollars for the establishment of a new federal agency, called Animal Damage Control. Its sole purpose: to eradicate "nuisance" animals on public rangelands. Throughout the 1960s, the ADC laced thousands of pounds of meat with Compound 1080, a substance that the Environmental Protection Agency has pronounced "one of the most dangerous [toxins] known to man,"[4] deemed by one of the ADC's own bounty hunters as "the most inhumane poison ever conceived."[5] The agency also set out over a million pounds of grain poisoned with the same chemical, to taint small animals that coyotes would prey upon. And over seven million strychnine pellets were scattered across the public domain, to be consumed by coyotes and whatever else had the misfortune of eating along that particular food chain.[6]

In just one year, these poisons killed 262 domestic dogs alone.[7]

Even so, the coyotes procreated more furiously than ever. As other predator populations plummeted toward extinction at the hands of the ADC, coyote numbers rocketed and spread. Within the hundred years during which the West was won, coyotes spread into British Columbia and occupied all of Mexico. By the 1990s, they had neared the Arctic Circle and settled into Central America—at the same time saturating every one of the lower forty-eight states. Coyotes have even been spotted in the suburbs of Los Angeles, and in New York City's Central Park. And in 1999, after decades of intensive efforts to eradicate them, of the 95,000 "nuisance animals" killed by state and federal wildlife-control programs, 85,262 of those animals were still coyotes.[8]

I ONCE ASKED my grandpa Blaisdell about the prolific nature of coyotes. He and the other Malad ranchers had just pooled their money; the man who shot the most animals would get to take the pot home. He took his time answering. My grandfather was a thoughtful man who always strove to do the right thing, but he once rode out to help a cow that was calving on the open range, only to find the coyotes had eaten the calf right out of the birth canal. It's hard to take lightly that kind of encroachment on one's livelihood. Finally, he shrugged his shoulders.

"They're uncontrollable," he said. "You've just got to keep clearing 'em out. Otherwise, they band together and take over everything you got."

When he said this, I couldn't help thinking about Mormons. Despite several decades of relentless persecution by Gentiles, despite the arduous conditions they had battled to settle Deseret, the LDS religion has become the fastest-growing faith in North America— and one of the fastest-growing in the world. Indeed, its membership seems to have strengthened and swelled in the face of adversity. This means that Mormons are not some fringe group to be ignored by the rest of the nation. In *Under the Banner of Heaven: A Story of Violent Faith*, Jon Krakauer quotes a prominent sociologist who calculates that Church membership will be nearly three hundred million by the end of the twenty-first century. Krakauer also points to a Yale scholar who believes that, before the year 2100, the nation will be ungovernable "without Mormon cooperation."[9] But here's where Mormons start looking truly coyotelike in their survival skills: the burgeoning numbers of faithful are due not only to the Church's expansive missionary program, but also to its members' procreative priorities—the state of Utah alone has a birthrate that is more than 50 percent greater than the national average.[10] What's more, if you look at a map of the original coyote homeland—the territory that *Canis latrans* occupied steadily from prehistoric times until the 1850s—you'll see that it looks a whole lot like Brigham Young's original vision for the Kingdom of Deseret. At the heart of both maps are the deserts of the Great Basin and the Colorado Plateau. At around the same time, both populations expanded from there, spilling into the West Coast states. And together they trickled into western Canada and down into central Mexico—the remote reaches of original coyote territory being the same places where Brigham Young established outpost polygamist colonies when the U.S. government began to crack down on the practice—colonies that still exist today.

It seems that nothing else besides sagebrush so dominates the Western landscape as coyotes and Mormons—and that it all comes down to extraordinary procreative strategies, one of which is best explained in terms of biology, the other justified by divine revelation. And just as the alpha male in a coyote clan begins to impregnate other females in times of stress, God revealed the covenant of plural marriage, or "celestial marriage," to the original prophet, Joseph Smith, about the time the Saints were beginning to take a little heat for their odd ways. The first known liaison outside Smith's legal marriage to Emma Hale took place while the Mormons were settled in Ohio, in 1831. The object of the prophet's affections was Marinda Nancy Johnson, a fifteen-year-old whose grateful family had taken in Joseph and Emma as boarders after Joseph cured Marinda's mother's paralyzed arm. When the community discovered that the prophet had bedded the young girl, all hell broke loose. Some forty or fifty outraged men stormed the Johnson house, vowing to castrate Smith. He was lucky to have escaped with only tar and feathers.

But the scandal didn't keep the prophet's pants zipped. In 1833, the Smiths invited to their home a sixteen-year-old girl named Fanny Alger, whom Joseph married that same year. He kept the marriage a secret, even from Emma, but eventually she caught the two in a compromising position. Despite Emma's furious disapproval, Smith went on to "marry" between thirty and fifty women, many of whom were adolescents. If his proposal was refused, the prophet often responded with threats. "If you reject this message the gate [to heaven] will be closed forever against you," he said to one prospect. Another he warned that the "salvation of [her] whole family depended on it."[11]

Most of the marriages took place between 1840 and 1844, and

largely contributed to the Saints' being chased from Ohio, then Missouri, and then Nauvoo. When the prophet was finally jailed, it was because he had destroyed a printing press that was publicizing his conquests and inflaming Mormon and Gentile sentiments alike. The press belonged to William Law, a confidant of Emma's, whose wife Smith had tried to seduce. From Smith, Law demanded a public admission of his improprieties, for, unlike other major doctrines that were revealed to the prophet during that time, Smith—believing that the general congregation was not ready for yet another radical lifestyle change—kept this revelation secret from all but a selected few of the most trustworthy Saints.

My great-great-great-grandfather Egan was one of those few.

Smith's instincts were correct—for not even all of those who had been entrusted with the revelation supported his conquests, Emma included. When her arguments against polygamy fell on her husband's deaf ears, she threatened to take a plural husband. But apparently polygamy was not a two-way street. To elucidate God's plan, Smith canonized his revelation in Section 132 of the Doctrine and Covenants, the Saints' most devoutly read text. The written version has God speaking directly to Emma, calling her a handmaid who, if she did not obey Joseph, would be destroyed.

Only after Joseph Smith was murdered and Brigham Young had led the faithful to the Salt Lake Valley was the covenant of celestial marriage revealed to the rest of the brethren. Some were mortified, and hightailed it out of Deseret. But most eagerly complied. The words were barely out of Brigham's mouth before men began taking up wives—often close relatives, even minors—and planting their seeds just as fast as they could get their trousers off.

It was following the region's postwar annexation from Mexico, when the U.S. took control of Deseret and began an intense series of efforts to end polygamy, that the Church finally denounced the practice. In 1890, after tangling with the nation's military and a number of increasingly ruthless congressional actions that culminated in a seizure of the Church's assets that left it nearly destitute, the fourth Church president, Wilford Woodruff, announced his revelation that the Saints were to "refrain from contracting any marriage forbidden by the law of the land."[12]

Today, the LDS Church excommunicates polygamists and vocally condemns plural marriages, but it is curious to note that, for a long time after Woodruff's retractive manifesto, Church leaders still lived as polygamists and performed plural marriage ceremonies for others. In the twenty-first century, the doctrine of polygamy remains in sacred Mormon texts, and the celestial kingdom is still known as a place where a man may have more than one wife. Every now and then, the Utah attorney general prosecutes a polygamist man for raping a minor, or beating a spouse, but other than that, it's almost as if there's a widespread unspoken approval for such a lifestyle, for the way it justifies keeping women from doing nothing but making babies, for the way it paints for men a sanitized and pious veneer across their animal appetites. Nothing more, really, than a euphemistic license to fuck.

I GREW UP around polygamists. I went to school with them. They lived in a compound near the house I rented in college. It was a polygamist man who repaired our family's appliances—until he became one of the few to be made an example of and was shot by authorities in a standoff over the home-schooling of his children. And there are polygamists in San Juan County—passels of children and women living on large tracts of land with one man. The state doesn't recognize their marriages, so all the "single mothers" can claim public assistance. A polygamist interviewed by Jon Krakauer for *Under the Banner of Heaven* characterizes it as "the Lord's way of manipulating the system to take care of his chosen people."[13]

There are an estimated thirty thousand to one hundred thousand polygamists dwelling today within the western United States, Canada, and Mexico. On Coyote Land. On lands that were once part of the original Deseret. These are the fundamentalist Mormons, who believe that the LDS Church has gone astray, that it sold out its most holy principle to be accepted by mainstream America. It makes sense to me that the men are loath to give it up: with all those women to do the work and care for the young, with the public coffers supporting their lifestyles, most polygamist men have it made.

It's funny, though—you can't really single out the males, who dress and move in the world as most any man would. But many of the women and girls look as if they are from a previous century; their fashion sense derived from a cultish, misogynistic culture that demands extreme modesty, chasteness, and obedience in its females—for how else could so few men control so many wives? And so they wear distinct dresses—long and old-fashioned, with high collars. Their hair is swept back in colonial-style coifs, their faces are undecorated by makeup or earrings. They are raised with little education, or any other form of outside influence, and to this day they are often married to uncles and other relatives while still in their teens. It is not uncommon for them to bear between a half-dozen and a dozen offspring.

The dress and manner of mainstream Mormon women isn't much better, and, together with the wives of the polygamists, they largely made up my role models for womanhood. So pronounced and pervasive was the cultural conditioning that none of us Utahns, no matter how far we stray from the Church, ever truly escapes its effects. In my case, fortunately, there was counterinfluence: There was Ada. And there was my mother, who may have sometimes tried to get us to church on Sunday, but for the most part dressed and did as she pleased. Still, these two were anomalies in the sea of women that surrounded me—women who were celebrated for their subdued and sexless ways.

I am certain it was this kind of cultural conditioning that shaped my father's weekday compulsion toward conservative civility—as well as his view of women. When I was thirteen, he met me at school late one morning to take me to the Rotary Club luncheon at the old Salt Lake Hilton Hotel. It was an annual Valentine's Day event, for prominent Utah businessmen and their daughters. It was a weekday, which meant my father was suffering a suit, and sober. In the school parking lot, he had ranted about my brightly patterned short skirt and bare legs—and it wasn't the fact that it was winter that made him object. He marched me home and demanded that I change into something more respectable. Along the way, he grabbed my chin and tried to wipe off the fresh coat of pink lip gloss. He wanted the earrings out of my pierced ears.

Despite my nerve-racking yearning for my father's approval, despite the awkward budding of my body, I stood my ground. In the past year, I had discovered that subscribing to a faith where my eternal life was expected to consist of nothing more than the role of helpmeet was the most boring and undignified thing I could imagine. Besides, I just couldn't reconcile this father with the one who had put me on skis at four years of age and pushed me off the top of a steep, snowy hill, yelling, "Atta girl, Amos . . . let 'em run!" So I refused the prim milkmaid dress with the lace collar he had pulled from the back of my closet; I left my hair down. He didn't speak to me all the way to the hotel. I was surprised he let me go at all.

We parked, walked inside the grand ballroom. The claret carpets and waterfall chandeliers were opulent. We approached a table of white linens and china—a red rose and a small box of chocolates on each girl's plate. Around each table were men from Tracy Collins Bank, Gump and Ayers Real Estate, men whose families had descended from old Deseret. No matter that some were now Gentiles; in this setting, they all looked and acted as if they were at church. Between the men sat their daughters—up to their earlobes in pink satin and red velvet. Their dresses were long enough that you could barely see their white stockings and shiny patent-leather shoes.

Their hair was swept back with ribbons and held hostage by hand-fuls of Dippity-Do. Hands in their laps, they stared at me. I could feel my father practically vibrating with what should have been mild embarrassment but instead was disgust and fury.

Soon I knew why he had allowed me to accompany him. Another man would have left such an unruly misfit daughter at home, especially if he shared my father's obsessive albeit episodic need to submit to society—especially one as conservative as Utah's. But my father held me at arm's length, an example of the wild and unrefined, and with that gesture he distanced himself from those very elements in his own character. If he couldn't transform me, he would instead make me his scapegoat.

When he introduced me, he put me out in front of him. His fingers clutched the back of my neck as if I were a ring-necked pheasant he had just retrieved from the brush. His introduction was spat out from between pursed lips.

This is Amy, my wench.

Standing at the tip of an equilateral triangle—balanced perfectly between the Church's trajectory and my father's—I was as much at odds with them as they supposedly were with each other. It was geometric schizophrenia, and it marked an escalation in my battle to belong—as well as an increase in my sudden detours into radical rebellion.

And there in the ballroom, as those trajectories converged on me, I could see just how similar the Church and my father really were. After all, Donald Irvine was the great-great-grandson of Howard Egan, a man who had been in the know of Mormon authority, who had suffered duty at the expense of himself, who had had it explained to him long before most Mormons the true place and purpose of women.

Egan himself took three wives in total. I read somewhere that this was the minimum requirement for achieving godhood in the afterlife. My guess is he would have taken more had his transient and demanding lifestyle allowed it. Or perhaps he was humbled by the realization that women have the same appetites as men, that they too can act on their desires. Perhaps that realization helped him to see that he already had more women than he could satisfy, for in 1849, when he returned from the California gold mines where he was working on behalf of the Church, one of his wives had given birth to the child of another man.

My great-great-great-grandfather put things right by following his wife's lover's wagon train out of town. When he caught up with the man in the hills above Salt Lake, Egan shot him. Placing a hand on his own breast, Howard Egan stood before the gape-mouthed wagon company and made what sounded nothing like a remorseful confession but was, rather, a proud declaration: "Gentlemen, I have killed the seducer of my wife, and vengeance is sweet to me."[14]

His trial was heard by fellow Mormons, who understood Egan's contract with God, the earthly entitlements it provided. Within twenty-five minutes, they acquitted him.

MY FORMER HUSBAND, Brian, was also raised as a Latter-day Saint; the degree to which he was immersed is exemplified by the fact that one of his uncles was a "General Authority," or one of the Church's Twelve Apostles. I remember the uncle, a tall and imposing man who came to our wedding. For a gift he gave us a signed copy of the book he had written. It was about marriage. It told me to serve and obey my husband.

By the time we met, Brian was no longer active in the Church. I can't help wondering if that denominator was just too common and served to snuff out between us anything that resembled passion. In other words, perhaps two Jack Mormons are a confusing and stifled mix. Perhaps we need a pure Gentile for a partner, to show us life on the other side. All I know for certain is that the time came when it became clear I would have to leave my marriage.

This knowledge came on a starlit beach in Costa Rica. It was the year before my father died. The year before I moved to San Juan County. The vacation was a trying one—a last-ditch effort to ignite something in our union. One night, we paid five thousand colons for the chance to see *la tortuga baula*, the rare leatherback turtle. After a two-hour wait at a jungle-side café, we were summoned by the graveled voice of the tour operator. The *ticos* who worked for him had spotted her; their excited, staccato words fluttered like bats in the night air as we followed them through the dense, vine-wrapped trees and down to the beach. It was midnight. There was no moon. Only the tour guide's flashlight shone—its beam muted by a piece of red cloth so it couldn't be mistaken for sunlight on the horizon, the turtle's beacon to the sea.

La baula was flat on her belly. Her body was over four feet in length and weighed close to a thousand pounds. At her sides, two sets of flippers splayed out like boomerangs. Her shell was long, nearly heart-shaped, the color of onyx. We gathered around her backside, away from her line of vision. Only inches from her tail, I dropped to my knees. The soft scarlet glow of the flashlight illuminated her barnacled topography, allowed us to see how her rear flippers scooped up sand and flung it off to the sides with surprising force. Beneath her, a perfect hole the size of a shoe box began to take shape. A researcher stepped in to measure the hole's depth and width. After recording it on her clipboard, she stepped back without ever having disturbed the turtle.

Marine biologists are trying to learn what they can from the last of the leatherbacks, for very little is known about these prehistoric leftovers. Most of their lives, they inhabit such deep waters that it has been difficult to obtain information about their behavior or movement, although we know that mating is polyandrous—that multiple males mate with a single female to ensure fertilization. Their migratory routes are a mystery. The turtles dive deep and can be off the radar screen for months; some that have been outfitted with radios in Central America have shown up as far away as Japan.

The researcher who worked alongside us was a toffee-skinned Costa Rican native who stayed out all night to collect data and to guard both mothers and eggs from poachers. She showed us the tag on the turtle we were observing, and explained how they are able to identify her every few years, when she returns to lay eggs on this very same beach—one of the last remaining nesting sites for Pacific leatherbacks. She went on to describe how the rest of the sites had been taken over by development—pointing across the bay to the very villas in which we were staying.

It took *la baula* nearly another hour to complete the hole. Many of the tourists grew bored and drifted off to gaze at the surf. My husband also wandered off—but because he was uncomfortable with the spectacle made of such an intimate act. Though I knew how he felt, I was mesmerized with the way her body hugged the earth, how heavy groans cracked the thin line of her reptilian mouth. Pulses of energy shuddered across her armor, and then engorged, leathery lips strained visibly beneath her tail. A glistening pearl of an egg appeared between them and dropped into the hole with a soft thud.

Another egg dropped. And another. In the best of circumstances, only one in a thousand leatherback eggs survives to become a full-grown turtle. And those that actually endure the gauntlet to adulthood stand a good chance of being made into black-market soup, or a purse handle. But there on the beach, for that night at least, each egg was a small sphere of promise. Finally, *la baula* swept sand over them, so they would self-incubate. Her task complete, she slowly turned toward the sea. I watched her go, black fading into black.

Later that night, at the rented villa, I had two dreams like none I'd had before.

The first finds me home alone, squatting on the immaculate white tile of the kitchen floor. I deliver a beautiful rose of a child, but I am outside my body, a casual observer to the event. There is no blood. No grunts, or sweat. I scoop up the infant, take it to the closet. I stuff it in a backpack, which hangs on a hook on the back wall. The child cries; I cry too, stroke its face, whisper apologies. Shutting the closet door, I turn up the radio and hurry to prepare dinner.

In the second dream, I am wandering through a red-and-purple canyon that looks like the chambers of a heart. I meet a wild man who stalks me, pads circles in courtship. When he pounces, I taste: Damp salty flesh. Clumps of hair. Sweet red earth. Then I howl. Shooting stars fill my belly.

After the dreams, I slid out of the hotel bed and across the Saltillo tile, out to the patio above the ocean. As the sky whispered the pale lavender of early morning, a western tanager landed in the fronds of a nearby tropical bush. His yellow body and flame-red head flashed like a semaphore: *Caution, Stop. Caution, Stop.* Over the next two months, the tanagers would make their way to my home state, their breeding ground. I would see them there, my harbingers of all that was about to change.

I stood on the patio, naked and shivering, as the mist from the sea drifted in and settled on my skin. I imagined the rumblings of a new life inside me, ran my hands over what would be the hard white lily ball of myself, touched what would be a mushroom-cap navel. Like a glacier in motion, my hip bones would shift and open. My tiny breasts would grow luminous and full, and lie heavy across the top of my ribs. Magic and electricity would gallop through my body.

There was the overwhelming urge to drop to my knees, to crawl across the sand. And there was the drive to move out, to seek uncharted territory. These impulses were pure instinct and biology. Nothing divine about them. Still, they were revelations—just not the kind that could be written down, canonized. And therein was the problem: How would I ever articulate this now present feeling, that to stay would be to live an infertile life?

THE END OF our first year, a community fitness center opens in a spare room at Monticello High School. Herb and I are eager to join; we had both envisioned rural living as having more opportunities for exercising outdoors, but there are many weeks when we work all hours, and plenty of days where the weather won't cooperate. The fitness center seems like a good supplement for the winter months ahead.

Before using the facility, we are required to attend an orientation. We enter the back of the school, near the gymnasium—which I remember well from my teen-age years, when we traveled by bus from northern Utah to compete against the Buckaroos in track, football, and volleyball. The workout room is walled in by painted cinder blocks, and between them is a neat row of exercise machines. It turns out that the orientation will be conducted by a city councilman—a short, red-faced man named Evan who knows Herb and me from a recent meeting at the Forest Service office. He had been there to advocate a solution to the drought—to propose an improvement to the town's water-catchment system on the north slope of the Abajos. We were there to protest the extras that had been thrown into the proposal. It was my first time speaking at a public meeting in southern Utah, in front of men who represented both public and private interests. I could feel their solidarity—for, despite their distinct roles, I knew they went to church together every Sunday. I could feel their authority—for they held the priesthood, I did not. So I wavered in my description of how other towns had lost their water-delivery systems when clear-cuts similar to what the city proposed had destabilized hillsides. In other instances, the drastic denudation had unleashed massive mud slides into the drainages that collected the water, destroying pipelines and choking off the towns' water supplies. I had said that taking out the Abajos' thousand-year-old ponderosa pines—the range's last-remaining old-growth trees, which about 150 vertebrate species depend on for at least a portion of their life cycle—seemed like a short-term sacrifice just because the logging company that was going to clear out the smaller trees on the slopes wanted to sweeten the deal.[15] In sum, I said, the whole thing sounded like a poor use of taxpayer money. The Forest Service representative had patted my head and told me that the mud slides in other town watersheds must have been caused by a different kind of dirt, and that the trees would grow back. The councilman had rolled his eyes and told me that my concerns were the most hysterical ideas he had ever heard. I had left the meeting in tears. It was further confirmation that I should stick to my original strategy for surviving in southern Utah: Remain out of sight. Off the radar screen. Otherwise, risk rejection, even annihilation.

Now, in the fitness center, the councilman walks a group of Monticello citizens through the machines. He shows us how each one works, what the safety precautions are. He banters easily with the others, but neither Herb nor I can get him to answer our questions with more than a curt "yup" or "nope." He won't even look our way.

Before we leave, we are told the fitness center's rules of operation and conduct. For starters, you have to use the machines in clockwise order. Every five minutes, someone will call "Time!" and, no matter where you are in your workout, you will be required to move to the next machine. We are also told the dress requirements: Nothing with bare bellies or shoulders. No shorts above the knee. Nothing tight or revealing. Herb shrugs his shoulders. He wears T-shirts and sweats for these activities. But, thanks in part to that standoff I once had with my father, I don't have a single piece of exercise clothing that will meet their standards of modesty.

I had already balked at the idea of shuffling around the room like a herd of bawling cattle being run, all too timely and uniformly, through a meat-processing line. But when I hear the dress code, my face must betray my indignation, for Herb laughs under his breath. He is the first to appreciate my style of dress, but he also doesn't think form should ever precede function. When we walk outside, he cups my chin in his hands and pierces me with ellipsoidal pupils.

"What do you think your pioneer ancestors wore to pull their handcarts across the plains—yoga pants and sports bras? They survived in long, shapeless clothing. So will you. In fact, the way you're dressing these days doesn't make it much of a stretch."

I open my mouth, then close it. It's hard to convey why the idea of acquiescing to these regulations and this routine sounds like a death sentence. I use the gym only twice and then stop going for good.

CHRISTMAS DAY COMES with a foot of new snow. There is also a new puppy, a border-collie mix named Ursa who is fearless enough to have earned the Latin name for "bear." She was rescued from a rancher who was preparing to shoot her—a man who had said it was easier to kill new litters than to take the mother in for spaying. We come across her in town, sitting with her siblings in box marked *Free*. I make the mistake of pointing her out to Herb, who takes her home without consulting me. When I push the issue, stating that this should be a joint decision, that it is after all my house, and that I will be the one to care for her when he is away, he grows outraged.

But the power struggle has faded as our attachment to the puppy grows, and by Christmas morning, we are laughing at her desperate attempt to reach the turkey we are stuffing on the kitchen counter. Our plan is to leave the bird to roast while we take the dogs for a cross-country-ski tour in the Abajos. We're just opening the oven when the doorbell rings—the second time all year. It is Afton, the tiny old woman from next door. We had only ever exchanged pleasantries in the driveway, but here she is, her head bobbing on thin, hunched shoulders as she extends a plate of sugar cookies wrapped in cellophane and red ribbon. Heady with holiday cheer, we thank her, and nod eagerly when she invites us over for clam chowder the following afternoon. Afton clasps her hands in delight. Then she asks, "Well, then, beforehand, would you like to attend Sacrament Meeting with me?" We are awkward, stumbling in our excuses for why we cannot join her. She accepts our apologies and teeters away, and it's not really clear if she'd still like us to come for soup.

WHAT WE CAN SEE of Blue Mountain Road is covered with a dusting of fresh snow, before it disappears into the dense clouds that veil the mountain. Halfway between town and the turnout from which we'll ski, Herb tells me to stop. He points to the side of the road. Strung across the fence is a dead coyote. Blood drips from a fresh wound, blooms like a red Oriental poppy in the snow.

I pull over. Herb is out the door and making wide strides before I can say how unable I am to face an open-flesh bullet wound. But, as always, my urge to follow this man overrides any other impulse. I sigh with resignation as I pull on my gloves and slide from the cab.

The body is still warm, its fur a palette of every desert color. The animal was shot at fairly close range, its neck ragged from the blast. We climb over the fence and then lift the coyote off the barbed wire. Herb carries him away from the road, back into a grove of oak trees. Among the oak stands a single piñon, and Herb lays the dog at its snowless base in a nest of exposed and tangled roots. I envision returning to this place later to find bare, bleached bones.

A much older version of such bones was found not far from here—near some of the oldest archaeological sites on the continent.[16] Those remains proved coyotes originated here in the Southwest, and evolved alongside the great mammoth-hunters of the Pleistocene. Together, man and dog endured the end of the era, survived the extinction of the woolly mammoth and other megafauna. Together, they adapted to the warmer, drier environment, to the foraging skills it came to demand. As the Desert Archaic way of life came into full swing, both man and coyote thrived. These hunters-turned-gatherers, along with the wily wild dog, represent the desert's true native denizenry, the only two groups of social beings to survive on the Colorado Plateau for over ten thousand years.

Herb gathers red and gold stones that lie scattered beneath the trees, shielded from the snow. He hums something unrecognizable as he places the stones in a circle, around the coyote. I kneel next to the creature's head, observe eyes the warm brown of maple syrup. Removing my gloves, I stroke the creature's fur. There is a flash of memory, of touching my father's body as it rested beneath a blanket in the mortuary. Of hearing the crinkle of plastic that filled the space where his heart and lungs had been. Of remembering his voice, saturated with both gin and genealogy, saying, *Young lady, you were put on this earth for one man and one man only.* Of remembering how, after he said that, my heart and body closed like a moonflower at daybreak.

Until the lion man. Until I hike with him into a canyon carved by Muddy Creek through the San Rafael Swell—at the northern end of the Colorado Plateau. It is only weeks before I leave my marriage. There he pulls me through willows to the water's edge, where our sweat shimmers in the sunlight, where from a cottonwood tree two ravens jaw approval. We walk downstream, find a beach of untouched slate-covered mud. He gives me that look, and I instantly know his wish. And for the first time ever, without the flame of obedience or rebellion licking at my heels, I can honestly name my own desire too.

Until we strip in silence. He dips his finger into the mud and begins with a turtle across the small of my back. I reciprocate with paw prints across his shoulder blades. Handprints are slapped onto buttocks, thighs, his chest, my breasts. We paint equations with our initials across our bellies and add war paint to one another's cheeks and foreheads.

All the while, the black-blue birds watch us. We know ravens are faithful mates for life. With a fresh handful of mud, he draws great wings across my shoulders.

Until I heave handfuls of wet earth high on his hamstrings and smear it down the backs of his knees, across his calves, to his Achilles. I am careful there, for he had said, *You could take me away.*

But we had both known that this coupling was not about that, not about making us proper or public or legal or certain in any other way.

Until we climb an enormous round boulder that stands tilted like a planet in the middle of the creek. Our limbs stretch upward, and the mud on our knees cracks, like raku pots fresh from the kiln. Then we shimmy down the other side of the rock, and I realize there are only the whites of our eyes and teeth. They reveal us to be anything but human.

Animals. Those who suspected muttered the word behind our backs. They were right.

Until he pounces. His weight forces me down deep into the mud. The wet earth sucks at our skin, and laughter is a spider spinning a web, entangling our bodies. We devolve even further, becoming the first proteins in the world, igniting evolution. We wrestle as if our lives depended on it.

My life, at least, did depend on it.

Until that final tackle, where we help each other up, wade to higher, drier ground. Every pore, every cavity is filled with mud. To anyone else we would have been unrecognizable. But we had never seen ourselves, or another lover, so clearly.

Until I hear the deep belly laughter, the water sliding over stones, the duet of ravens and burping mud. The sound waltzes across the canyon walls.

Until, with gentle strokes, we wash each other off in a putty-colored pool. We dive under, and the mud falls away in pieces, dissolving in the current. *This*, I realize, *is total submersion.* And this time no part of me feels compelled to stay above the surface.

AND SO, at the end of my first year in San Juan County, when we squat over the lifeless coyote, the struggles for sovereignty pale in comparison with what binds us. Still, things are in stark contrast to the year before—the year that included the inspiration and exhilaration of Costa Rica and Muddy Creek. This year, it began just as it ends now: nose to nose with violent death.

A truck hauling bales of hay approaches—a rancher most likely taking winter feed to cows still in the foothills. He sees my truck, comes to a stop, and with his eyes follows our footprints into the woods. We can see him, but the trees obscure us from his view. Just then, a small herd of mule deer jump the fence and bound across the road in front of him. He turns to watch. As the deer brush through the trees on the other side of the road, the boughs sift sugar snow, and a flock of dark-eyed juncos rushes out.

In that moment, the man's expression is both serenity and delight. It is the look of a man who loves his place in the world—a place he knows in his bones and would do anything to defend. And in him I can also see a certain knowing: This is a man who will do his chores and return to his family—an entire tribe of grandparents, aunts, uncles, cousins, wife, and kids. They will share the holiday, and tomorrow they will go to church. There they will mingle with the greater tribe like their own, whose men will drift off to speak of the land, of the good God that gave it to them, and make arrangements to help the man get his cows down into the low country before the big snows hit.

Standing in the trees, watching him, I ache with envy. And I realize: In order to survive, I must expand my territory. I cannot continue to lurk at the periphery of this desert. I will have to creep in, find openings for some semblance of acceptance.

It will require camouflage. A masquerade as successful as my father's suit and business card, one with enough fabric and manners and credentials to hide all that burns beneath. I hope I won't catch my costume on fire—or, worse yet, extinguish the flames entirely. I hope Herb and I will survive my pretense—for my need to have what I see in the man on the road is about the only thing that competes with my desire for him.

But here in the wide-open space of this place, I can also see that there will be plenty of time to contemplate the complexities. For now, it is enough to know that the coyote is off his crucifix. And that, at least within this tree-shrouded, makeshift gravesite, concealed from his persecutors, there is a prayer of a chance that he might be allowed to remain in dignified repose, ears and all.

6

Forage

S PRING AGAIN. My father has been dead for over fourteen months. Ada, who finally succumbed to Alzheimer's in a nursing home in Salt Lake City, has been gone for twelve. And my divorce is now final. What persists is paradox: Stay, go. Comply, rebel. The things that brought me here to San Juan County in the first place, one year ago. Still, we manage to buy the cabin on the rim of Lila Canyon. The move itself is paradoxical: It is a move that takes us out of town, drives us deeper into the arms of the desert. And yet it is a move that plants us firmly as official residents of San Juan County, gives us a sense of permanency and belonging that I'm not certain how to manage.

The broad promontory on which our new home sits forms the northeastern rim of a boulder-choked drainage that originates on the flanks of the Abajos, before it runs southeast and bisects 191, halfway between Monticello and Blanding. From the highway to our house is three long and meandering miles of dirt road; the property is closer to the end of the point; just below the point Lila Canyon joins with an even larger drainage before spilling right smack into the Four Corners.

Plateau. Chasm. Plateau. Chasm. The contrast of high and low country, its undulating oceans of slickrock and sagebrush, is any-thing but redundant. The cabin's view of them—four states' worth—clinches this real-estate transaction. The deal is as rash as my first entanglement with the lion man. As impulsive as my move from the city. And it is prompted by little more than a morning's walk: I had taken Pablo and Ursa along the perimeter of the golf course, up into the foothills of the Abajos. I hadn't walked that way since the previ-ous autumn, when the first snows had hit. A warm spring wind had turned the snow to mud, and as we tramped our way toward the woodlands, it sucked at my boots and the dogs' paws.

Negotiating the mud demanded all of my attention. So, when I finally looked up, for a moment I thought we were lost—for there were no woodlands. Then I remembered: the city of Monticello had torn them up in order to make way for nine new holes—an expan-sion funded by the EPA tailings clean-up.

There had been public discussion about what to do with the money, and I knew the golf-course expansion was one possibility. But in my determination to lie low, I hadn't gotten involved. Be-sides, I figured that no one in his right mind would vote to spend such badly needed money on sprinklers and sod—not when Main Street was in collapse, not when the school district's test scores were so low and the senior-citizen programs were flailing. Truly, it seemed unthinkable—in a place as dry as this, and in the middle of a long-term drought.

Then, when the expansion had been approved, I had shrugged my shoulders. I assumed that the city would use the former tailings pile, a large, nicely contoured chunk of land already denuded, ready for seed, and immediately adjacent to the existing course. I figured that, under the circumstances, it was the best use of the place. But the city left the site bare. Instead, it razed the foothills on the opposite side of the existing greens, and obliterated the route of my morning walk.

I had gawked at the orange survey stakes—*Hole Ten, Hole Eleven . . . Hole Eighteen*. Around them were acres of arboreal anatomy: The trunks and limbs of Douglas fir, Gambel's oak, piñon, and juniper protruded at odd angles from bald, raw mounds of earth. Wilting clumps of sagebrush and yucca lay in repose across the debris. And where there were once stout bunches as thick as fox tails, wild grasses were strewn in single flaccid strands—no match for the fertilized, hybridized turf that would replace them.

I saw then why my eyes had stung all winter long. The city had been burning the downed wood and vegetation in big slash piles. Everywhere, thick gray streams of smoke rose from the landscape like mesmerized cobras, and yet it seemed there was still an endless amount of wood to burn. The dogs' noses twitched as their eyes peered through the dense air in search of wildlife—on that walk, there had always been a jackrabbit or a deer to give chase, but the land was vacant now. The occupants had departed in search of a residence with the essentials: food, shelter, concealment.

A single command spun the dogs on their heels, and we headed home. Herb had looked up from his work as I stumbled through the door. On that day, he was not so engrossed that he failed to miss my consternation. When he asked what was wrong, I searched for the right words to describe what I had seen.

"It's a goddamn bone yard." This was all I could say.

The rest of that morning had been spent buried in the *San Juan Record*. What began as a belated effort to educate myself on the golf-course project ended in the classifieds, where I stared at a picture of the cabin. *Very rustic*, the newspaper read. *Needs work*. By early afternoon, I was standing on the property with the local real-estate agent, trying frantically to reach Herb by way of the agent's cell phone. Within the hour, he had joined us, and we had written an offer on the hood of the car.

THE ASKING PRICE was fifty-five thousand dollars—for the cabin and ten acres of land. Included in the deal is a metal pole planted in the middle of the yard; it bears a large, tilted frame fitted with four photovoltaic panels—each one the size of a small window. We quickly discover how most financial institutions categorize our home: *High-risk*—for San Juan County property values are abysmal. *Unconventional*—for the house is powered by sunshine. And we will discover that banks balk at a dwelling that draws water from a cinder-block cistern stored in a basement made of red earthen walls; that utilizes a pump the size of a Pringles chip container to distribute the cistern's contents to a sink, shower, and toilet; that requires the homeowner to haul a thousand sloshing gallons from town and deposit them underground by way of gravity and a garden hose.

There is only plywood for siding. And the roof is a dried, curling layer of tar paper that looks like the skin of an onion. The cabin consists of one big room—only the northeast corner is divided, to create a small bathroom that includes a plastic trailer-size shower stall. There are steep, code-violating stairs that lead to a sleeping loft. The dwelling's heat source is a wood-burning stove, which is connected to a large drum that heats water by circulating it through a pipe running through the stove's belly. In the corner designated as the kitchen, two-by-four studs hold slats of wood for pantry shelves; a battered curtain, years of red dust clinging to its folds, hangs as a door to the only closet in the house.

But the light comes in at all angles. And a landmark is framed in every window. Facing into Utah, the Abajos, Cedar Mesa, the Bears Ears. Looking out into Arizona, the Carrizo Range and Monument Valley. New Mexico: Shiprock. And Colorado: Sleeping Ute Mountain and the fourteen-thousand-foot peaks of the San Juan Range. Each view is an excuse for why it never occurs to us to consider how we might acquire financing. Why we forget to ponder how we will haul water to fill the cistern, or if the solar panels will generate enough power to run my computer.

And it certainly never occurs to us to consider the weeds. Immediately surrounding the cabin are two acres, fenced off from the rest. The remains of old desiccated cow pies divulge the area's former life, pre-cabin, as a small stockyard—a place where the previous tenants' livestock ate or trampled every growing thing within its perimeter. The next resident, the man who built the cabin, had done so fifteen years ago—sans animals. But even now the yard is void of vegetation—in a place like this, soils and native grasses can take decades to reestablish themselves properly. There is one exception, though: a monotonous fuzz known as cheatgrass.

Cheatgrass is only interesting-looking in spring, when it briefly shimmers deep violet and emerald green—its large broomlike tops hang like ripe heads of wheat. But as the summer bears down on the desert, the grass fades and turns dry as straw. Even at its best, it provides only scant nutritional value for wildlife or domestic livestock—which means the animals avoid it unless they are desperately hungry. It was inadvertently transported among grains brought to the western United States from Europe in the early 1890s—and in its new digs, the plant thrived, especially in areas disturbed by farming, grazing, or the passage of wheels. It wasn't long before it had begun to overrun crops; then it crept out of cleared fields to choke out neighboring native vegetation. So virulent was the spread that Aldo Leopold was inspired to write that it was as if "one simply woke up one fine spring to find the range dominated by [the] new weed."[1]

As an attorney who works on public-land issues, Herb knows the havoc cheatgrass can cause. Much of his day is spent writing appeals to protest "public range improvement projects," which are little more than open invitations to host this aggressive invader further. Executed by the BLM on behalf of ranchers who hold grazing permits on the public domain, these projects involve the use of a hydro-mulcher—a monster-sized weed-whacker that indiscriminately shears away trees and ground cover over a large area. The tumulted land is then reseeded with more bovine-friendly feed—native forage is often replaced with exotic grasses. Once the cows graze down the plowed site, cheatgrass tends to spring up with a vengeance, and eventually it stifles anything else that dares to crop back up. Even on a personal level, cheatgrass is intensely invasive. A single walk through desert that's been grazed, and its seed heads will find you. They will work their way into your pants, lodge steadfast in socks and underwear, and become one with car seats and sleeping bags. They jab mercilessly at your skin, and bury outright between dogs' toes—where they sometimes fester to the point of abscess.

But Herb and I are willing to live with two acres of cheatgrass—although I am already dreaming of an attempt to reclaim the yard so it looks like our other seven acres, beyond the old stockyard's fence. Just past those demarcating strands of barbed wire, we now own additional groves of oak and a whole host of common high-desert evergreens—including a small stand of young ponderosa pines. In most places, the soil is untrodden and lathered in silvery, savory sagebrush, interspersed with cactus and wildflowers. Among them is a regal, snapdragonlike flower that will soon bloom into the endemic ghostly-lavender petals known as Abajo penstemon.

The land beyond the fence also bursts with clumps of tall native grasses. Needle-and-thread: this hardworking plant produces seeds *twice* a year; the sharp-nosed awns, encircled by graceful, curling tendrils, feed deer in spring and elk in autumn. Sand dropseed: its delicate, bobbing tassels belie a stout root system, designed to anchor sandy desert soils that would otherwise be carried off by wind and rain. And Indian ricegrass: its wispy strands yield papery bells that drop large, tar-colored seeds in autumn, when wild animals are storing up for winter and can use its dense nutrients. Ricegrass seeds were also foraged by the prehistoric hunter-gatherers of the Archaic period; they were ground into a protein-rich meal that became a staple in a diet whose proportions of meat had been scaled down with the extinction of Pleistocene megafauna.

We hop the yard fence and wander the outer seven acres. We marvel at the thick and diverse ground cover—these days, such a strong representation of untouched native plants is called a *relic community*. And though I can see how such a landscape—pre-cows and pre-cheatgrass—would have supported a great deal more wildlife and people, it is still hard to fathom the shift in diet for ice-age hunters-turned-foragers. One might think that such a shift—from mammoth meat to seeds the size of a pinhead—would have been costly. It is easy to imagine that the transition must have invited malnutrition (if not famine) and required exhaustive amounts of time and energy to gather enough calories to survive. But deep ecologist Paul Shepard points to studies showing that hunter-gatherer groups have rarely suffered from more than local vitamin deficiencies, and that their food-getting requires far less time and energy than are spent by those who rely upon agriculture for sustenance.[2] For one thing, living off of such a broad food base (hunter-gatherer cultures have been known to use more than fifty kinds of plants and twenty species of animals) meant that, no matter what the season, no matter what the nutritional need, there was a wide range of items available for sustenance during the Archaic period. And because hunter-gatherer populations remained stable (birthrates in such cultures are generally limited to replacement rates), the environment's supply could almost always support the people's demands.[3] What's more, the remains of such cultures have shown that hunter-gatherers didn't just survive, they often thrived—a fact evidenced by "excellent bone structure, heavy musculature, and flawless teeth."[4] And it is largely a myth that such populations had a shorter life span—that trend came into full swing only after agriculture was introduced. In earlier times, individuals that survived the first three years of life—a time when nature did its sorrowful but practical business of ensuring tribal strength by weeding out the less hardy—tended to live nearly as long as we do now.[5]

Of course, there must have been local variations in these general findings about hunter-gatherer life—especially on the Colorado Plateau. And as I wander along the outer perimeter of the property, I wonder why the people stayed—why they didn't migrate to someplace more forgiving in climate and in food and water sources. But here I am, forsaking even the automatic heat and lights I had in town—the luxuries of my city life fading into the part of the brain that stores distant memory. Most people I know would call it regression, or even masochism. Of all the people close to me, only my father and the lion man would understand.

I turn to Herb, to plan the reclamation. But he is talking about the BMX track he will build for his son, who will come from Moab to visit. By his guess, in a year he'll have put in the gardens and an orchard. While he's at it, he'll also put up a volleyball court, a chicken coop, and a hot tub with a tiki bar. He even dares to utter the words "palm trees."

I stare at him, wait for him to finish his declaration of things to come. Then I say, flatly, that I want nothing cleared. Only in its undisturbed state does this land harbor any real possibilities. And as I describe what that means, I am suddenly standing in the backyard of my childhood, staring out at the ten acres of open woodlands behind our home in the foothills of Salt Lake City. Beyond them, near the mouth of Millcreek Canyon, the neighborhoods picked up again—but as a young girl, I felt those woodlands were an endless wilderness at the edge of the earth. I first disappeared into them to nurse my pangs of jealousy over a new sibling, and by age six I was spending entire afternoons there. Some days, I waded through the chest-high grasses of open fields, sun-kissed and buzzing with grasshoppers. On other days, especially at summer's apex, I played beneath the dark canopies of scrub oak, clustered so tightly that the elements barely penetrated. It was within one such dense thicket that I made my first crude camp—complete with a fire ring and a lawn chair for reading.

At first the fire ring was just for show, but then there came the summer after my eighth birthday, not long after my father first refused me a Mormon baptism. It was the same summer when my mother cultivated my sister's and my love of books. Every week, she turned us loose in the children's section of the downtown library to gather our quota of reading materials. But I was a precocious child. Often I ended up in the main library, exploring the world of books beyond my years.

It was from them that I discovered magic. And from my lawn chair in the oaks, I read about casting spells and brewing potions. My fingertips sizzled with the sensations of power and possibility. I came to believe that, with the proper enchantments, I would be able to fly. And if the spell worked on me, I figured I'd move on to others: Make my father stop drinking. Create harmony in our home. And I would create a protective ring around the fields—one that no matchstick or bulldozer could penetrate. Already, the neighbor boys had caught them on fire. And rumor was that new homes would soon be built in their place.

All this, from incantations muttered over sticks and stones. The prospects were intoxicating. Even more appealing than the promise of ruling a planet in eternity.

One day, I asked the librarian to help me locate an occult book that provided information on how to fly. The woman who helped me took my request very seriously. In hindsight, I wonder if perhaps she was Mormon. After all, among his kind, Joseph Smith had lent the occult a lasting credibility. But by dabbling in it—seeing prophecies in stones, divining treasures with a tree branch—he had also made the religion he founded seem, to outsiders, nothing more than the high jinks of charlatans. Latter-day or no, the librarian found what I was looking for, and, the following Saturday afternoon, while my mother cleaned and my father napped off the combined effects of a late-night binge and an early morning of fishing, I quietly stole things from the kitchen: A small pot. A thermos full of tap water. A book of matches. I also took a jar of Schilling cinnamon sticks, for good measure. Into the woodlands I scurried, to my crude camp among the oaks. From the ground beneath the trees I scraped up duff as dry as paper, set it and a stack of twigs amid my circle of stones.

One match was all it took. I set the pot full of water on a flat stone, placed close enough to be licked by the flames—the way I'd seen my father do it when we were camping and he forgot fuel for the Coleman stove. While the water heated, I laid out the items I had scavenged the day before: a snail shell, a magpie feather, three acorns, the legs of a beetle, and a dandelion root.

I had improvised a bit. The book had called for an owl feather—not an easy find for a young girl. Magpies, however, were ubiquitous in our neighborhood. To acquire its plumage, all I had to do was wait for one to land on the patio furniture. Before it could leave a stream of bird droppings, my mother would pick it off with a BB gun. And I was supposed to have gathered the root of something whose name I could not pronounce, let alone identify. For some reason I can no longer recall, a dandelion seemed like a safe substitute.

The spell book said to bring the concoction to a "rolling boil," and when this was achieved, I threw in the cinnamon sticks, which bobbed frantically on the bubbly surface. Having forgotten a cup, I drank straight from the pot. The recipe hadn't said anything about dancing around the fire, or taking my clothes off and painting myself with bat's blood—actions I had imagined that witches and other summoners of magic used to invoke the supernatural. But already I had strayed from the original recipe. Instead, I sat back on my heels and waited, picking beetle legs from between my teeth.

The afternoon passed. No wings sprouted from my arms. There was not even the slightest levitation. Finally, once the ashes of the fire were cool and the first crickets of the evening began to chirp, I headed home. As I walked, I decided that my potion hadn't worked because I had failed to gather the precise ingredients required, or I hadn't cooked or drunk them properly. After all, I knew how little one could stray from the Book of Mormon if one wanted to make it to the top tier of the afterlife. On that day, I deduced that all rituals—and the beliefs that inspired them—must be rigid and precise in order to be effective. And with that deduction, my ability to improvise, to make up my own rules, diminished even more.

When I reached our backyard, my mother was standing there sick with worry, and scolded me for staying away so long. She ushered me down the hallway to my room, where I was to contemplate my thoughtlessness until suppertime. My father was still snoring away on the couch. He would wake later to catch me returning to the kitchen the items I had borrowed. He squinted his tired, blood-shot eyes and looked from the scorched pot to the matchbook, and I braced for a stern lecture on the dangers of fire followed by another march to my room. Instead, he grinned proudly. It was a totally inappropriate response—especially in contrast to my mother's earlier effort to instill in me a sense of responsibility. But for a young girl fearing punitive action, his reaction was pleasing. It was also one of the last times he would look at me like that, or speak with such encouragement.

Atta girl, Amos. I love that my girl can make and tend her own fire.

IN NO TIME, the Arizona man who has grown too old and feeble to visit his cabin getaway accepts our offer of fifty thousand dollars. Combined, Herb and I have only thirty dollars in our checking and savings accounts. After we have been turned down by financial institutions across the state, a bank just over the Colorado state line accepts our loan application—but only with an outrageous interest rate. We drive to Dove Creek, sign on the dotted lines, figure we'll find a way to refinance soon. Before the ink is dry, the bank president reminds us we'll need proof of homeowner's insurance—another detail that we had failed to consider in our excitement. Over the next twenty-four hours, we will learn that house insurance is hard to come by when you have no water and live more than fifteen miles from the nearest fire station. We will learn too that only the Farm Bureau will insure such a place. And a few days later, when we walk into the office of the local agent, he will be unable to hide his astonishment. It isn't every day that he does business with tree-huggers.

If we are going to buy the cabin, there is no way around the hypocrisy of the situation. The Farm Bureau is at complete odds with our efforts to designate wilderness; the organization views Western public lands as little more than free range for domestic herds. Regularly ranked by *Fortune* magazine as one of the twenty-five most influential special-interest groups in Washington,[6] the Farm Bureau often lobbies aggressively to weaken federal laws that protect public lands and any native species that might serve as competition or threat to livestock. It promotes itself as the farmer's and rancher's representative to big government—yet the majority of its five million members are uninformed, nonvoting members—mere holders of insurance policies and financial products. The national federation is committed to less government regulation and more local control, but the Utah chapter of the organization is especially anti-Federalist—its public-land policies are actually prefaced with a demand for "the immediate relinquishment of land and water owned by the federal government."[7] And, to achieve a safe and tame range for livestock, the Utah Farm Bureau revels in coyote bounty hunts—these public predator-control efforts, the Bureau insists, should be run "without interference by environmental groups." And if the coyotes still get the cows, well, then, taxpayers should compensate ranchers for their losses—although the Bureau opposes public disclosure of the costs of such taxpayer-funded programs.[8] The Utah branch also demands that taxpayers pay for forage eaten by any form of wildlife.[9] If forage deteriorates so there isn't enough to feed the cows and sheep, the organization's solution is not to remove the livestock, or to practice forage-and-soil conservation techniques, but instead to initiate a "reduction in wildlife, wild horses, and burros."[10]

And so Herb and I stand shame-faced in the doorway of the insurance agent's office. The agent looks equally awkward. A nice young local man, he quickly recovers his shock and politely asks how it is, given the nature of our beliefs, that we've come to find ourselves in need of his services. The curiosity in his voice is genuine, and without judgment.

I root desperately for a response—diplomatic words that will nourish some sort of understanding. I have dressed for the occasion, and hope that helps too. Since the day when we laid the coyote to rest, I have been seeking out opportunities to engage with the locals, to make friends, but each encounter has felt contrived. Already, this encounter feels no different, and it occurs to me that perhaps my intentions are too convoluted to result in anything else. Given this heightened state of self-consciousness, it eludes me that I am ferreting out the right thing for this man to pass on to the locals, once they discover we have actually purchased a home in San Juan County. Also eluding me is the possibility that perhaps this man won't want to act as our liaison, that he might prefer his neighbors not know he has done business with us.

Amid all my social gymnastics, the man asks a question.

"So this work you do—are you guys range specialists or something?"

"Well, uh, no. Herb has a law degree, and I just write."

He looks quizzically at me.

"You know, foundation proposals, newsletter articles, stuff like that."

Now the agent looks truly perplexed. I scavenge for more words.

"We believe wilderness is the truest form of the land, and the one that will best serve the needs of the community by maintaining an enduring, high-quality way of life . . ."

We believe. The truest. Missionary-speak.

"We just want to create dialogue with the locals . . . to really integrate with the community . . ."

Dialogue. Integrate. He was the salesman, but I was the one making the pitch. I could see in his face I had just sown the seeds of mistrust.

"We share more common ground than you know . . ."

Common ground. When I had used these words on my mother's family—nearly all of whom are loyal members of the Farm Bureau—they had rolled their eyes and laughed.

"Get some pictures of the structure, will you," he says, standing up and extending a tentative hand, "so I can send them to the underwriter."

BY THE FIRST WEEK of May, the Farm Bureau has approved us for coverage, and the bank has wired funds to the title company. The cabin is officially ours. We remove the cap from the bed of my pickup and load it with a teetering stack of belongings; six trips transfer everything from the blue house out to Lila Canyon. Closer inspection shows our new land's outer perimeter to be squared off with rotting fence posts cut from old juniper trees. The rusted barbed wire that once strung the posts together now lies mostly in tangles on the ground—only the fence around the inner yard of two acres remains intact. First thing, I say to Herb, we should restring those fence lines. He looks perplexed. To keep out the cows and the riffraff, I say. Herb throws his head back and laughs.

"Sweetheart, we are the riffraff."

We dump the last load and take off to explore. Near the property's northeast corner, we find an old outhouse buried in the trees— an ancient thermometer nailed to its weather-beaten exterior. A rattlesnake, fat from the mice that leave the outhouse after a night of shredding an old yellowed roll of toilet paper, lies curled in a depression of dirt just beneath the door.

Next we venture out on the dirt road that passes by our house, to see where it will end. With the dogs sweeping wildly through the brush on either side, we find that the road connects with other faint tracks—barely distinguishable for lack of passage and an overgrowth of vegetation. It's clear that there's not a lot of traffic out here, perhaps because the promontory is mostly private property—fenced parcels of ten, twenty, and forty acres dotted with a handful of hunting shacks, cabins, and trailers. Only eight of the more substantial dwellings appear to be used with regularity. In a few weeks, we will be able to count our neighbors on two hands. Two of those, in all the time we live there, will refuse even to wave when we drive past. But we will also find that not one of our full-time neighbors is Mormon—even the two who seem least happy about our arrival. Somehow, we have unwittingly managed to move into what is San Juan County's minority neighborhood.

Just before dusk, we find the BLM boundary nearest our house, above a small and subtle finger of the main canyon. We stand above its head, on the lip of a pour-off that looks as if it runs with ferocity when it rains. In the dwindling light we can just make out a small spring below, encircled by a grove of aspen—an anomaly this far below the Abajos. Later that night, we lay our mattress out on the west porch and celebrate our new abode with a good bottle of wine—another anomaly in these parts. Beyond Cedar Mesa, the sun singes the horizon. The bladelike wings of nighthawks slice the air, and somewhere on the fringe, coyotes heckle a rising moon. The howls nudge Pablo and Ursa onto the porch, next to our bed, and finally onto the foot of the sleeping bags. And as Herb curls his sleek, bare cat-body around me, as the moon casts aluminum light across the desert that is now officially our home, I think how my father too would have sold his soul, would have suffered any contradiction or exile imaginable, to inhabit this piece of heaven.

THE FOLLOWING WEEK, I see Nora at the Laundromat. She looks as tired as the last time I saw her. I tell her we have moved, describe our new place. In the process of moving, I say, I have cleaned out my closets. There are boxes of clothes for her girls, if she'd like them. I give her the number to our new cell phone, the only form of communication we have at Lila Canyon. She calls the very next day.

"My husband, he wants to know if we can come out for a visit. Pick up the clothes, maybe cut down a few of your trees for firewood. We go through so much of it, you know—and there's no more trees on the Rez."

Forage, according to Webster's:

Food that wild or domestic animals take for themselves.
A search for provisions.
To wander in search of food.
To secure forage by stripping the country.
To rummage. To ravage. To raid.[11]

Over the past year, I had heard the local Anglos refer to the culture of local Indians. In that world, when someone needed something, he simply asked it of the person who had what he was looking for. And that person always provided. In this way, the tribe's needs were met.

"I am so sorry," I say. "But we don't want to cut down our trees."

Silence.

"Uh, there are plenty of places to cut wood on public lands; why don't you go there?"

More silence.

"Nora?"

"What do you mean, *public lands*?"

I snort. I think she is joking.

"You know, Cedar Mesa is BLM land; the Abajos are managed by the Forest Service. You could get a permit to cut in an area that has burned, or needs to be thinned. Or how about getting the okay from the golf course to take away some of the wood they've got piled for burning?"

Silence again, and then, finally, a question saturated in incredulity.

"Why would anyone need a permit to gather the gifts of the earth?"

AFTER I HANG UP, I look out the window to see that the cows from the grazing allotment in the canyon below have somehow clambered up onto our mesa. They are roaming our pristine seven acres—their slick pink snouts root furiously among the bunch-grasses. My dogs whirl in circles and yip frantically, all the while looking anxiously to me for direction. Despite their herding-dog genes, they have no idea how to round up cattle.

Still clutching the cell phone, I march to the edge of the yard and shout encouragement at them. Then I look down at the extraordinary technological instrument in my hand. Its screen registers 2:36—the number of minutes and seconds that it took to say no to Nora. I urge the dogs out past the fence, then right up to the fat, manure-crusted hind ends. And when the dogs start nipping the right places, when the bovines start stumbling away, I point in the direction I want the dogs to send them. But the dogs are too excited, and run the interlopers in circles. I start to dial the sheriff, to tell him we have livestock in trespass. Then I remember that county law is on the cows' side, not mine. I stand there helpless, watching the tall grasses diminish before my eyes.

I have scavenged for ways to put down roots here. I am performing the precise rituals required. Still, I have no idea how to claim the promised land, to gain any semblance of acceptance among its people. And I realize this is probably how I will always live—slinking around the margins—even on my own property.

My mind compensates through fantasy: Wearing nothing but a rabbit skin that flaps from my waist, I squat in the dirt and rummage for stone. From a stout piece of flint, I fashion a point—not quite as big as a Clovis, but still fairly substantial. I attach it to a spear with animal sinew, and creep forward. Suddenly I sprint from the sagebrush and pierce the hide of an unsuspecting, wayward cow. I am flooded with a sense of power brought on by the kill, with the possibilities that come with the knowledge that one can fend for oneself.

And here's the psychic reparation: no matter that there's no band to butcher and transport the carcass—I could roast it right there, not far from my new home. After all, I could make and tend my own fire. And if I could scare the cows away before they ravaged my land, there'd be plenty of ricegrass left for a side dish.

7

Shaman

THE PICKUP CAREENS toward the man standing at the intersection where the gravel county road meets the two-track leading to our property. But the man stands composed, confident that we will stop in time. Between bad brakes and three hundred gallons of water sloshing in the plastic stock-tank in back, Herb and I aren't so sure. When we finally begin to slow, we are close enough that I can read the caption on the man's red, white, and blue T-shirt: *God, Guns, and Guts Made America Great.*

It isn't my truck. I had begged Herb not to haul water with my only vehicle—even hid my keys when he had waved me off. So we are driving Herb's latest acquisition—a red '87 Ford F-250. The auto mechanic in town who sold it to Herb was careful to tell him that what we were paying for was the new engine, nothing else. And as we hold our breath and wait for the truck to stop in time, as a blue electrical wire that dangles beneath the dash throws sparks at our toes, as I move my foot to avoid the sparks, only to catch sight of the dirt through a rusted-out hole in the floor, we understand precisely what the mechanic meant.

We are grimy from the past few days' efforts. Herb has been out in a remote corner of the county, looking at a new road that was carved through a proposed wilderness area. He is planning to sue the county for the intrusion, and at the same time force the BLM to reclaim the fresh bulldozer scrape—before it welcomes ORVs deeper into the desert and renders the area ineligible for wilderness designation. Meanwhile, I had taken time off to unpack boxes in our new home. I have also spent the time hanging Ada's art on the walls. After she died, I acquired so much of her work that, by the time I placed the last piece, hardly an inch of the tongue-and-groove could be seen.

The pictures I have hung are mostly serigraphs, for which Ada was best known. Later in her career, she had become obsessed with the form—a process in which razor-cut stencils, often thirty or forty shapes, are arranged on a blank canvas. A single edition can include fifty to three hundred prints, and for each and every print in that edition, the artist must adhere one stencil at a time. Then, for each stencil, a squeegee is pulled across a stretched screen of silk, forcing through it the color of paint chosen for that particular stencil. It is a painstaking effort, requiring a great deal of vision and patience. The number of signed prints in the final edition is determined by how many prints took the color and technique well—although no two prints will ever be exactly the same. The silkscreen technique of the serigraph gave Ada an almost supernatural ability to cast color and shape—to alternate opacity and transparency, to mix geometry with fluidity. And despite their contemporary and abstract character, most of her work somehow conveyed the natural world in a substantial yet most sensual way. The overall effect is utterly organic, and the titles of the editions follow: *Wheat. Autumn. Color Country. Canyon.*

Ada died the year before, only a few months after my father—and his memorial service was one of her final public appearances. There, on the front row, she had sat blinking with incomprehension. Shortly before that day, I had taken Herb to the rest home to meet her, and there she was, in the same black shirt and slacks she had worn for two weeks—despite my uncles' wives' attempts to dress her in something more fresh and vibrant. It was a Sunday morning. We found her sitting in a chair in the sitting room, only a few feet from a wide-screen television that was broadcasting a Mormon service. There was yellow pudding caked on her face and in her hair. She looked vacant, and miserable. I stormed the nurses' station, told them that under no circumstances was my grandmother to sit through any sort of religious program.

"She's an atheist, for God's sake," I muttered, from between clenched teeth. The two women in the station glared at me, as if they were the ones to have been offended.

Herb was already helping Ada to her feet when I returned to the sitting room. She was telling him that she didn't know why they were keeping her there, that she had a perfectly good husband at home. But my grandfather had passed away several years before. And as she spoke, the pudding on her cheek cracked. Of all the losses and changes in my life that year, Ada's death was the least complicated.

WHEN WE PULL UP to the man at the intersection, I do a quick check. We are wearing old jeans and flannel shirts to keep a brisk morning breeze at bay. The only thing that reveals us as something other than good local country folk is that our dogs are squeezed between us in the cab. They have never traveled in an open pickup bed—only beneath a bed cap, curled up on blankets. Any real cow dog would be in back, in the open, deftly balanced atop the stock tank. Quickly I make a mental note to train the dogs to do the same—to ride, at least, without the cap. The note gets tacked to the mile-long list of ways to improve our chances of fitting in— something I started on Christmas Day. Herb thinks I am crazy, but he's a gregarious soul and goes along with some of the more social aspects of my plan. Today, he has tucked his hair up under a ball cap, and has traded his thongs for work boots. I sit up and smile as the man approaches the vehicle.

"You must be the folks who bought old Bill's place," he says. "Welcome to the neighborhood."

We thank him, and ask where he lives. As the crow flies, he is our closest neighbor. His name is Robert, and he and his wife's family, whose various members have lived out here for more than twenty years, have tens of acres. Through the course of introductions, we gather that they are able to live largely off the land. They are so self-sufficient they even school their kids at home.

He offers his help—his son's too—with the move-in-progress.

"Any day but Saturday," he says.

It turns out they are Seventh-day Adventists. Herb and I are both mildly surprised. It must have registered on our faces, for the man grins.

"Yup, was raised LDS but have since seen the light."

My heart leaps. A kindred spirit. What luck to have such a neighbor in San Juan County. But as I relish this idea, he is already asking Herb what he does for a living. And before I can soften the delivery, Herb replies unabashedly that he works for the Southern Utah Wilderness Alliance.

Robert's eye travels to the back of Herb's neck, where his hair snakes up and out of sight. He looks at the dogs, panting away in the cab. He takes a step back.

"Well, now. I'll act Christian and all toward you, for that's what the good Lord intended. But I've got to tell ya, my employer and yours don't see eye to eye."

Herb is looking right at him, his fat-cat grin unwavering.

"Really, sir, and who is your employer?"

"The San Juan County Road Department."

———

BY MEMORIAL DAY WEEKEND, we are fully settled into the cabin. For these few days, Herb is as surprised as I am to find himself unoccupied—for his work schedule has grown increasingly relentless. Even up on the plateau above redrock country, the days have grown warm, and we fear that the move may have caused us to miss the best temperatures for hiking in the desert below. Still, we load both gear and dogs into the back of my truck, then head to the southwest corner of the county. We follow what was once the Hole-in-the-Rock trail over the Clay Hills Divide by way of Highway 276, an especially stark stretch of desert that must have incited near madness in the starving and weary Bluff-bound pioneers. I think of them from the cushioned cab of my air-conditioned truck, where a small cooler of chilled drinks sits behind the seat, a bag of gourmet potato chips lies open between us, and an old Johnny Cash tape croons across the speakers.

We have the luxury of admiring our surroundings. It occurs to me that it is the same perspective from which some people have the pleasure of admiring a good work of art. I think about my two grandmothers. Ada lived in relative ease. Even raising four boys, she had ample leisure time in which to retreat to her studio. She had Lee to thank, for he made a good living overseeing Utah Lumber Company. Together my grandparents cultivated for the whole family a life saturated with the arts—literature, dance, opera, music, visual art, and architecture. During the days when I was intent on getting baptized, I remember my uneasiness when Ada and her sons joked about the dull and redundant design of Mormon churches, which they likened to tin-can factories. But then, at nineteen years of age, I traveled the European continent and saw even the simplest country village graced by a beautifully designed and crafted house of worship—each one a profound gesture to the divine. When I returned to the States and attended a relative's wedding reception at a Mormon ward house—a building for nontemple activities, such as regular Sunday meetings and various social events—I decided that, if I were God, I would be tempted to throw the Mormons out of heaven just for their lack of good taste.

Then there was my grandma Blaisdell—a rancher's wife. Other than a few hours for Church meetings, she didn't stop working all week on practical matters—she rarely had time to enjoy even a sunset. Her artistic sensibilities extended as far as the Kleenex-box covers she made at Relief Society—the Mormon women's auxiliary group, which gathers weekly in ward houses everywhere. She must have knit three dozen of those covers—each one a crocheted mass of pastel yarn that flowed over the box like a ballroom skirt. Atop the skirt, just behind the opening for the tissue, protruded the trunk and head of a Barbie doll. The most elaborate one sat on the back of the toilet in my grandparents' bathroom. Perhaps it was the artistic snobbery I had inherited from the Irvine side, but even as a young girl I was bothered by the legless, Kleenex-guarding Barbies. When my grandmother gave me one for my bedroom, I promptly stashed it far in the back of my closet, out of sight.

I AM STILL THINKING about my grandmothers when we turn off the highway onto a dirt road that quickly gets us axle-deep in coral-colored sand. Herb shouts to hold the gas pedal steady as I steer frantically to keep my pickup from bogging down. Both dogs and water jugs slide wildly from one side of the truck bed to the other. I panic, say we'll never make it. Well, don't stop now, Herb retorts, and I plow on through the dunes, the blooming purple sage a blur in each window.

Finally, the rim of our intended canyon appears in the foreground. At its lip we park on a slab of slickrock and step out onto what looks like the only solid surface for miles. Everywhere there is sand. And an enormous tongue of it—perhaps a thousand feet long—connects the stone rim beneath our feet with the circuitous chasm below, before the canyon slithers away into the western horizon like an enormous sidewinder.

Sunscreen and wide-brimmed hats are applied; day packs filled with several water bottles and food are hoisted. And then, by way of the sand slide, we stumble into the canyon depths; the dogs tuck and roll to protect their paws from the blazing-hot granules that give way beneath the weight of our descent. At the base of the slide is a sign posted by the BLM asking that ORVs be ridden responsibly. Herb kicks the signpost. Until recently, this route was impassable to vehicles—it was only when advancements in ORV technology made the slide accessible that the BLM fenced it off. Within days, the locals had torn the fence down and blazed their way to the bottom. The BLM had capitulated—effectively legitimizing the incursion by adding the sign at the bottom. The agency then told Herb that it could do nothing, that San Juan County had declared the sand slide as well as the canyon below an official road under local jurisdiction. Rumor had it that the route was being touted to visiting recreationists too, and that the canyon had become a bit of a motor park.

On the way here, it became apparent that Herb had suggested this canyon as our weekend destination so he could kill two birds with one stone. For work he needed to investigate the damage in this area. But he also wanted to go somewhere that I wanted to explore, for he was trying to repair the small fissure that had appeared between us. Already he was trying to spend some time at home, but what he couldn't see was that all that time seemed to be filled with projects—planting tomatoes, erecting a tree fort, building storage bins for the back of my truck. It was all for me, for our life together. And the thought of him standing out in that yard, suffering that small field of cheatgrass, bent over my tailgate wielding a Skilsaw and wearing nothing but a tool belt . . . He didn't seem to understand that I wanted him, not all his projects—no matter how they contributed to our life. And when he came in at sunset, his rear end burned strawberry red, he had suddenly realized how delinquent he was on paying bills and returning phone calls. Before I knew it, it was midnight, and I had fallen asleep waiting for him. I wasn't prepared for how much I missed his original attentions, how little else there was to fill my days.

So I am both encouraged and relieved that he has proposed this outing. We hold hands for the first half-mile of the hike, crossing a wash bottom that is little more than parched sand and sun-scoured stones. The dogs are not happy, and seek relief in the scant shade cast by a few stray tumbleweeds. The air is stifling, and a blistering heat convects between the soaring canyon walls.

I grow uncertain about our chosen adventure. But we continue on, for Herb is certain it will get better. And, sure enough, saturation begins—the steady work of seeps and springs. Then, suddenly, cottonwoods and willows spring from the sand, their leaves gyrating into a byzantine mosaic of greens. Birds, frogs, and insects trill out brilliant improvisations—a kind of critter jazz. And as the water gathers substance, there is the ballet of tadpoles and water skeeters across the face of clear pools.

The dogs drink and cool their pads. We squat and scoop water over our heads to cool our scalps, then recline beneath a dense, low-lying awning of trees. At that moment, a parade of ORVs appears. It looks to be an entire extended family—mom, dad, aunts, uncles, cousins, even grandparents. A baby is strapped to the front of one machine, sans helmet or sun hat. Already her white cheeks are scorched. The other machines carry coolers, lawn chairs, and large, soft bodies.

Hidden beneath the trees, we are invisible to them—even when they grind through the water just beyond our toes. And though their passing is swift, it is enough to obscure the mosaic, to silence the music, to still the dance. I want to run out and scream at them to stop. But I remain hidden, and it occurs to me that this is how I have come to live every day in San Juan County—inoffensively incognito. When the air clears, the mud reveals the flattened body of a collared lizard, its lustrous turquoise torso and golden head still twitching in a tire track. Herb gets up with a large flat rock, puts the dazzling reptile out of its misery. I lean back again, stare up through the leaves. The red rectangle of wall above pierces an oval of blue sky.

I cannot get past the hard edges—their basic geometry, the primary colors. Perhaps this is the curse of the desert: It reduces you. And you reduce it in return—diminish it to something so basic you can hardly see it, let alone imagine its gorgeous and abstract possibilities. It happened to my great-great-great-grandfather, during his record-breaking mule ride across the Great Basin: He had traveled for many hours without sleep. At one point, he entered a steep side canyon, where delirium caught up with him:

> It appeared to [Egan] that he was going through the street of a large city. The buildings on each side appeared to be of many shapes, and some of many stories high, and occasionally a bridge would span the street, and so low down that he would duck his head to ride under them. Some of the houses seemed to be lighted up. He could see the lights in many windows, but there was no sound.[1]

Even Egan's eye—stung by sun and wind, dulled for want of rest, water, and food—failed to see the natural world in its complex design. Instead, he defaulted to simpler, man-made representations, comforted by their basicness and familiarity. Surely his limited sight was no different from what the pioneers experienced when they came across the continent: At the beginning of the journey, the scenery would have been a blank canvas upon which they could endlessly paint their future, and the array of colors, textures, and shapes was infinite. But as time wore on and their boot soles wore away, their outlook was also pared down, made a two-dimensional black and white. At first, sagebrush was a plume of silver-green smoke, rising up fragrant from burning embers of red soil—a symbol of the wide ocean of divinely pledged frontier that swam before them. After a while, sagebrush would have been just sagebrush—an encroaching shrub that flourished in the place of much-needed food and forage.

I fear that I too am losing my broader perspective. I squint, try to view things as my grandmother would have—for whatever reason, she never gave in to the desert's reductionist tactics. Too soon, my eyes are closed. And I sigh, for there was a time when I would have pressed for creative vision, when the genetic hand-me-downs of Ada would have eventually sparked some great and fanciful imagery. But nothing changes.

I have known this void before. Sometimes it struck me as writer's block. And always it struck me within the walls of my childhood church. But never before has a canyon failed to move me, and the fact that this one does not alone tells me something is gravely wrong, tells me that somehow, over the course of this year of life in the desert, I have become less of Ada's granddaughter.

After a brief rest, Herb and I continue downstream, but we play leapfrog with the family on wheels, which stops to spin donuts on the stream banks. And with each encounter, both sides cast glowering looks of suspicion and annoyance—apparently the feeling that our experiences are incompatible is mutual. Finally, we turn back up-canyon. We drag our feet in hopes that the sun will drop onto the horizon before we have to trudge up the slide's hot, merciless face: the more arduous the climb is, the more smug the riders will be when they pass us.

But the ORVs make the climb only after we have topped out and cooled off and fired up the stove for a dinner on the rim. Surprisingly, they stop, and they are smiling—albeit sheepishly. They ask if we have any water, for the baby girl is suffering from heat exhaustion. We open our water jugs for them after learning that all the party has in its coolers is Mountain Dew and Red Bull, and the little girl revives a bit.

Later, after the riders are gone, we sit in lawn chairs on the canyon's rim, which turns a vein-engorged violet in the day's last light. The dogs press their bodies into the rapidly cooling rock and lick their sore paws; Herb pulls my feet onto his lap and rubs them. Then he leans over and kisses my sand-caked eyelids. As we fall asleep beneath stars that by midnight are veiled in fine clouds, as traces of gentle rain dampen our sleeping bags—I think that there's still hope, for at least I still respond quixotically to the man next to me, and to the sharp metallic scent of rain-smacked stone.

THE FOLLOWING MORNING flares with heat the moment the sun cracks the horizon. We pack up quickly, then, on the shady side of the truck, make deliberations for alternatives to hiking. We decide on a trip to the end of 276, where, at a place known as Halls Crossing, the highway runs quite literally into an enormous and unlikely body of water.

Lake Powell is actually a euphemism for the United States' second largest and most popular man-made reservoir. Its naming is an irony—apparently meant to honor the one-armed major who had explored the very canyon sacrificed for its creation, a man who had cautioned strenuously against irrigating the arid West. In 1963, three years before I was born, the Bureau of Reclamation closed the floodgates of a massive dam at Page, Arizona. The dam stood eight miles south of the Utah border, and from its immensity, the labyrinthine landscape of Glen Canyon began to fill with the backwaters of the Colorado River and all its tributaries—including both the Green and the San Juan. Over the next decade, the dam backed up the flows of the Colorado and San Juan rivers—186 miles and 72 miles respectively—creating 1,960 miles of shoreline and eight hundred megawatts of hydroelectric power for the sprawling subdivisions that were cropping up in southern California and Las Vegas. The whole project had been clinched by the cooperation of the Navajo Nation, which waived forty-three thousand acre-feet of water rights to thirsty downstream entities and basically gave away fifty-three thousand acres of reservation land along the Colorado River.

Since then, the "lake" has stood as the centerpiece of Glen Canyon National Recreation Area. Its annual visitation ranks not far behind that of Yellowstone and Yosemite Parks.[2] As out of place as it is, the appeal is not hard to appreciate: The main channel is flanked by some of redrock country's most magnificent sandstone cliffs, and in most places they rise straight out of the water for hundreds of feet. Boats can maneuver the endless maze of side canyons, where they are almost sure to anchor upon a private beach of pink sand beneath sculpted alcoves frocked in hanging gardens of monkey flower and ferns. It is a comfortable place, even luxurious, all thanks to an artificial abundance of water. Lake Powell is paradise manipulated— the desert made palatable for the masses.

Lake Powell was really the only place in redrock country my father ever took to, the only place within its expanse where he could still have his bourbon on ice. This was thanks to Ada and Lee's boat. For years they had a small cabin cruiser, an Owens with turquoise trim, which was launched just as soon as there was enough water to float it. The first day, the boat was lowered into the water without a drain plug. To everyone's horror, the boat sank up to its windows. The watermark that stained the curtains remained an embarrassing reminder of that day, and mimicked what the Irvines and other Powellites would call, after only a few years on the lake, the "bathtub ring." This solid white line ran horizontally across the sandstone that rose out of the lake—the result of minerals that leached from the rock at the most frequent water level. The ring quickly became an indicator of what kind of trip boaters were in for. When the ring was visible, it meant the water level had dropped enough to expose the trash and human waste that had settled in the shallows—a situation that made for most unpleasant camping. If the ring couldn't be seen, then the beaches would be in good shape. And after those early years, the bathtub ring would grow to be even more portentous: thanks to the beginning of a long and sustained drought, the ring was soon seen more often than not. At first no one though much of it, but over time, as the ring crept up the cliff wall, progressively higher than the waterline, it became apparent that, beneath the relentless desert sun, the reservoir was evaporating faster than it could fill.

In typically modest and agnostic Irvine fashion, my grandparents never christened the Owens—for years it was simply called "the boat." It was powered by two small outboard motors and was just capable of pulling a water-skier. Belowdecks was a small galley with enough elbow room for whoever was on dish detail, and in the hull was a bed where Lee and Ada slept. Everyone else spread sleeping bags up on deck—although many opted to sleep on the beach where the boat was moored, after the night my father's youngest brother sleepwalked off the boat, right into the water.

For many years, the boat resided at Bullfrog Marina, just across the San Juan County line, in neighboring Garfield County. Early on, the Irvines could easily access the few of Glen Canyon's treasures that had not yet been entirely inundated—like the waterfall at the back of an especially gorgeous alcove named Cathedral in the Desert, or the picturesque mouth of Davis Gulch. For a short while, Lee could even drive right under Gregory Arch. But the year came when the boat could no longer fit beneath the stone curvature. And then, the next year, the lake was full, and the arch was no longer visible—at least not until the drought kicked into full effect a few decades later.

What I have seen of Glen Canyon is like having seen the tip of an iceberg. The top of only the highest cliffs remained above water after the reservoir was completely full. Those who knew its depths say Glen Canyon rivaled the Grand Canyon in both beauty and majesty—so much so that entire books have been written by those who have lamented its flooding. In *Desert Solitaire*, Edward Abbey perhaps best summarized the dirges: "To grasp the nature of the crime that was committed imagine the Taj Mahal or Chartres Cathedral buried in mud until only the spires remain visible." But Abbey went on to make an important distinction between such monoliths: "Those man-made celebrations of human aspiration could conceivably be reconstructed while Glen Canyon was a living thing, irreplaceable, which can never be recovered through any human agency."[3] What Abbey meant was that, in the flooding of Glen Canyon, some of the world's greatest natural architecture was lost forever, never to be replicated—not even by an architect who possessed Ada's organic artistry.

What many of Glen Canyon's mourners fail to mention is the enormous loss of human history—for Glen Canyon was not only beautiful, it was also an archaeological hotbed, a point of convergence for several distinct regional influences within Anasazi culture. Unfortunately, the archaeological survey that was undertaken prior to the canyon's demise was, at least from the Bureau of Reclamation's point of view, largely perfunctory—a mere legal requirement to be met in order to get the turbines up and running. Yucca sandals and gypsum arrowheads were hastily unearthed and cataloged—quite literally as the concrete was being poured into the dam forms. Overworked and underfunded, the sound of the government clock ticking in their ears, two devoted teams of archaeologists from the Museum of Northern Arizona and the University of Utah tried to record what they could. Nearly two thousand sites were noted, but only dozens were ever excavated and studied in detail. Probably thousands more were never even discovered.

Though tools and trinkets were dug up and removed, there was really no way to save the ancient artwork—including hundreds if not thousands of prehistoric petroglyphs and pictographs. Many were the products of the Desert Archaic period—the long-lasting pre-Anasazi era. Given the dearth of other artifacts to study from this time period, such artwork becomes invaluable. An abundance of Archaic panels could have shed light on the most poorly understood yet arguably most successful period of habitation in the history of humanity.

Southwestern archaeology has never been as enamored of Archaic study as it has been with that of the more illustrious, relic-rich Anasazi—so it's not surprising that more effort wasn't made to document its remnants in an already impossible situation. But what if researchers and funders had better appreciated that all-too-distant period, and the spare lifestyle that defined it? After all, as Richard Manning writes in *Against the Grain: How Agriculture Has Hijacked Civilization*, "Our kind has spent at least 290,000 years as hunter-gatherers, [and] only 10,000 as agricultural people, making the latter way of living a relatively brief and novel experiment."[4] It probably wouldn't have hurt to take a look at what worked so well for so long.

Had there been the time and inclination to study more seriously the varieties of Archaic art panels before Glen Canyon flooded, Glen Canyon Linear would have been the most intriguing. Of the five rock art styles identified, this was the most localized, as well as the earliest in origin—and can most certainly be attributed to the pre-agricultural times of the Archaic period. It has been observed in only a few other river canyons, and was largely abstract in its symbolism—a trait common among Archaic-style rock art throughout the world. Wavy lines, dots, rakes, and zigzags are interspersed with animals represented by large geometric bodies and small appendages. The animals frequently flank similarly abstracted anthropomorphs—beings whose large cross-hatched bodies lack significant legs or feet and seem instead to hover in space. One might be tempted to call these drawings crude, as if their creators were incapable of the skills necessary to convey a more realistic representation.

But many of the anthropomorphs wear elaborate headdresses, which suggests more exacting detail—in which case, limited artistic ability can't be called the limiting factor.

There are other noteworthy characteristics of this rock art style: Anthropomorphs without headdresses instead sport horns, or antennae, or a series of concentric circles. Also prominent in many of the figures' hands are scepters—each one an expression of something significant in the natural world. Some look like lightning bolts, some like snakes; others burst from the fingers like stalks of ricegrass. Colorado Plateau rock-art expert Polly Schaafsma has interpreted these figures as otherworldly—drawn by shamans in isolated and special locations, seemingly as part of a ceremonial retreat. Schaafsma and others believe that the style reflects a spirituality common to all hunter-gatherer societies across the globe—a way of life that appreciates the natural world and employs the use of visions to gain understanding and appreciation of the human relationship to the earth. Typically, Schaafsma says, it is a spirituality that identifies strongly with animals and other aspects of nature—and one that does so with an interdependent rather than dominant perspective. To underscore the importance of art in such a culture, Schaafsma points to Aboriginal Australians, noting how, in a so-called primitive society, where forms of written and oral communication are considered (at least by our standards) to be limited, making art is "one means of defining the mystic tenets of one's faith."[5] In such a society, the task of recording those tenets is taken very seriously, and thus the task is assigned to only a select few. Those selected are highly trained and skilled at shamanism, which has been called "an ecstatic technique at the disposal of a particular elite,"[6] and which allows those induced to travel "into realms above and below."[7] On these travels, they glean understanding from ancestral spirits and the deities who embody the natural world; then they return to their people to share what they have learned. And one way they convey the wisdom to the masses is to etch symbols into stone.

I remember that when I learned about shamanism I couldn't help drawing parallels between it and Joseph Smith's encounter with the Angel Moroni, who directed him to the site of the golden plates. It was with that spirit's guidance that Smith was able to translate the symbols inscribed on the plates, the revelations he then published as the Book of Mormon, which he proselytized to people far and wide. And in that comparison, I can't help appreciating the Mormon prophet's euphoric state, his ability to engage with otherworldly beings. But I am left wondering: perhaps it was the hard, material making of words, the tedious task of translation, the labor of language that drained the artistic abstractions, but it seems that things got boiled down to a level so fundamental that they lost their color and complexity.

And perhaps this is why Mormon buildings—ward houses and temples alike—leave something achingly, longingly, viscerally to be desired.

I HAVE AN OLD, yellowed photograph of Lee and Ada, standing alongside my mother and father, on what was once a cliff bench above the Escalante River, not far from the river's confluence with the Colorado and the original descent through Hole-in-the-Rock. The year the photo was taken, the water had backed up from Glen Canyon proper, over portions of the historic trail, and into the Escalante and its tributaries, and the bench on which my parents and grandparents stood had become a beach where they could anchor the boat. They stood only a few yards from the shoreline, beneath a shallow alcove. It was the year before I was born, and the lake was still on the rise. The camera captured Lee and my mother pondering in fascination the rubble of an Anasazi dwelling, while my father stares straight into the lens, his face in a wildly exaggerated grimace. With eyes crossed and mouth smirking, it is the look of someone barely civilized, someone constrained beyond capacity. This is in contrast to his mother, who stands in the foreground with a contained and graceful ease, gazing at symbols on the caramel-colored wall that swoops over their heads. Her look is almost rapturous.

That look is what I remember most about my grandmother. It crept across her face whenever she was working on a serigraph, or when she read to me from *A Child's Garden of Verses*. I saw it every year at Christmas, when she took me to see *The Nutcracker* ballet, and I observed it when we heard Jean-Pierre Rampal play his golden flute with the Utah Symphony. The last time I ever saw that look was when Ada and Lee took Paige and me aboard the Owens for the first time. By then my sister and I were older kids, for my grandfather didn't allow anyone to board the boat who couldn't swim the length of a swimming pool and perform a perfect dive from a diving board.

Paige and I were so excited. Our parents had made many trips to the lake, and we were anxious to experience it ourselves. By the time we were ready to go, the trip to Lake Powell had almost become too much for Lee and Ada to manage alone. But I think they made the effort to get my sister and me away from the tension at home—which was mounting in direct proportion to the increase in my father's drinking.

The boat had suffered electrical problems, and we didn't leave the marina for two days. Finally, Lee got us out into the main channel, and eventually moored us on a beach at the end of a silent little box canyon. Paige and I followed Ada off the boat onto the sand; drifting alongside us was the smell of freshly caught bass on a grill tended by my grandfather. The early-evening light was diaphanous—like a wraith pressing through loosened molecules of sky, stone, and lake surface. I turned to my grandmother, who had dropped to her knees and was sketching furiously. Her skin was practically pulsing with elation.

Wind. Water. Stone. And light changes everything. Shortly after that trip, Ada would begin a slow but steady decline—first her eyesight, then her mind. That evening on the beach was the last time I ever saw my grandmother look at the world so easily, with so much vision. In hindsight, I can't help wondering if those physical and cognitive degradations were signs of permanent flight to another reality—some internal means of escape from the growing embarrassment of her eldest son, and from the disappointments she was beginning to feel about the rapidly changing world in which she lived. There were clues: Having never uttered a single smite against a person, she began to tell me that perhaps my father was inherently lazy. And she kept saying how much had happened in her lifetime.

Bombs. Cars. Television. Rockets. Computers.

It's too much, too fast. And there's no beauty in it.

Her words haunt me now.

ONCE WE REACH Halls Crossing, it's astonishing how far Herb and I must walk from the general store, where we have purchased a six-pack, to the ferry dock. The two were once in spitting distance of one another, but the dock has been moved to reach the new water level—which has hit an all-time low. Herb laughs and recalls how, at a recent meeting to address concerns about the drought's economic impacts on lake-related tourism, San Juan County officials told the National Park Service staff that manages Lake Powell to "just keep chasing the water."

The bathtub ring is twenty feet above the water's surface, but that fact has failed to deter holiday visitation. The entire bay at Halls Crossing is propeller to propeller with watercraft. There are speedboats that look like they were used in a Jason Bourne getaway, houseboats larger than most of the homes I had ever lived in, and Jet Skis as advanced as the ORVs that navigated yesterday's sand slide. The bay sloshes violently from shore to shore, and I recall another family photograph from these same waters: It shows the water still and calm—except around the Irvine men, who have been caught in a rare moment of abandon and are making waves in the process. My father is hunched over, mid-grunt. With his hands he scoops water up into his armpits. His youngest brother, David, brutishly swings a driftwood club at him. Both are looking out the corners of their eyes at Lee, whose hands are clasped in delight. All three are waist-deep, while my mother looks on from the shore, dressed smartly in navy Keds, a nautically inspired T-shirt, and cut-offs. Ada is the only one whose feet don't touch land. Out in the deeper water, she floats, and one can just make out beneath the surface the dark, round sphere of her trunk, the pale limbs spread out and undulating. She wears a bright yellow bathing cap and smiles radiantly at her family.

Facing the sights and sounds of today's Halls Crossing, I have the sudden urge to resurrect both that version of the reservoir and that version of my family. I look for a place to wade out into the water, to reenact with Herb that Kodak moment. But there is no place to swim without the risk of getting mowed over by a watercraft of some sort.

Later, I will be glad not to have gotten wet. When we return to Monticello, I will hear from the bank tellers how, after the big holiday weekend, practically half the town was bedridden—some even hospitalized—with illnesses contracted from human sewage.

All from swimming in the waters of paradise.

IT IS the summer solstice, the first one celebrated at our home on the edge of Lila Canyon. Herb is gone again, and his absences have become so frequent that this time I can't even remember where he is. I am sitting on the couch staring at one of Ada's paintings. The print is little more than a large, shimmering square, awash in an ethereal blue. In terms of form, I had always thought it to be one of her least interesting works, but I loved the quality of the color. It had always struck me as a piece in which to daydream, and as the afternoon fades away, I swim in the blue, contemplating the shortening of days and knowing how suspiciously my attention to this holiday would be viewed by most of San Juan County.

Pagan, Earth-worshipper. Dirty words, on their tongues.

Suddenly the serigraph comes into sharp focus. I now see what Ada intended: The vague and shimmering square of blue is Lake Powell. The orange flames that rise up from the water and reflect off the surface—more like apparitions than geology—are the crests of Glen Canyon's walls. And beneath the water's surface, dappled by rays of light and stifled currents, one can see the sandstone sarcophagus—the rest of the canyon's entombment. It is a brilliant orange; in some places it is opaque, and in others it is porous and inundated by the blue.

The name of my grandmother's rendition of Lake Powell, her lament for the lost canyon, is *Illusion*.

THE LAST TIME I went to Lake Powell was without Ada. I was about to graduate from high school, and my grandparents had sold the Owens. This too was a Memorial Day weekend in San Juan country, and for this trip, my father had rented a houseboat for us and his friend—who also had two teen-age daughters.

Water was water. And rock was rock. The sole thing on my mind was the recent words of my father—which, ironically, were some of the last words I had heard from the Church before I had dropped out.

You were put on this earth for one man and one man only.

These words made me stave off the boy I loved for a year and a half, until finally he convinced me that he was the one. Then, one night, the boy pulled up to the restaurant where I washed dishes for spending money. He waited until I came out the back door and coaxed me into his slinky blue Corvette to profess apologies—for I had caught him at a party running his hands and lips across the body of another girl. He asked me to show him forgiveness, no, really show him—really bow to that feeling of absolution. I did, and when I came up red-faced and sputtering, there was a vacant look in his eyes, and his keys were already turning in the ignition. He didn't speak to me again for years.

A month later, my father had taken us to Lake Powell. I did nothing but lie on the top of the houseboat under the pretense of working on my tan. I was intent on burning—a concentrated effort to scorch every nerve ending in my skin. My goal was never again to feel desire, or pain, or any other kind of vulnerability. And all the while, I tried to make sense of those words of indoctrination, to see how they shaped the threshold of womanhood. But I couldn't figure out to which man I was meant to belong. What I saw was not that I had picked the wrong guy, but that I hadn't been worthy of his devotion.

Baking in the desert sun, my body limp against the boat's rocking motion, I began to wonder. Perhaps there was a Heavenly Father after all, and He was punishing me for not living righteously. And so again, one last time, I tried to talk to Him, to his big, white, long-bearded image. I had defaulted to what was basic and familiar, and the image, as unappealing as it was, was something I could get my head around.

While I waited for a reply, my father and his buddy stood reeling drunk at the wheel below, and were intent on steering the boat into a frighteningly tight canyon. I sat up just as the cold shadow of the encroaching walls hit my seared skin, just in time to see my father run the houseboat, full-throttle, high onto the beach.

The impact was extraordinary. I pitched to the front of the boat deck, where the guardrail broke my momentum. I heard the cupboards below fly open and dishes stamped SHATTER-RESISTANT hurl across the cabin and smash against the far wall. Then there were the sounds of the engine grinding out in the sand, and my father's snorting laugh. Next I saw my father and his friend, cocktails in one hand and cigars in the other, stumbling onto shore—leaving behind their four daughters to contemplate the mess.

It was the last trip I ever took with my father. And it was the last time I tried to talk to God. From then on, there was retreat—into remote and beautiful locations. But there was no ceremony or vision. I traveled only horizontally, hidden beneath a canopy of tightly clasped petals. It wasn't until I met the lion man that I was ready to bloom again, and I did so—for a time. But eventually, we revert to what we know. And what I know is this: Going deep is to enter the dangerous underworld of the heart. And rising above is to risk cracking my head on the white-tiled floor of the celestial kingdom.

OF ALL THE TIMES my father had driven drunk, the day he ran the houseboat aground in Glen Canyon stands out. On that occasion, he stumbled away from the wreckage, and when he returned, something torpid had settled over him. I knew it later that night, when the hair-raising swoop of a horned owl over our campfire failed to thrill him. And the next morning, when the leap of feeding fish and the waterfall notes of canyon wrens failed to wake him. That afternoon, he didn't even comment on my bikini—an article of clothing that, before that day, would have been completely off limits.

I think the change was the result of oversaturation. With each drinking binge, he had imagined he was inviting some heightened state of consciousness, but really he was slowly killing his essence— something both wild and divine—the thing that made him spring to life in anticipation of the hunt, the thing that made him feel reverence and grace in the muddy, salt-crusted marsh of the Great Salt Lake. Until that point, he may have struggled with outward appearances, but ultimately his viscera quivered with what Paul Shepard says are "more than dim reflections of outmoded customs from the ice ages," or the deeply original tendencies that express themselves as optimal human physiology and psychology. Exercising these, Shepard says, is required for a vibrant and healthy life. The trick is, they must be exercised within the "functional equivalents of the environments in which . . . the human organism evolved."[8]

Houseboats were not at all my father's style. They were too big, too pretentious, too clumsy in design—and they were too removed from the gorgeous world in which they floated. His renting one should have been my first clue that something drastic had changed, that he had lost his view of things. And, sure enough, after the houseboat trip, his life stagnated. He no longer put on his business suit, for he was no longer trying to appear as if he had a job. He lived off Lee and Ada's refrigerated leftovers, and any financial donations he could talk them out of. When his car was repossessed, he borrowed Ada's maroon station wagon. Sometimes he drove it places he shouldn't have, just as he had the old family car of the same make. But mostly he drove aimlessly around Salt Lake City. On a few occasions, friends confessed they had seen him at the bars—so drunk he could hardly stand—and had both paid his tab and given him a ride home. I couldn't help turning away. Drunk or sober, he had become a constant embarrassment, and utterly depressing to be around. And it wasn't that difficult to avoid him, for he rarely called or made plans with his daughters anymore.

But I saw him from afar. I worked at a retail shop in his neighborhood, and on my way to work, I often saw him parked in front of the liquor store, waiting for it to open. The car was trashed—there were dents everywhere, and the muffler dragged on the pavement, throwing sparks. Fortunately, my grandmother had long ceased to drive and probably didn't even remember that she owned the vehicle. And his retriever was always sitting in the front passenger seat, a sight that prompted my father's friends to nickname the car "The Red Kennel."

It was as if my father's vastly complex and beautiful view of the world had faded. He couldn't imagine a life more invigorating—a rapturous combination of things both primal and spiritual. Even the idea of shooting something fresh for supper did not stir him as it used to. It was as if his perspective had been reduced to the way the engineers looked at Glen Canyon and saw only storage, the way a weary Howard Egan saw skyscrapers instead of sandstone.

God, Guns, and Guts.

I realize now that my father stilled his heart all the way back then, that he was dead years before he shot himself.

THE FIRST DAY of deer season at Lila Canyon. Pulling off our property in my truck, I see a man I've never seen before, parked on a shiny new ORV, dead center in the road. His gun is propped across the handlebars, and his feet are kicked up and resting across the gun. His Day-Glo orange vest has creases in it; his matching cap sports not one speck of dirt or stain of sweat. He is talking on a cell phone. To pass him, I am forced to pull my truck off into the brush. I want to flip him off, but his barrel is pointed my way.

Turning out onto the main county road, I find another orange-frocked man parked on his ORV, but this machine is perched in the back of a pickup bed. The man that straddles the machine also has a gun laid across his handlebars; his gaze is upon the open bean field spread out below the road. He is waiting for a buck to wander into the clearing; it is obvious that when he gets what will be a ridiculously easy shot, he can back the ORV down a ramp propped against the open tailgate and drive through the opening in the fence to retrieve his kill. In the process, his feet will touch the ground only once. I drive past, gawking—for the scene did not qualify as anything I knew about hunting.

I BELIEVE THAT it was his hunting life that kept my father alive for so long—despite his drinking—for it was on foot that my father tracked his quarry, hauled his kill. Indeed, studies show that food-getting for most hunter-gatherer societies requires only about three hours per day, or three days per week.[9] Sure, procuring food would require more effort in more extreme environments, in a place like the San Juan country, but the idea is that these groups are fit—from running away from predators as well as running after prey—far more fit than their agricultural and industrial counterparts, who suffer more readily from cardiovascular problems like heart disease and thrombosis.[10] Such health, and the well-being it inspires, coupled with the honed and heightened senses of living vigorously, would have surely inspired creativity. Indeed, in *Against the Grain*, Richard Manning describes how the hunter-gatherer's ability "to live off hundreds of species of plants and animals required an attention to color, light, shape, and motion that must have bordered on obsession," adding that it is "no wonder we began painting in such fine detail so early in the course of human events."[11] It comes down to *arousal*, says Manning, a state that is primarily induced by food and sex—our most primal drives. In his view, the arts perform the same function—stimulating our sensibilities and stirring our psyches. Arousal adds vibrancy to both body and psyche, organizing life not only for survival but for higher, more esoteric purposes as well. A state of arousal, then, is a state capable of elevating and elating the consciousness. This means that it isn't only the shamans of hunter-gatherer cultures who enjoy divinity, it's the whole tribe. The concept is not too far-flung from Mormon doctrine, which says the priesthood makes spiritual revelation available to the male masses. But I have to say, arousal is not a state I witnessed on the church pews or in the neighborhood—not ever. As I creep past, watching the lazy hunter, I think how at least, even in his most moribund days, my father was never reduced to this blood sport.

MY NEW VENEER and diplomatic efforts about town have finally paid off. My reward is an invitation to a gathering of local women. I dress mildly, make a list of topics not to broach. I am careful to bring finger food that won't seem too uppity.

To my surprise, the women are drinking wine—decent wine. There is a selection of imported cheese on a platter, and fine blues guitar coming off a turntable. They tiptoe a bit carefully around me, the newcomer. But the group is easygoing and genuine. One woman singlehandedly runs her own ranch; another is married to a man who will soon tell me that if my earth-worshipping friends and I try to drain his lake he knows where to find me. Another is a teacher who will be run out of town for letting her seventeen-year-old daughter drink a birthday beer in their own home. For me, in San Juan County, it is the first evening of its kind. I grow heady with the camaraderie and the ambience, and I begin to think there is hope for a life here.

But then I have a second glass of Merlot. My mouth opens like a pent-up river, and the veneer I worked so carefully to build recedes like a drought-stricken waterline. I flood the room with my politics, inundate senses and sensibilities. It's too much too fast, and there's no vision.

The women are gracious, and let me have this moment. When it passes, when the words that I've used so many times they've become rhetorical lie strewn about the room, someone passes the Stilton. Another recites a poem. Sighs and shivers fill the room. I, for one, am finally speechless.

When I walk out into the night, I see how the trees scratch their own architecture in the star-soaked sky. The cool air licks the nape of my neck, my heart pounds and the blood rushes just beneath the surface of my skin.

One man and one man only.

I hope he isn't old, with a white beard, standing expectantly on a white tile floor. I hope that he has long red curls, and that tonight I find him at home, waiting.

8

Ghost

J une 1847: *From the saddle he guided the wagons in until they formed a tight, defensible circle around a large ash tree that stood rooted in the middle of a clearing. It was standard procedure at night, to stay that close and well guarded. Not that they'd had any trouble—in that first crossing of the plains, the entire party had lost only four horses to Indians and not a single Saint had died. In fact, during the next twenty-some years, of the thousands of Mormon pioneers that would follow in their footsteps, only six Saints would ever fall prey to the natives. Nearly eight times that many would die from self-inflicted accidents—like the misfiring of their own guns.[1]*

The wagon train had just crossed Rawhide Creek, which drained into the North Platte River not far from Fort Laramie. That first day in June put the fourteen companies of ten less than two months away from their first glimpse of the new Zion. As Howard Egan turned out his company's livestock—Brother Kimball alone had five horses, seven mules, six oxen, and two cows—he could see the fort to the southwest. If he looked north, he could see less scabrous shapes, dark and soft—the Black Hills of South Dakota. Straight ahead, the western horizon was jagged now, where the

Rocky Mountains slashed the sky. And everywhere, the cedar groves thick-ened—forerunners of the higher elevations and rugged country ahead.

By his count, 541 miles of flat earth and seamless skylines stood be-tween him and his two wives, who had remained at Winter Quarters with the rest of the brethren. But he didn't think of Tamson or Nancy now; he would pray for them tonight, and soon enough he'd be returning to the settlement to retrieve both spouses. In that moment he thought only about the variations in topography, how they delivered such palpable re-lief from the monotonous country behind him.

Standing in such proximity to fourteen-thousand-foot peaks, Egan knew that the promised land was near. Not that he knew exactly where—even Brother Brigham didn't quite know the specifics yet. Their new leader may have been a brilliant and pragmatic strategist, but he was not as prophetic as Joseph Smith had been. He knew only that the new Zion lay somewhere beyond the Continental Divide—that their quest would take them "out from this evil nation"[2] and into lands ruled by the distant and indifferent arm of Mexico. But for that first train of faithful Saints, this was good enough to go on. They already based their faith on many things not readily apparent.

They had come this far, with this much ease, thanks largely to Egan's quick mastering of frontier life. The brethren could count on him to feed the entire camp, to get the wagons across even the most swift and swollen rivers. And he could deal with the Indians in a manner that rarely ended in gunfire, despite the natives' relentless demands for supplies. Brother Brigham had admonished Egan and the others to get along with them, had counseled specifically that it was better to feed an Indian than to fight him. After all, the goal was to convert them all to Mormonism. Without the natives, they could not fulfill the prophecies that would usher in the last days on earth.

Indeed, Egan had done his best. His trigger finger never strayed far from his holster, but he remained generous with the savages—giving freely from the wagon train's stores of tobacco, flour, and ammunition.

And for each band they encountered, Egan was the perfect diplomat. He sought quickly the names of the headmen, learned their greetings, and studied closely the forms of etiquette and protocol that varied so greatly from tribe to tribe.

That evening, from the encampment around the ash tree, the words in Egan's journal are those of a content and grateful man. "The Lord has blessed and prospered us in our journey,"[3] he writes. He then describes in detail the Saints' campsite and its extraordinary views. In these passages, the man sounds fresh and relaxed. And in this state, he can see the complex wonders around him.

His descriptions take up an entire page. At the end of that page, he mentions briefly the ash tree around which 140 Mormons are gathered for the night. He notes that the bark has been peeled away, and surmises that it is to prevent wolves from climbing its trunk. For, tucked in the tree's branches, for all the camp to see, is the corpse of an Indian baby, wrapped carefully in animal skins. "It is said," he writes, "that this is the mode of burying their dead."[4]

That is all he writes about the dead infant. In fact, Egan uses just three sentences to describe the great tree and its haunting contents. He doesn't ponder how the child met its demise, doesn't name the tribe to which it belonged. He doesn't describe why such a ritual was performed— or how such a custom might assist a spirit into the afterworld. It's as if Egan's cultural curiosity extends only to realms necessary for peaceful passage and the hope of conversions. It's as if the camp circle was oblivious to the human body in the tree, as if it was nothing to go on with the business of baking biscuits and greasing wagon axles in the shadow of a dead and decaying child.

JUNE 2001: A temperamental summer afternoon, and Abajo Peak gathers clouds like the robes of a reeling dervish. Layers of steel blue and ribbons of spectral gray swirl around the mountain. Herb is out in the Canyonlands Basin, investigating some new ORV routes that have mysteriously appeared in what was previously untouched desert. I worry that his Volkswagen Beetle will get stuck on the way out there, for it's an afternoon ripe for flash floods. As I stand at my north window, the swirling raiments grow thick and heavy, enshrouding the mountain entirely. An all-too-near flash of lightning, and I decide it is not only an afternoon to stay out of wash bottoms and off unpaved roads, it is also a good day to stay off the computer. It seems the only option left is laundry.

The Monticello Laundromat is empty save for the two Mormon missionaries who knocked on my door the summer before. I walk past them, to the next available machines. Our eyes meet fleetingly; the young men quickly return their gaze to the folding of two perfect and identical piles—white shirts, white socks, white briefs.

There is no doubt they remember me. But after a year in the field, they are now seasoned veterans. To maximize conversion rates, they have learned where to focus their energies. This means they have learned that Jack Mormons like me are a much tougher sell than those who have had no prior involvement with the religion—in fact, we're mostly a waste of time. Of course, slamming the door in their faces didn't do much to encourage any future encounters. For nearly half an hour, the Laundromat suffers along in awkward silence. There is only the rain pummeling the roof, and the intermittent snarl of thunder.

As my machines begin to agitate, the front door bursts open. In strides a man who is larger than life, who looks and acts as if he were walking into the saloon on a spaghetti-Western set. He sports spotless Lee jeans and an unsoiled white Stetson. The kind my grandpa Blaisdell and my uncles wore only when they went to the fair, or rodeo.

With an air of familiarity, the man slaps the missionaries' backs, bellows, "Good afternoon, elders." The boys look up, their faces suddenly animated. They respond to the cowboy with wide grins and a flurry of greetings. He banters with them as he moves down the row of washers, before setting down his laundry basket on the table nearest me. He tips his hat my way.

"Are the elders giving you any grief, ma'am?" His eyes sparkle in jest.

"Not today," I reply.

"You let me know if they do, and I'll set 'em straight," he says, winking at the boys. I smile, and apologize for taking up so many machines—once again I have waited nearly four weeks to wash our clothes. I had vowed to be more regular, but moving farther out of town has only made the task easier to put off.

The cowboy shrugs. He says he needs only one machine, since he is doing what he calls his "bachelor laundry." I smile, and offer assistance with temperature choices and soap measurements.

"So—where you from?" he asks, dropping quarters into the machine's slots.

Sizing me up, he seems to have found me to be a nice young Mormon woman. I suspect this because he speaks with a familiarity only one step removed from the tone he used with the missionaries—a knowing tone that Mormons reserve for people they don't know but have pegged as brothers or sisters in the eyes of God. I am pleased. It means the look and demeanor I have been cultivating all year long are beginning to pay off.

Not that I'd made any real inroads yet, but there was progress: My neighbors were friendly, even stopping by to check on me whenever Herb was gone. The women who invited me to their party had invited me to another one. In September, we had even been invited to a backyard barbecue hosted by BLM employees who were saying farewell to a few seasonals. Most of the evening was filled with bureaucractic double-speak, but at least I had met another nongovernment Gentile, a young woman named Jessica who had lived in the

Central American rain forest, where she trained with a shaman. Now she was raising her two small children in Monticello so they could be in proximity to their grandmother.

Herb could see that Jessica and I had made a strong connection, and so, other than bringing me a cold beer, he left us alone under a willow tree. She entrusted me with two things: One was that her mother was here on a sort of incognito basis, for in her former life she too had been a wilderness activist and had been run out of another southern-Utah town, but not until her windows had been shot out, her well vandalized, and her children beaten up. The other thing Jessica told me was how, in the spirit world, each person had spirit guides to help him or her through life. If a person asked it of her, she could journey into the spirit realm and receive information that would help the person in need.

"It's amazing," she had said to me. "There is so much going on that we never see." I was actually relieved when her loose black hair had fallen across her eyes, for their green luminosity seemed to glimpse things in me that I myself had never looked at. Still, Jessica was utterly delightful to spend time with, and I began to drive into town to visit with her several times a week.

Besides my social calendar's filling in, there were other signs that I had achieved some sort of initial acceptance. On a recent day, as the chill of winter had descended on Monticello, I had gone to the local dentist's office, where the hygienist had commented on the pretty trim on my garments. She had assumed I had on the underwear worn by Mormons who have gone through the temple rites—a vast expanse of filmy white polyester that covers the entire trunk of both men's and women's bodies, kept on by some even during sex and gym workouts. I couldn't bring myself to tell her that what she saw sticking out from beneath the collar of my sweater was actually the white trim of my thermal underwear, for I knew that such a confession would replace her warm and intimate tone with one of distant formality—the tone reserved for Gentiles.

And now the cowboy has accepted me, and I am congratulating myself on my conformity. Not that it was ever a stretch for me to appear Mormon. There are my fair Aryan looks—for most ancestors of Deseret originated in the British Isles, or Scandinavia. There is my Mormon patois—like Charity's—which unleashes itself whenever I encounter fellow Utahns. But now there is my dress—also like Charity's. It buttons up over my collarbone and hangs straight off a high empire waist. It is so billowy that walking in it feels like floating across the floor. I have grown my hair out too, let the trendy cut and color fade into long, soft tresses of natural dishwater blond. And gone are the makeup and jewelry. Living out at Lila Canyon—where we don't even own a mirror—we hardly seemed to have a reason for such details.

The cowboy before me is immaculately groomed, and shares with me the classic Utah stock features of fair skin, blue eyes, and blond hair. He looks to be about my age.

"I live here," I reply.

He turns abruptly toward me, his eyebrows raised high to demonstrate his profound sense of shock.

"Now, why haven't I seen you around? I know everyone in this town."

"Oh, I don't get out much," I answer.

"So how long have you been here?" he asks.

"Little over a year now," I say. "I moved down here from Salt Lake."

"To Monticello?" he asks. "What brings you here? Seems no one comes here unless they got family or a government job."

"I love this landscape," I say. "And I wanted to get out of the city."

I give him the easy pieces. I leave out the part about moving to be near a man he surely knows and whose work he most likely resents. And I leave out the part about my father, how I left to avoid duplicating his fate. Quickly I ask the cowboy about his life—not only to deflect his questions but also because I find him endearing.

Despite his Hollywood showmanship, he has that clean-cut cowboy handsomeness that reminds me of my male relatives in Idaho.

He tells me he was born and raised in San Juan County, served in Chile, and returned to move north as a newlywed. My second clue that he has accepted me as one of his own is that he mentions his mission without ever actually saying the word—assuming I would know what "served" meant. And he says "move north" without saying where—knowing that I would envision somewhere within the territory of Deseret. He goes on to say that after his divorce he returned to help his father on the family ranch. I know who his father is. He has many of the grazing permits in the Abajos and down near Canyonlands National Park. His father is a man who hates environmentalists and says so at every public opportunity.

Then the cowboy asks the inevitable question.

How do you make a living here?

Avoiding the part about working part-time for an environmental group, I tell him I'm a writer. He smiles. Says he loves a good book every now and then. He wants to know what I write about. I hedge, making a vague and lighthearted reference to "topics that aren't too common in these parts."

"And those would be . . ."

Now I fumble, for I still haven't perfected this part of my masquerade. I say "conservation issues," and avoid the poker-hot words like "wilderness." I am hoping this will be enough to squelch his curiosity.

"Oh, that's cool," he says, with a wave of his hand. "We're all conservationists down here. We love the land more than anyone."

These are precisely the words my grandpa Blaisdell had said whenever we debated land-use issues. I look down at my long, loose dress. It reminds me of the thick living-room drapes I hid behind whenever my father came home drunk. The collar claws at my neck. But the cowboy had said, "That's cool," and those words are the sweetest music to my ears.

Cover. I'm in.

The fantasy begins: I will be invited to the cowboy's next family barbecue. I envision his father pulling up a lawn chair beside me, welcoming me to town. Over homegrown hamburgers and Jell-O salad, we'll discuss ranching. On desert public lands. Even wilderness-designation. The talk will be congenial, for I will drive home the point that cows are still allowed in wilderness. That we are not out to shut down the ranching lifestyle. That my mother's side of the family has made its living in the same manner. Then I'll take a big bite of my burger and say, See, I eat beef too. And by the time we have homemade ice cream with fresh peaches from the orchard, we'll have met in the middle—for I will have done a better job at keeping my opinions palatable than I did at the last social gathering I attended. The rancher will see that I'm not so bad, that perhaps we agree on more than he realized. He'll promise to talk to other cowboys, tell them the tree-huggers that have come to town aren't so different after all. And he'll invite me back for the big drive, when they move the herds down to winter pasture.

In the fantasy, I am of course wearing the same dress. And in the Laundromat, the cowboy is still talking.

"As long as you're not trying to lock up everything—to keep us from making a living. You're fine by us so long as you're not like those wacko extremists from SUWA . . ."

The machines gurgle as they drain soapy water. Lightning scurries across the sky, and the fluorescent tubes sputter above our heads. The cowboy's curiosity about me has been sated, and he saunters back to the missionaries. Draping an arm over each shoulder, he pulls them in close like football players in a huddle. Like wagons circled against a savage world.

On the opposite side of the room, I stand watching the men across the tops of the machines. They are engrossed in commonalities: A departing elder's farewell gathering. The potluck on Saturday, after the wards play softball. The week's baptism schedule.

Despite my dress, I have now been fingered as Not Quite One of Them. A Mormon woman of my age would have supplied different answers—she would have been married, would have had children dodging in front of the dryers, would have most likely not had a job outside the home. It would have been a real stretch for her to say she was a single freelance writer. To move to the desert only for the sake of scenery. To say she wrote about conservation issues. And so now, immersed in their common culture, the cowboy and the missionaries are barely aware of me.

A year and a half in San Juan County, and now Herb squints at me every morning, trying to find some sign of the woman who once howled foul words across a canyon just to hear the raucousness of her own voice. The woman who ran naked with him across a field of oil rigs. Last year I had tried to be anonymous—to lie low, marinating in isolation. This year I have attempted integration by pretending to be something more palatable to the locals, something that even my father would have approved of. I look down at the dress again. I've got cover, all right. Whatever the cowboy sees, he isn't seeing me.

Suddenly the mass of fabric is unbearable. I tear at the top buttons, pull the collar away from my neck. A current of air moves down my chest, across my belly. I stand up straight and square my shoulders. Already the men have turned to look at me—and their faces are not unlike my father's on that Valentine's Day when I stood my ground and declared that I would wear whatever I damn well pleased.

When I speak, my voice emerges with a substance that startles me. It carries over the rumble of the machines, over the rain spattering on the glass.

"Actually, sir, I work for the Southern Utah Wilderness Alliance."

The washing machines have hit their spin cycle. The missionaries are stuffing their clean clothes into duffel bags as fast as they can.

The cowboy's eyes meet mine. I brace for reprisal. But his face curves into a question mark. He scratches his brow.

"But you seem like such a nice girl . . ."

He paces back and forth on the linoleum. I count the footsteps—nineteen before he turns to face me. Then the sermon begins: How cattle have actually *improved* the condition of the land, how it's the blankety-blank (that's a Utah euphemism for "goddamn") earth-muffins who are the problem, that they go out and camp on public lands like they own the place, and while they're there, they take drugs and have sex and shoot cows dead on the spot. Then they go back to their big fancy cities and drink their cappuccinos and cast votes for East Coast liberals—pretty boys who think that the prime rib served at their fund-raising dinners grows on trees.

His fair skin is bright red now. He stops to catch his breath. Then he says that his family is native to San Juan County, that the good Lord gave them the land to use, and it would be in fine shape except for the darn elk that are eating and trampling everything in sight. He says we ought to kill 'em off, they don't even belong here, they aren't native critters anyway.

"Besides," he says, "if you people had it your way, you'd have us running around in loincloths and grubbing for roots. But let me tell you somethin'—even the Navajo and Ute don't buy that crap anymore."

In response, I have my own quiver of litanies: Since cattle were introduced to the West, at least 50 percent of desirable native plant species have been eliminated.[5] A recent EPA report says that, thanks to cows, Western riparian corridors—those slender ribbons of water that alone sustain the Western landscape—are in "the worst condition in history."[6] It's not liberal politicians putting family ranches out of business; without federal subsidies allocated by Congress, most small operations couldn't afford to graze a cow and calf for a year—which, on public lands for that time period, costs less than feeding a pet hamster.[7] To epitomize ranching as the essence of

Western life is to ignore U.S. Department of Interior findings show-ing that an elimination of public-land livestock grazing would result in a loss of only 0.1 percent of the West's total employment.[8] Finally, there is the fact that most of the small independent guys simply can't compete with corporate agriculture. Family ranches account for less than 0.13 percent of BLM rangeland, because most grazing allot-ments are now controlled by major corporations.[9] And one of the larger corporate permittees in the nation is owned by none other than the cowboy's beloved Church of Jesus Christ of Latter-day Saints.[10]

But I don't say any of these things. Perhaps I am not yet prepared to reveal myself fully. At least I know that I will never again wear this dress.

I also know that to speak directly against cattle ranching in Des-eret is to speak against my mother's family, people whom I love. Un-til now, for the sake of getting along, for the sake of limiting the severity of my betrayals to blood relatives, I have talked out of both sides of my mouth. And I could get away with it: the Wilderness Act allows grazing in designated wilderness areas, thanks to an eleventh-hour compromise struck in the back hallways of Congress.

But in the end, I say that I don't shoot cows.

And then I say, "You forgot the Paiute."

The cowboy blinks. "What?"

"The Paiute. When you mentioned the Ute and Navajo being in accordance with your ideas of modern living, you didn't mention the Paiute."

He tosses his chin to the side. "Well, they're mixed in with all the others. Just poor relations to the Ute, you know."

His remark reflects how most folks have come to think of the San Juan Paiutes—if they have ever heard of them at all. Even the most detailed and credible accounts of San Juan history hardly dis-tinguish between the region's other Native American cultures and the most original of southern Utah's historic tribes. Unlike the Ute and the Navajo, who migrated into redrock country *after* history was being committed to paper, the Paiute made their regional debut in prehistoric times.

This is significant: it means the Paiute overlapped the Anasazi by about two hundred years. The two cultures, however, were headed in vastly different directions. The Paiute lifestyle emulated the hunting-gathering era that dominated the Colorado Plateau and the Great Basin for at least ten thousand years, but by the time the Paiute arrived on the scene around A.D. 1000, the post-Archaic Anasazi had already evolved through the Basketmaker stage and were well into the Pueblo period of cliff-dwelling. The Anasazi were probably once like the Paiute—and evolved out of a nomadic, foraging lifestyle because the success of it eventually allowed their numbers to bulge with infants and elderly, making it much harder to roam the countryside in search of food. The idea is that they probably settled in, first learning intensive farming techniques and the weaving of fine basketry. Later, they developed masonry skills to erect stone housing.

So while the Paiute moved in, camping in temporary shelters on the heels of game herds and otherwise ferreting out the desert's rather subtle abundance, the Archaics-turned-Anasazi were beginning to hunker down inside their stone palaces—dwellings that declared permanence, territoriality, and in some cases paranoia. They kept a watchful eye on both crops and storm clouds, and hoarded possessions and food stores. They did not get out and actively seek their sustenance; instead, they bent over in the fields for hours at a time. After a long day's work (which, by most estimates, was more than twice as long as that of hunter-gatherers), they sat stiffly in ceremony, praying to gods who gradually began to embody not so much the spirits of animals, trees, and mountains as human likeness. To curry favor with this new brand of supernatural beings—some of whom could singlehandedly make the harvest more bountiful—their rituals appear to have grown dogmatic—and, in the cases of cannibalism and human sacrifice, perhaps even desperate.

Meanwhile, the Paiute continued to wander the land in relative peace, carrying little more than the atlatl—an updated version of the stick used by the Archaics to hurl spears at game, which had evolved to be more sleek and swift than Pleistocene megafauna. Wherever the Paiute made camp, they left behind only the stones on which they ground their seeds into flour and within which they burned fires—and perhaps a few bones from a recent feast of meat. So adaptive, so perfectly synchronized with the desert was the Paiute life, that even when a great drought drove the cliff-dwelling farmers from the region, the Paiute managed just fine. But the Paiute's story has a great irony—almost identical to that of the Desert Archaic period: Despite the enduring success of this lifestyle, it left an imprint that was nothing more than a whisper upon the landscape. Indeed, its traces are so difficult to discern that one might wonder if the prehistoric Paiute were ever really there at all.

Historic times changed the Paiute's fate, but not their low visibility, even though by the mid-nineteenth century they had formed at least sixteen bands throughout the Colorado Plateau and the Great Basin—the very lands that would soon be claimed by the Mormons for Deseret. And although the world changed dramatically around them, even as other Indian tribes moved into the Four Corners region and increasingly assimilated into the Anglo cultures that had descended on the West, the Paiute remained fiercely loyal to simplicity and nomadism. Eventually, though, the outside world encroached on the Southern Paiute. And of all the bands, the one who suffered most in the face of that encroachment was the San Juan band.

This was largely due to the presence of the Ute. Close relatives to the Southern Paiute, the Ute had become skilled with both horses and weapons—acquired from seventeenth-century Spanish explorers. By the nineteenth century, they had mastered a more aggressive style of culture, and the only common denominator that remained between the two tribes was the mutual intelligibility of their Numic languages. Ultimately, the difference was this: whereas the Paiute maintained their status quo of resources needed to get by, the Ute had found that, from astride their saddles, the San Juan country was theirs for the taking. Soon the Ute were in full-time cahoots with the Mexicans, who claimed the region from afar. Showing no loyalty to their pedestrian cousins, the Ute kidnapped Paiute women and children and took them south—to be sold as slaves.

Infiltrating Anglos also mistreated the Paiute largely because they failed to appreciate the Paiute lifestyle. Very early on, derogatory portrayals of the tribe led to a widespread prejudice against their kind. Captain John C. Fremont called them "diggers" and "lizard eaters" who lived "in the lowest state of human existence."[11] Another white traveler characterized them as

> the most degraded and least intellectual Indians known to the trappers. They wear no clothing of any description—build no shelters . . . They provide nothing for future wants. And when the lizards and snails and wild roots are buried in the snows of winter, they are said to retire to the vicinity of timber, dig holes . . . deposit themselves in them, and sleep fast until the weather permits them to go abroad again and hunt for food.[12]

It was the Mormons who finally came to their aid. The bands had been seriously weakened by disregard and exploitation, and the earliest Saints responded with food, clothing, and shelter. They also responded by outlawing Indian slave trade throughout all of Deseret. In gratitude, the Paiute sought to help Mormon settlers. Their intimate knowledge of the desert and its resources proved invaluable to the pious newcomers, so much so that by 1859—a mere twelve years after Howard Egan and the first wagon train arrived in the Salt

Lake Valley—the Mormons were able to establish in Paiute territory more than a dozen settlements.

During that time, the Paiute in the southeasternmost corner of what is now Utah continued to languish. The reasons were many: The first Mormons would not penetrate the Hole-in-the-Rock for a few more decades, so Paiute there would not receive the aid that other bands received. At the same time, large non-Mormon cattle operations had infiltrated the San Juan country, and Athabaskan-speaking Navajo—having migrated from Canada—punched into the region with their sheep and goats, looking to escape ongoing conflicts with the U.S. government. Indeed, in 1868, Washington resolved to end those conflicts on lands it thought no one in his right mind would want to own. And so, without consulting the Indians who already lived there, the government awarded the Johnny-come-lately Navajo a vast tract of San Juan Paiute country, which is now part of the Navajo Nation.

Then the Mormons moved in, and, through a series of wheelings and dealings, acquired all the big cattle companies' herds. Between those creatures and the Navajo's sheep, goats, and horses, the desert was stripped bare. The Saints' numbers burgeoned, and the piñon groves that had supplied a nutritious and sweet-tasting nut as a staple to the Paiute diet were felled for homes and firewood. Water sources were drained or diverted, and game disappeared. Seriously weakened by the depletion of resources they had relied upon for almost a millennium, the Paiute began to die from an assault of Anglo germs.

The Mormons responded with empathy, and, just as they had done in so many other parts of Deseret, they took in the destitute natives. But in doing so, they tried to convert those in need, and the Paiute soon found the limits of their gratitude. For the purposes of school and land use, they had been lumped together with Indians whose cultures were unfamiliar and adversarial to them, and they resented it. More adamantly than the Ute or the Navajo, the Paiute resisted assimilation, and eventually the Mormons became frustrated with their incorrigible and incompatible ways, ultimately proposing to the federal government that the Paiute—along with the other tribes—"be put on a reservation . . . and taught something of civilization."[13] To the Paiute especially, a people who had been told by Coyote that they alone were meant to live in this desert at the center of the world, reservation life seemed a fate worse than death. With hardly anything but the breechclouts they wore, the last-remaining San Juan Paiute made themselves scarce, and vanished into the deepest recesses of the San Juan.

They inhabited the margins like ghosts. One group remained in a remote location at the base of Navajo Mountain. By 1960, the unassimilated Paiute were only eighteen in number, and yet, as if to erase their traces further, the U.S. Census listed them as Navajo. The only other group of Paiute that remained in the southeastern corner of Utah were those that had been rounded up and moved to a sliver of land called White Mesa Reservation—the place where Nora lived, a place now adjacent to a disposal site for radioactive waste. Forever after, this group has been referred to as "Ute," even in prominent historical records.

Staring at the cowboy, I remember my last trip to the Laundromat. It had also been my last encounter with Nora, which took place before I had understood the distinction between Ute and Southern Paiute. As we waited for our clothes to dry, I had remarked how outraged the White Mesa Tribe must be that the Nuclear Regulatory Commission had approved the processing of massive amounts of hazardous waste atop Ute burial grounds.

It had seemed almost perfunctory, the way she had corrected me.

"Actually, I'm Paiute." Then she rolled her eyes and shrugged her shoulders. "Whatever that means."

OUTSIDE, the rain hasn't really let up at all. More thunder, which competes with the next thing I say to the cowboy.

"And, besides, the old rock art in this area shows elk."

"What?" he says.

"Too much antler to be deer. Means they were here in prehistoric times. Before your family. Before your cows."

I am breathless with the boldness of my statements. But my resolve strengthens with each word, and his responses intensify accordingly. We're barely looking at one another, so rapt are we with the sound of our own voices, with the sweet righteousness of our positions. He says "Church" with a capital "C." I say "Wilderness" with the same emphasis. We continue right through the stalling of the cowboy's machine, a load unevenly distributed.

Mid-sentence, the cowboy stops.

"You single?" he asks. He's staring at me now.

The missionaries hightail it out the door. In their haste, they leave behind a box of Cheer.

"You know," I say, "I think your dad would disinherit you if he knew you were hitting on an earth muffin."

He shrugs his shoulders. "Can't blame a guy . . . As long as she's Christian, and she loves the redrock country, I figure we got somethin' in common."

He has assumed that I am at least a Christian. Perhaps he thinks I am just one small step away from conversion. And it is here that I realize just how much I have duped this man with my superficial subduedness. How I have proved again the extent to which I am my father's daughter. How I live a double life, and how miserable and dishonest that duality is.

"Yes, I bet we see a lot of things in the same light," I say, still struggling for some sense of diplomacy. Old habits, I suppose, die hard.

He's listening.

"Well, not only do we both love this corner of the world, but we both want it to remain unaltered by the outside world."

He nods. "Yeah, but the other day I was up on the mountain, fixing a fence line that some jerk-off dirt-bikers from Colorado had cut, when this tree-hugger drives up and asks what I think about opening a ski area up there." He laughs. "It wasn't too good of me, but I didn't tell him that we already had one in place—one that ran back when we used to get enough snow."

"What gave you the idea that he was a tree-hugger?" I ask. "If anyone tried to put in a ski area here, I'd be fighting right alongside you to stop it."

"Come on. You people love Robert Redford, and he owns a ski resort. Besides, the guy was driving a big SUV—Japanese model, with a mountain bike strapped to the top. That's a dead giveaway for sure."

The cowboy steps back, sizes me up from beneath his Stetson. This time, he's really looking at me.

"You sure you ain't single?"

I stand there, uncertain what to say, and consider how my masquerade has made me not more familiar but in fact less tangible. In this time, the cowboy's face changes, darkens like the sky over the Abajos. After a moment to think things through, he eyes me with suspicion.

"Do you *really* think cowboying is okay?"

I tell him that as a young girl I didn't play much with dolls, that instead I preferred Cowboys or Indians. I invented personas whereby I could imagine a life lived freely, roaming the open land. My father had cobbled together for me a costume for each game—my cowboy outfit was complete with a red felt hat and a cap gun; my Indian getup included a beaded headband with a feather stuck in it. What I don't tell the cowboy is that, when the rest of the neighborhood played Cowboys and Indians combined, I bowed out. To play them together would have required that I choose a side.

And here it is before me—the realization that will shift how I inhabit redrock country. I owe the cowboy more than this tiptoe double-speak. It is time to make an appearance.

And so next come the words that I know would break my grandpa Blaisdell's heart. But I must say them. I can no longer hover between worlds.

"Actually, I'm not sure that cows belong on arid public lands."

The cowboy stiffens. To bolster the strength of my statement, I quickly add my credentials: A sixth-generation Utahn. A family of ranchers. A meat-eater . . .

He interrupts. "You eat meat? I thought you people were vegetarians."

I tell him I would rather eat an elk—not the farm-raised variety, but a wild one—than a cow. But, I repeat, I would never shoot his livestock.

We stand looking at each other. Then, slowly, he nods. But before he can speak, the door opens and a woman walks in.

"Sister," he says, touching his hat. As she shakes the rain from her hair and shoulders, they exchange pleasantries. Then she bends to pull clothes from a dryer, explaining that her dryer at home is on the fritz, how the kids have no clothes for the coming week.

The cowboy looks from her to me and back to her. And he suddenly interrupts her.

"This young lady lives here in town, *and* she works for SUWA. Can you believe it?"

The woman coils back from the dryer as if she's just encountered a snake den. She whips around, and her eyes form a bead on me. Her face hardens, and her body stiffens.

"You people . . ." she seethes.

"Now, wait a minute, Sister. This gal seems pretty reasonable. She says she don't shoot cows."

"Yeah, well, why did you move here? Would you ever listen to our views, or are you here just to spout off your crazy earth-worshiping ideas—to tell us to put snails and slugs before humans?"

She snaps a pink pillowcase so hard I think it's the lightning outside, cracking open the sky.

"We've got our ways, and they work just fine. And I don't care a bit to know about yours—so don't even try."

The missionaries are back, to retrieve their soap. The woman and the cowboy turn to acknowledge them. Through the Laundromat's glass doors, I see blue-gray still billowing against the dark mountain.

I want to run out into the rain. To recede into the landscape. To disappear entirely. It's an exit my father made every time things got too tame for him. An exit he perfected in his final earthly act.

I thought moving here had largely been a gesture of love. For the desert. For the lion man. But in that move, I was looking at the horizon, and my imagination ran romantically wild. I forgot how tightly people drew together against everything outside themselves. And I hadn't realized how ethereal things were—my identity, my beliefs, my life.

With a long deep breath, I step into the circle of blue eyes like my own. I skip the Gospel of Wilderness—dogma that is scientific, economic, even aesthetic. Instead, I go straight to my infidelities—to God, to my former marriage. I tell them that I know I'll never get to the celestial kingdom, but that's okay, because anything terrestrial sounds heavenly.

They stare in disbelief, as if they've just seen an apparition. They are trying to envision how such a nice girl, raised with such good values, could have devolved so far.

From "white and delightsome."

To "dirt digger" and "lizard eater."

I am thrilled with their curiosity.

The woman folds the last of her laundry, then picks up the first basket of clothes and takes it out to her car. The missionaries' mouths hang like hammocks, but the cowboy grins wide.

"Boy, if there are more girls like you," he says, "I'd sure like to meet 'em." He slips me his phone number, then winks. "Guess I admire a girl with strong opinions."

He opens the glass door and is gone.

The woman returns for her second basket. She says goodbye to the missionaries, says she'll see them at Sacrament Meeting. They actually nod a farewell to me as they leave. I find myself smiling, waving back. I'm standing there looking after them when the woman walks right up to me and sets her basket down. Her hair is windblown, and her glasses are wet from her first dash to the car. She peers over the rim, with one eye closed, like an owl. I study the raindrops on her face.

She actually takes my hand.

"You seem like such a nice person," she says. "I realize I haven't been very Christian, just hating and judging all of you people without ever having known you."

THERE WAS isolation, from which it has been hard to emerge. And then these miserable attempts at assimilation, which feel like self-immolation—an offering made to appease the horned gods. And whether or not they are satisfied, remains to be seen. But what is already apparent is the keen sense of suspicion that all my earthly acquaintances—even the lion man—have about the truth of my existence.

I am my father's daughter. In time, I will see how those who reach out to make contact with my vague form are left wanting.

The woman squeezes my fingers. I wonder if she can feel the bones, how pliable they are in the meaty palm of her hand.

"It's actually been nice meeting you," she says. Then she's out the door, into the rain.

PART III

⊰ BASKETMAKER ⊱

⇥ 9 ⇤

Mano

SEPTEMBER AGAIN, and the best season for desert wandering commences. All across Cedar Mesa, along the tributaries of Lake Powell, and throughout the Canyonlands Basin, canyon pools have been recharged with the monsoon rains of summer—although the water has hardly been enough to offset the drought. And as the desert weather phenomenon that provided the replenishment recedes back into the Gulf of Mexico, so goes the threat of flash floods. What remains is an afternoon sun that concurs perfectly with your own body temperature. Bullion blooms of rabbitbrush. A frame of redrock and blue sky made almost unbearably vivid by the angled light.

Living at the edge of Lila Canyon is an entirely different thing from living within the Monticello city limits. It's strange to be paying for and sleeping under a roof that is smack in the middle of a landscape that was once strictly a destination for primitive leisure— a place to which I once brought only a backpack, a pair of boots, and a water bottle. My new home's appointments are, by modern standards, crude—where they exist at all. But the place is a far cry from the tent I used to sleep in when in San Juan County, and it has changed considerably my relationship to the desert. Now I avoid the national parks, the monuments, the wilderness areas—even the well-known BLM lands of Cedar Mesa. Instead of visiting the county's crown jewels, I wander no farther than the little-known canyons that flank the mesa where my house sits. And my forays are shortened. They are designed to return me to the house with plenty of sunlight left in the sky, for there is much to be accomplished before winter hits. The stovepipe, thick with pine-pitch resin from the last cold season, must be scoured. There is evidence of termites in the crawl space, and they must be made unwelcome before they invade the wooden beams that uphold the floor. The roof needs patching, as do the window screens—whose holes are large enough to let in the droves of local hummingbirds. Sprinting after the fragile, frantic creatures who find themselves inside has become almost a daily chore; I have learned to trap and remove them safely by casting a bedsheet across their flight paths. The mice would be a problem too, but for the four-and-a-half-foot-long bull snake that lurks in the rock outcropping off the front porch. The snake is a valuable amenity, for he eats rattlers too. But there is the occasion when he tries to slither through the dog door and gets stuck halfway. At that point, the effort required to reverse his line of travel makes me wonder if I'd be better off just setting traps, or acquiring a cat.

Then there is the constant hauling of water. And wood that needs to be cut and stacked before the days get any cooler. With Herb gone so often for fieldwork and meetings, these two tasks feel overwhelming. I can't shake the feeling that the snow will hit early and hard—and soon I am riddled with anxious, incessant urges to stockpile resources. But when I express my concern, Herb just scoffs.

"You know damn well I would never let my woman go thirsty or freeze."

And there he is at midnight, after a fifteen-hour day at his office in town, draining water from the stock tank into the cistern by headlamp. It's not enough to last the week, but Herb is sure that it will get me through one shower and a few days of dishwashing, that it's enough to last me until he returns from his next journey. And by 6 a.m., he is out on the far corner of the property, where the Ipps beetle—an opportunist who settles into drought-weakened trees— has decimated a stand of about forty small piñons. For several hours I hear the chainsaw whine without pause, doing the thing I had told Nora we don't do, and then, suddenly, Herb is approaching the house, Cheshire-cat grin preceding a red plastic snow sled full of freshly cut beetle-bored logs. Together we stack the firewood on the east porch, and I thank him profusely. But in my head I am measuring the supply, counting the number of days it will last. I can't get past November—only two months away. One look and Herb knows the calculations that are under way. He rolls his eyes.

"Do you have to live so far in the future? I'll cut more soon. I promise there will be enough."

I'd make up the difference in both water and wood, but he refuses to let me use either the red truck or the chainsaw. Says that there are certain jobs that a man feels are his alone, that he likes providing for me. I want to tell him how bogus and controlling that sentiment is, but he is already off again: First to see his son in Moab, then to a meeting in the central portion of the state. He'll stop to visit friends before crossing the county by way of Highway 95, where he'll turn off at Butler Wash. There, along the soft and sandy curves of this ephemeral streambed, he'll examine a place designated by the BLM as a "play area" for ORVs. It is also a place where prehistoric artifacts are scattered visibly in the tire tracks, a place one BLM archaeologist has told him is most likely an ancient burial site. The thing is, no one knows for sure, because the agency never properly surveyed it before building a kiosk and inviting the motorheads to *Ride Responsibly*.

He wants me to join him. And he rolls his eyes again when I tell him that I can't go, that I have too much to do. I try to explain that this settling in has shifted my relationship to the land. No longer am I passing through as the desert's spectator, I say. No longer am I simply an admirer of its aesthetics. Instead, I am its consumer— one who must store its water, gather its timber. I say it's not just the long list of house chores that I must fit in around my day job. In addition to my occupation as a protector of Utah's public lands, I now have a preoccupation with defending my own turf. That vigilance against wayward cows and ORVs, against invading cheatgrass and termites—they add up. I tell him that, though I remain devoted to both causes, the constancy of such a defensive posture is exhausting.

The man who has always seen the world the way I have just stares at me as though I am speaking in tongues.

IT IS my new stay-close-to-home policy that lands me in a nameless side canyon behind our house, a place I seek out after meeting my neighbor Robert's brother-in-law the week before. Howard is a tall, lanky man who lives on a piece of land between Robert and his in-laws, Harmon and Verna. The government contracts him to replant trees in the aftermath of wildfires, and Howard takes great pride in his job—in being what he calls "God's gardener." When he stopped by to welcome us to the neighborhood, he described with zeal the natural wonders that the good Lord had placed in our very backyard. In the process, he mentioned a pour-off that marked the head of a certain canyon where a ruin lay, and the old cattle trail that was used to access it. There was a month's work to do in northern California, but he promised to show me the place upon his return.

The next week arrives, and Herb is in Butler Wash—while I am fed up with both my paid and unpaid jobs. Besides, learning the lay of the land seems as vital as paying the mortgage. And so I go looking for the canyon alone. By little more than dumb luck, I find the cattle trail, a vague and treacherous route that no cow would have negotiated without having a bossy horse bearing down on its hind end and a herding dog nipping at its legs. It's not surprising, then, that the route is wide open, that no barbed wire crosses its path. One good look into the canyon and I see how narrow its floor is, how little forage grows—except where a small spring bubbles up from what was once a patch of thick, lush grass, now mowed down and trampled. The sight leaves no doubt that the bovines that have appeared on the mesa originated from here—that out of hunger they scale this impossible trail. I sigh. More vigilance will be required.

Beneath the pour-off, a ruin lies protected from the elements—and this is what I have come to see. As far as ruins go, it is fairly unimpressive. But my intrigue lies in the site's proximity to my home, as well as in my newfound grasp of the word "stratigraphy," the study of layers of artifacts and burials. The soil depth from which a relic or a corpse is retrieved can reveal a great deal about the period of time and the culture from which it came—especially when compared with relics and bodies buried above or below it. According to Howard, this site was a most literal example of stratigraphy—a place where an archaeological dilettante such as me might learn something about the past.

I immediately see several subterranean stashes, unearthed and emptied of the contents. Called *cists*, these storage pits were made by the Basketmaker Anasazi, who would have inhabited the cave as early as 1200 B.C. Then I see what Howard meant about layered evidence: an enormous slab of alcove ceiling lies embedded in the sandy floor. My neighbor had explained to me that at some point, either during or after the Basketmakers' occupation of this particular site, the huge hunk of rock had come loose and crashed to the floor. Many of the Basketmaker remains were entombed beneath the great slab of rock. Later, around A.D. 750 to 900, the Puebloans moved in, and erected a few stone structures right on top of the ceiling-turned-platform. Their pottery sherds—geometric black-on-white and red-on-orange—are scattered around the slab in mounds of soil that had, at some point, been dug up and tossed aside to expose the earlier Basketmaker cists. Among them is an anomalous chunk of lapis blue—a piece Howard had mentioned, a piece he believes is early Navajo in origin. This is curious, he had explained, because the Navajo usually avoid Anasazi sites—for fear of offending the ancient spirits. In general, it is only their medicine men that enter, and then it is only with great reverence and ritual. Otherwise, to disturb a ruin in any way, or to take anything from it no matter how small or insignificant, is taboo. Tribal culture has generally reinforced this, and as a result, southeastern Utah's Anasazi sites remained intact—until the Anglos became interested. Today, it is estimated that 90 percent of the hundred thousand Anasazi sites in San Juan County have been looted.[1] What's interesting about this modern trend is that sometimes anonymous boxes containing pilfered artifacts are returned to local BLM field offices. Many of them are sent with unsigned notes, explaining how plagued with misfortune the sender's life has been since he or she first absconded with the goods.

The way the slab hides the Basketmakers here, just beyond my backyard, is sort of symbolic, for the Basketmaker world remained buried beneath later artifacts, hidden from archaelogists for a long time. When their existence was finally discovered, it was right here in San Juan County. The year was 1893, and Cedar Mesa was already known for its dense and fascinating array of Puebloan ruins and artifacts. For Colorado cowboy Richard Wetherill, finding new sites and sharing them with the public came to mean more than running cattle, and his knowledge of the area, coupled with his desert outfitting skills, made him the perfect tour guide for East Coast collectors. Some archaeologists criticize Wetherill's crude excavation techniques, saying his methods prevented more sophisticated findings later on. Still, there is no doubt that the cowboy contributed mightily to the emerging field of New World archaeology; Wetherill was most likely the first to employ stratigraphy to distinguish between prehistoric cultures in the Americas.[2]

It was in Cave 7, in Cedar Mesa's Grand Gulch, that Wetherill found what he originally coined "the Basket People." Sealed away in cists used to bury their food, which Basketmakers were beginning to grow instead of gather, Basketmaker relics were found three feet below artifacts belonging to the already recognized Puebloans, and Wetherill quickly noted them to be "a different race from anything I've ever seen."[3] The Basketmakers had distinctly smaller skulls than the Puebloans, and they used fine handwoven basketry for storage vessels—as well as to enshroud the heads of the dead. This helped Wetherill and the others understand the vast variation in prehistoric dwellings they had encountered: now they understood that some were far more crude than others because they were built by Basketmakers. The rooms were a step up from the ephemeral shelters of the Archaic period—and included rooms built in caves as well as brush-covered pits—but they were not the elaborate masonry of the later Puebloans.

Finding the Basketmakers was significant, because they were a people of great ritual, adornment, and possession. Despite their relatively crude and distant past, these people left behind a wealth of material for examination—far more than the Desert Archaic hunter-gatherers before them. And with the aid of the dry San Juan air, the way that material was socked away had preserved it perfectly. When excavated, it explained unequivocally that the early phase of the Basketmaker world—from about 1200 B.C. to about A.D. 50—marked the transition from nomadism to agriculture. It was the beginning of village life, of life lived in one place.

I pick my way through the alcove and sit on the edge of the ceiling slab. I stare at the bits of relics scattered around—corncobs, pottery sherds, bits of rough cord, and coal from long-ago fires. The transition from one life to another—no matter how gradually it occurred—must have been profound. I envision a late-Archaic woman living here, where I live now, living as women lived for thousands of years before her. She isn't always down in the canyon; she is up on the mesa, moving, walking vast expanses. She is right on the heels of her mate, stopping to forage whatever the desert offers up at the time, but ready to respond if her mate makes a successful kill. Then they work together, peeling fur or feathers, dressing the meat with the savory goods she has gathered along the way. Later, there is the building of the flames, the dance of thanks and reverence before the feast.

All this she does with a child strapped to her back. Such a load, over long distances, might seem a burden—especially since she carries her offspring for its first three or four years of life. Sure, her feet get sore. And there are cold winters to wait out. But, like all the people in her tribe, she knows with a deep intimacy the surrounding landscape. On the coldest days, she knows where to find a shallow south-facing alcove that holds the most sun rays. Where to drink from a spring that runs cool and deep, even in the hottest, driest months. Where to eat when drought has withered most everything in sight.

As a result, she is a woman of relatively few worries, for there is a calmness in knowing that there is always shelter available, always something growing that will nourish, or heal. She knows hundreds of places of refuge, hundreds of medicinal herbs, hundreds of food-stuffs. For any reason, if one goes belly-up, there are more to choose from. It's a diverse portfolio, and all she has to do is go to the right location, at the right time, to gather from its sound returns. The act of walking there—its impact on her heart and lungs—only enhances the effect.

As for her child, until he is old enough to walk on his own and consume the same foods as the tribe, he needs nothing but his mother's milk. For him, nursing exclusively for such an extended period is more fortifying than other foods, and his mother's efforts at food procurement and preparation are greatly lessened by this arrangement. The extended nursing also reduces the number of times that she ovulates. This in turn ensures that her pregnancies are widely spaced, that she is rarely overburdened with more than one dependent child. And so the woman moves easily across the landscape. Her hands are available to stop and gather whatever the earth yields beneath her feet, whatever is bountiful in that particular place and season. Her senses, then, are unoccupied to appreciate the wondrous world around her. And her body—it is free to enjoy both the journey she makes and the pleasure of her mate's company.

But then *maize* arrives—most likely through trade with Indians from Mexico. Perhaps it brings with it such seductive ceremonies and mystique that her people are enthralled. Perhaps they are ready for a new taste. Or perhaps the drought gets so bad that traditional food supplies are greatly diminished. Whatever the reason, she begins to stay more frequently in one location—hunched over a certain set of stalks, a certain patch of soil. When the corn is harvested, she grinds it into a meal with the aid of a *metate*, or rock slab, and a *mano*, or handheld grinding stone. The woman is used to the feel of the mano; she has used one all her life to grind down wild nuts and seeds. But this meal is different—she can grind it soft enough for even a baby to gum down, and so her infant is weaned from her breast earlier than her previous children. As a result, she ovulates with much greater frequency. More babies are born—even though she spends far less time with her mate. While she runs the homefront, he is away, having to go farther each time to scare up a rabbit or a sage grouse. But the forays are necessary—for his family needs meat to make up for the lysine that is scarcer in their new domestic diet. Big game once provided plenty of this important amino acid, but it's not hunted so often anymore. The large ungulates may have dwindled because of environmental change, or because of overhunting, or perhaps the new tasks of planting and harvesting compete with the year's best hunting seasons. Whatever the reason, the San Juan woman is left with that wanting that comes from lack of adequate protein. Droughts, pests, and other invaders leave her anxious about whether there will be enough food to harvest for the days ahead. All this worry, combined with an increased workload and the toll of more children, begins to alter her health and her psyche. An inclination toward hoarding is spawned. In response, she crafts a larger mano, to grind larger amounts of meal. She weaves fine, impenetrable baskets, which she fills with what she grows. The baskets are then cached in the cists she has dug—her insurance for the lean times she has come to anticipate.

This shift to planting domestic cultigens occurs in the San Juan region just as it does across the globe, among other cultures, within approximately the same time frame. But whereas other cultures continue—for a while at least—to supplement their crops with large amounts of wild foods, for some reason the early phase of Cedar Mesa Basketmakers almost completely replace their traditional hunter-gatherer menu with the new Mexican cultigens.[4] And as they toil over their crops, their hearts and lungs grow flaccid from lack of aerobic use, and their muscles pull short and knotted from a dearth of limb-lengthening movement. And their senses change— they lose touch with what the desert offers, fail to recognize within the portfolio of hundreds—hundreds that provided returns in almost any market—more than a handful of items of sustenance.

The San Juan woman's world changes more than her husband's. Hers is reduced to little more than the homefront, where she softens and stagnates, pregnant more often than not, tending to food and children alongside the turkeys and dogs that now inhabit her hamlet. And despite the way it confines her, makes her life more arduous, she welcomes the extra offspring, because more hands are needed to manage the workload. Her mate needs the help too, because this new arrangement means that there are more mouths to feed, and that his woman is no longer available as hunting companion. Burdened with responsibilities, their children grow up hard and fast. For everyone, there is little time or energy for play, or laughter, or pleasure. There is more land to be cultivated, more water to be diverted for irrigation, and more seeds to be sown and tended.

But there is another amendment to the San Juan woman's life,

and to her mate's—one that we never read about in the studies of archaeology or anthropology—and it is a change that must have re-
configured the Archaic world as much as anything: At the end of the
day, with so many people to cook and care for, with so many chores
having been completed—and all with such a weariness for want of
meat—the lovemaking between the woman and her man must have
been, at best, mediocre. For, in the process of stepping up and separating the worlds of men and women, the two mates must have
grown distant, must have come to know one another less as lovers
and traveling companions. In other words, perhaps the greatest loss
suffered at the dawn of agriculture, at the beginning of life lived in
one locale, was the loss of good sex.

I stand in the alcove and think what a shame it is to live in a
place like this and not have the energy to be turned on, not have the
time or inclination to feel pleasure or passion or wonder. A dimin-
ishment in sexual appetites, the loss of companionship—these seem
reason enough to fight the winds of change. But perhaps the change
came too slowly for anyone to notice its effects. And perhaps people
were tired and too anxious to care.

I sigh. I may as well be contemplating my own life of late.

THE NEXT DAY, the cistern runs dry. The pickup truck that holds
the stock tank won't start. Herb isn't due back for two more days, so
I call Robert, offer him twenty bucks to bring me a load on his way
home from work. He's got enough to do, hauling water for his own
family and animals, but he agrees. And that evening, when he's
backing out of my driveway, when I try to pay him for his efforts, he
holds up a hand in refusal. Says that a good Christian always helps
out a neighbor—no matter what their differences—and that he
wouldn't think to profit from someone in need. Says he'd rather see
us get our share of town water anyway—rather than watch the new
golf course guzzle every last precious, drought-forsaken drop on

nine holes' worth of new sod. And it is on this point that I reach agreement with my neighbor, for I have seen the new sprinkler system running at high noon, in the blistering heat of summer, and often in thirty-mile-an-hour winds. Together we shake our heads about how quickly the spray evaporated in the air above the new turf, how it never even touched the grass at all.

The camaraderie of the moment is exquisite. The words and ideas exchanged are the kind I had wished for with the Blaisdells, with my Mormon neighbors in childhood. There is a glimmer of homecoming, as if I am a seed that has been blown, then dropped, in perfect soil conditions. I feel as if I am taking root.

And then my neighbor speaks again.

"Just don't go makin' a big deal out of it," he says, as he puts his truck into reverse and guns the engine. "I probably wouldn't get a lot of points for havin' helped out the tree-huggers."

THE FOLLOWING MORNING, an ancient, rusted-out Toyota Corolla rolls into my yard. I answer the door in the leopardskin pajamas I had been wearing at the computer since daybreak. On my porch stands an old man, who holds out between liver-spotted hands a large Mason jar full of amber-colored honey. It is Harmon, Robert's father-in-law. Next to him stands a tall woman with a long gray braid down her back. He introduces her as Verna, his wife. Their clothing is from an earlier decade than their automobile, but they don't so much as glance at my attire.

The old couple have gathered the honey from their own beehives. They tell me there's more where it came from, and that the fig tree in their green house is about to bear fruit. They tell me I must come over and taste one. I squint in disbelief. A fig tree in a greenhouse sounds like something you'd see in the backyard of an expensive home in the Hamptons, or the Berkeley hills. I cannot imagine such a fine thing out here, on this mesa of sand and cheatgrass and abandoned trailers. And later, when I see the structure, built from a rather ingenious patchwork of plastic gathered from the landfill, shored up by old railroad ties and recycled car tires, I'll realize that, no matter how well it grew exotic fruit, the greenhouse would indeed be barred from most neighborhoods throughout the nation.

Harmon asks how I like living out at Lila Canyon. I tell him that I'm not used to spending so much time in one place, that I didn't anticipate the amount of hands-on manual labor required for day-to-day living. I explain that I don't mind really, that I am growing accustomed to the extra tasks I must perform around my paying job. What I don't say is how lonely I am, how much I miss Herb, and how separate our lives feel. And as they step off the porch, they reiterate their invitation—adding that I should call if I need anything, especially when my husband is away.

Cohabitation is neither common nor condoned in Utah's more remote and rural corners. But I have promised myself: no more concealment, no more obfuscation. Besides, these folks seem like a good bet—like Robert, they don't seem to wave the same bright flag of judgment that Mormons often do. And so I am calling out after them, clarifying in a most self-conscious and conspicuous way, that we are not married. To my relief, Harmon and Verna seem unfazed. But it doesn't change the fact that, as I walk back inside and close the door, I lean into the heavy wooden planks and feel, quite literally, that I will die.

THE FOLLOWING MORNING finds me back at the ruin behind my house. By coming here I have temporarily distracted myself from the chores and work deadlines that await me at home. When I enter the alcove, it is early, and the sun has not yet filled it with rays. For desert air, it feels surprisingly cool and damp.

I examine more closely the shorn slab of stone that fell from the alcove lip. It is lodged front and center in the shallow cave, and whatever Basketmaker relics were buried beneath it would stay there forever. Strewn on its cleanly cut top surface, the few Puebloan-built rock walls are the remains of more complete dwellings that have been somehow toppled and lie mostly in rubble heaps. I peer over the walls at what was once the interior of someone's home. In it are sizable cow pies, and more loose stones. It doesn't take much to imagine how one of the resident herd's more adventurous members, after running out of forage on the canyon bottom, heaved its mass up a few ledges, into the alcove. It was probably worth seeking one last patch of grass here, before resorting to the hellish scramble up the stock trail to the mesa top. And once up on the great rock platform that was formerly the alcove ceiling, the animal must have worked its way between the walls. The next feat—putting that great backside in reverse—would have been an even tougher struggle than the bull snake's efforts to back out of my dogs' swinging door. In the process, the cow must have bumped into the rock walls, sent the upper layers toppling. And then, among those ancient remnants, came the untimely need to relieve itself.

In righteous indignation, I wrinkle my nose and step off the platform toward the back of the cave, out of gravity's way. The cave floor is covered with coarse sand, and pocked with exposed Basketmaker cists. I peer into the slab-lined holes, and make a mental note to ask Howard if he knows who opened them and when; if he knows the fate of what they once contained. Had they been emptied by an old-timer like Wetherill? Or had the BLM, in an unlikely display of timely concern for the resources in its care, excavated and archived them? Of course, there is always the chance that absent artifacts of any sort have disappeared into the knapsacks of looters, but at the time I am naive enough to think that this site is so out of the way, so unimpressive in the grand scheme of Four Corners' archaeology, that looters would never find their way here.

Walking back out to the front of the alcove, I drift to its eastern corner, where the walls are more vertical than overhanging. There lies a large mano. To my untrained eye, it would have been unrecognizable as the indispensable Anasazi tool that it was, would have looked like nothing more than a smooth river stone, had it not been lying next to a large boulder whose convex top had been worn down into a smooth trough. The boulder's depression had been made by the mano, held by human hands that ground it back and forth in seemingly endless repetition, until the meal was easy enough to get down the gullet.

And above the grinding implements, on the vertical wall perhaps twenty feet over my head, there is a large hole. Directly beneath it leans a long two-by-four—not exactly an original piece of the ancient record before me. I test it and find it solid enough to shimmy up, and the board's length gives me a direct look into the hole in the wall. The hole opens into what must have been used as a small storage chamber, dark and musty, with a flat floor and relatively uniform walls. It has obviously been hollowed out by hand. Rock-hard corncobs—a small variety unfamiliar to contemporary eyes—are scattered everywhere. When sealed, the hole must have served perfectly as a pantry, for no rodent could have gained access, and the cool, dry temperatures would have preserved the contents within.

The darkness, the odor, they remind me of my grandma Blaisdell's food storage—a concrete closet in her basement that was so unfinished that it smelled of the damp, mildewed earth pressed up around it. On hot afternoons I would cool off in there, and gaze at the rows of canned goods—peaches, raspberries, beets, and pickles. I'd scan the labels of tins—Dinty Moore, Van de Kamp's—and finger bags of potatoes that had been dug from the field across from the house, and baskets of apples off the tree in the backyard.

Even as a child, I found something reassuring about amassing so much food. And knowing we didn't have anything like it in my own basement just filled me with apprehension—for Mormon scripture admonished the faithful to "be prepared in all things against the day when tribulations and desolations are sent forth upon the wicked."[5]

The Last Days were upon us, and nearly every other family in the neighborhood had a full year's supply of food in its basement. After all, building up such a reserve was as important as paying 10 percent of your income as tithing, or serving a mission. Sure, my family's house had a freezer full of meat, fowl, and fish, but when Armageddon hit, what if the electricity went out and all the freezer food spoiled? Indeed, my mother joined my grandmother and aunts every July to make jam from Bear Lake raspberries, but you could be sure that my father, sister, and I had cleaned out every jar long before the next summer's batch was ready. I remember trying to pace myself, hiding a few jars to see us through the world's end, but ultimately I gave in to my cravings and ferreted out the stash. Not that jam alone could have seen my family through hungry times. There were nights I lay awake wondering if God would forgive our family's short-sighted ways. For a time, I even prayed that if the Last Days caught us unawares, perhaps God would be merciful enough to send down at least a pizza or two.

In the time I have spent in the alcove, the sun has reached around and made its heat known. I hoist myself off the top of the leaning lumber and into the hole, and scoot myself back into its recesses. I stare at the corncobs, and contemplate a leaner, simpler diet. It reminds me of a story in Howard Egan's diary, one of my father's favorites. It involved a return trip from California, when Egan found himself camped somewhere in the Great Basin, near a small spring. He was in the company of his son Erastus and several other Latter-day Saints and nothing more—the immediate desert in which they found themselves was almost as bare as a bone. The group scavenged a pile of greasewood and had managed to get a fire going when two Paiute Indians appeared. The newcomers were dressed as desert natives tended to dress—in nothing but grass breechclouts.

The Indians came close to the fire and stood "still as posts." From beneath black hair "the size of a bushel basket" they watched the Saints pull their dinner from the flames. Appetites evaporated when the Mormons realized that a live rattlesnake dangled from the fist of one of the Paiute. The reptile writhed ominously against the man's bare leg, but he seemed oblivious to it until he kicked a few hot coals out of the fire with his bare feet and tossed the snake across them. Skin sizzling, the reptile managed to crawl off, but the Indian simply picked it up and set it on the embers again. Several times it tried to escape, and each time the Indian replaced it, effectively cooking the snake alive. When it was roasted to his satisfaction, the Indian took it from the fire. With his fingers, he pinched off the head, which he tossed into the dirt. Then he broke off a piece of the body and "commenced eating it like a boy would a carrot." The other Indian ate too, and when they had finished, it was noted by the onlookers that they licked their fingers "as if they liked it."[6]

My father must have liked this particular story not only because he loved meat, any meat, cooked over an open fire, but also because of his pride in being able to make a meal out of anything. No matter how bare our cupboards got, he could still lay down a mouthwatering dinner. The menu was often daring, especially by the standards of modern Utahns and young girls. On my plate it was not uncommon to find frog legs, or elk liver. My father had even been known to steal into the woodlands behind our house and nab a few quail, whose tiny bodies he'd wrap in strips of bacon and roast to perfection. And so, despite all his shortcomings, despite his inability to get out of bed and go to work, for a long time this knack of his gave me great confidence in him as my provider. I had the feeling that no matter what happened we'd always be able to eat, and eat well. It wasn't until I was old enough to understand the Mormon sermons about storing a year's worth of food that my faith in his capabilities began to crumble.

And sitting there in that ancient pantry, just out of reach of the sun's rays, I can see how it's happening again:

God. Father. Lover. For each shaken source of faith, I have hoarded a seismic sense of hurt—a sensation that led to spiritual starvation.

What I can't yet see is how I tend to topple what remains.

LATER IN THE MORNING, I emerge from the canyon and realize I am going to be late for a lunch date in town with Herb. In my rushed state, I fail to notice how quiet the skies are, how not a single jet contrail laces the atmosphere. It is only when I climb in my truck and turn on the radio, only when I arrive to see the post-office flag already at half-mast, that I understand just how different this day is from other days.

Herb and the others in his office building are gathered in its common area, their eyes fixed on a television. No one looks up when I enter; they all seem unable to miss a single replay of the airplanes striking the towers, of the buildings crumbling into a fine gray dust. Herb, though, feels my approach, reaches out to draw me in against him. But we never touch. I am already backing away, repulsed by the possibility of glimpsing a single image. He calls my name, but I am halfway out the door, headed to the truck, headed back home. When I get there, I stand in the middle of the yard and feel in this desert a blaring new quiet.

I whistle to the dogs and flee back to the ruin. They sit quietly below the alcove while I scramble back up on the ledge. Out of the sun, I squat in the sand and look out at the small spring—a mere gurgle from the throat of the earth. The air in the alcove has grown cloying in the midday heat. I get up and move farther back, to the place where the most interesting pottery had been.

The blue chip is gone.

I can envision ancient Anasazi spirits following the thief back up the cattle trail, then proceeding to wreak total havoc on the culprit's life. I take great pleasure in this thought, especially knowing that the thief most likely passed through our neighborhood—perhaps even our property—to gain access to the canyon. On any other day I would be outraged. Today, however, outrage is not a response I can muster. I contemplate contacting the BLM's law enforcement to report the heist. But I know that there is a single officer for the entire county—for over two million acres of public lands—and that the chances that this will ever be investigated are nil. Instead, I sit for hours, scarcely noticing how the shadows move like clock arms with the sun's voyage across the canyon. The dogs wait faithfully, getting up only to chase shade or to drink from the spring.

THE SUN HAS DISAPPEARED behind the canyon's west wall when Herb appears. Uncharacteristically, he has arrived home from work while there's light in the sky. He guessed where to find me, and somehow produces two bottles of beer from the back pockets of his jeans. For a while, we sit on the ledge of the alcove and sip them in silence. Finally, Herb turns and quotes what he has heard our leaders say on the radio. Their responses are almost primal.

The President: "We will hunt down whoever did this . . ."

A U.S. General: "We will track them . . ."

And a U.S. Senator: "We should tear their guts out . . ."

When Herb reaches for my hand, I don't move. I feel him bristle at this rebuff, but I don't care. I may have made an effort to reveal more of myself to the rest of the county; with my mate, I remain enigmatic. I have cached away affection as a gesture of retribution for his absences and dismissals. Moments pass, and neither of us makes a move. There is the obvious stress of the day. And there is the fact that we are both too tired from working so much. Finally, he gets up, brushes himself off, calls the dogs. I listen to the crunch of pebbles beneath paws and boots as they disappear up the trail.

The air hangs in the shadowy canyon like a smoky quartz, in contrast to the last bit of sunlight bearing down into the ruin, which bathes the steepest, smoothest part of the alcove in pineapple light. I turn to admire the cave wall's brilliance. On its surface—which I have now gazed at all day—there is a sudden display of hands. The prints are small, almost child-size, imprinted on the stone surface with a rust-colored stain. They are faint, ghostlike—visible only at a certain time of day, in a certain kind of luminescence.

And color. It shifts.

I look at my own hands. Oh, what these appendages can do. And I am back at our round Formica kitchen table: I was sitting at five o'clock from where my father was seated. His third drink was before him. My mother was at a bridge game, and my sister and I watched as my father sank into a melancholic nostalgia that had become all too predictable. We were required to take note of all that had slipped away: The Ivy League school he had been unable to attend. The hunts in Alaska he had never been able to experience.

His eyes got their far-off, watery look, but we knew the routine. We had grown deft at reeling him back in. All we had to do was ask him questions. The questions that worked best were those pertaining to the natural world, to the tangible sciences that governed it.

Dad, how do fish breathe? How come we can't see stars during the day? Why do geese fly in a V?

These were the lifelines we threw to him; otherwise we would have been required to absorb his grief into our own small skins. But that night was different—he was exceptionally downhearted. It wouldn't be long before my mother would kick him out. And so, when our line of questioning failed, we moved into things about which he had deep philosophical convictions.

Dad, how come you hate Mormons? How come "God" is spelled with a big "G"?

These questions roused his passions—which had long been stifled by the surrounding culture, and then, more recently, in his failing marriage. When I went to bed, he followed me, sat down, and patted the mound of my body beneath my pink gingham bedspread.

I could feel his hands. Hands that had steadied a gun against my shoulder. Threaded a worm on the end of my fishing rod. Collected fresh huckleberries from streamside and then blended them into golden pancakes.

Hands that had hunted for me. Gathered me. Sustained me.

Bourbon. Water. Tears—his and mine. It's not a clear mountain stream, but a murky, silty desert river, one that disintegrates solid banks of stone and carries them away in granules. Somewhere on the surface I can see the hall light, and my sister's tiny silhouette—backlit, like a cardboard cut-out doll. When she turns sideways, I can see how she wrings her tiny sister hands.

I prayed to God in earnest. But there was no reply. There was only my quavering voice, raining like small pebbles when it uttered *No.* And then there were my hands on my father, who swayed like a tower when I pushed. There was the *thud* as he hit the floor. Paige and I watched in awe as he picked himself up, smoothed the front of his shirt, shuffled and swerved out of the room. He never once looked at us.

There is only wind, water, and stone. The pieces are carried off in the current, or taken by others as souvenirs. Either way, continuous cohesion is futile. The record incomplete. Things remain impossible to see for what they really were.

The Mormons may have taught me conformity, but my father taught me invisibility.

Light changes everything.

Alcoves. Airplanes. The sky is falling.

⊰ 10 ⊱

Burial

T HE DUST HAS BARELY settled in New York when armies of oversize pickups rumble into Monticello. On the corner where Main Street and Highway 666 intersect, the vehicles engulf the Texaco parking lot. While their tanks fill, the drivers congregate inside the mini-mart, wolfing down bad coffee and microwaved burritos. As in any small Western town, it is commonplace to see pickups and men gathered, but this congregation is different: the way big-industry names blaze expertly from the trucks' side panels, the way the men sport the same logos on spotless, well-made field jackets. And the rigs: They lack bales of hay, cow dogs, stock tanks. Instead, they are loaded with technical equipment—highly sophisticated stuff that requires the drivers to be well-schooled men. For the rest of the month, when I finally begin again to wander away from home, I will see these same pickups crawling across the desert. Sometimes they will stop, and the drivers will get out and spread maps of Utah's public domain across the hoods. They will consult Global Positioning Systems, and other instruments. All this to get the lay of the land—land that they have most likely never seen before and have known only as a contour on the map, a point on a GPS unit, and as a parcel leased from the BLM during a quarterly sale posted on the Internet.

I pull over and watch the newcomers. Herb has been fighting to keep them out of town ever since it was made known that the U.S. Department of Interior had posted all-time record sales of oil and gas leases. Most of the transactions had been concluded earlier in the year, but the recent breaches of national security have ignited worries about dependence on foreign fuel sources. In turn, the oil-and-gas industry has taken this opportunity to exploit domestic development, and, in a course-altering memorandum, the federal government has responded by instructing the Department of Interior and its underling, the BLM, to "examine land status and lease stipulation impediments to federal oil and gas leasing and review and modify those where opportunities exist." The memo concludes with the word "expedite."[1] In turn, the BLM has told its state office to make such projects the "number one priority."[2] This meant projects were being approved, with little public review, for the most special of places: Dome Plateau, an untouched mesa that filled the space beneath the most widely photographed natural arch in Arches National Park. The rim of Fish and Owl Canyon Wilderness Area on Cedar Mesa, one of the most beautiful backpacking areas in the region. Lockhart Basin, at the edge of Canyonlands. And the Book Cliffs, amid southeastern Utah's densest concentration of black-bear dens.

The clincher is that Utah's public lands only account for 1.1 percent of the total U.S. oil and gas reserves.[3] Still, the locals are delighted. They see the possibility of desperately needed new jobs, and an infusion of cash for related services rendered in their sputtering economy. Herb, on the other hand, is furious. And exhausted—every day, he must drive farther into the desert, looking at lease after lease, exploration project after exploration project, drill rig after drill rig. There was a time when I went with him on such investigative outings. But more recently, there have been confrontations with the security details that are now posted at the sites. They appear about the time that SUWA catches wind of a supposed memo to agencies concerned with national security—allegedly issued by the U.S. attorney general—admonishing that domestic environmental groups seeking to affect national energy policy should be watched and treated as a possible terrorist threat.

FINALLY, there comes a Sunday when Herb announces that he will remain at home for a day, that he will tend to the house and more woodcutting. A wind—unusually cold for this time of year—has descended from the north, scattered papery oak leaves across the property. I wrap a scarf around my neck to fend off the air's icy hand and try to adjust my equilibrium. Apparently I am the only one who has noticed how the planet has tilted, how precarious the day feels. For, despite his frayed state, Herb has declared it a beautiful morning, and says he can't wait to stack another wall of firewood against the house.

We are just finishing breakfast and tuning in to public radio when the dogs announce a visitor. I open the door to find Robert, his face sagging like heavy snow on branches. Dark crescents cast moon shadows beneath his eyes.

"Sorry to disturb you so early," he says, as the dogs tumble over themselves to greet him. "I've come to tell you Verna's died. Last night. Over at the Cortez Hospital. She got real sick all of a sudden, and when they opened her up there was cancer everywhere."

He takes off his oil-and-sweat-smudged cap and runs his fingers through his hair, tugging tufts of it as though the gesture might wake him up.

"We got permission to bring her home, but the state says we got to bury her today. So we're havin' a service at two o'clock, under the big yellow-belly pine. The men from our church just finished the casket and are digging the grave now. The women are fixin' her up. Harmon would sure appreciate your company, if you can make it."

In the doorway, we nod, mouths open. Behind us, the radio announces that the U.S. has bombed Afghanistan.

BY ONE-THIRTY, we have done our best to find warm and appropriate funeral attire: I am dressed in long underwear and boots beneath an ankle-length wool skirt. Herb wears his grandfather's cowboy hat with an old houndstooth blazer that is too short in the sleeves. We pick our way down the dirt road toward Harmon and Verna's place, squinting into bright sun and sharp air. Each of us carries a basket of hastily baked muffins covered with a dish towel. Other neighbors converge on the road in the same sort of practical attire; we nod to one another and comment on the unseasonable chill. I note the patterns on the dish towels that cover others' culinary offerings: Sunflowers. Gingham. Stars and Stripes.

Harmon's house sits up on a knoll, the backyard sloping gently downhill toward a colossal ponderosa. Even from up at the house we can see the casket beneath it—a simple roughhewn box perched on cinder blocks. Next to it, a mound of fresh red earth blossoms alongside a deep hole. Dogs and cats scatter as we file down alongside an orchard full of old and stout fruit trees, rows of squash, and a tangle of trellised grapevines. Given where we live, the harvest is unbelievable—achieved only because of a clever system of pipes and barrels that catch and store rainwater. We pass the greenhouse; I nudge Herb and point to the fig tree that springs from the ground at its center. Hens and roosters strut around its sprawl of exposed roots, pecking for insects.

Herb stops for a moment, takes it all in. Then he whistles under his breath.

"This is my idea of paradise," he announces. "This is exactly how I want to live."

These words come from a man who is resourceful and unafraid to work his fingers to nubs. In many ways, he'd make the perfect farmer. But I want to remind Herb that, as cheerful as he is about chopping wood on occasion, there's a reason that his backpack is never unpacked, why it never even leaves the back of his car: he can't stay put. He's home for two days, and then he's pacing the floor. I am certain that, after a week of being bent over one plot of ground, he'd be prowling the perimeter of his garden like a caged animal, looking at the canyons beyond, the horizons even farther on. And he'd have to go. Only his grand visions would remain, overshadowing the rows of budding produce until they at last withered.

I don't mean to condemn him. It's just that, since its advent, the farming life has tended to bring out the worst in a man. The prehistoric Southwest, with its subsequent post-Archaic population boom and diminished travel schedule, ushered in a period characterized by archaeologist Steven LeBlanc as one of "endemic warfare," a time of widespread, persistent violence not confined to a few isolated incidents.[4] In Cave 7 alone, where Richard Wetherill first made the distinction between Basketmaker and Puebloan Anasazi, ninety-seven corpses were unearthed, of people who had apparently perished on the same occasion. Six of the bodies had stone spearheads buried in them, two of which had been driven deep into the spinal columns. Others' breastbones had been penetrated by spear points and daggers; many of the individuals displayed broken arms and smashed skulls. In a departure from what would soon be understood as Basketmaker tradition, the bodies were not found in positions of respectful repose, nor were they decorated with parting gifts of honor. In fact, cut marks about the ears and hairline suggest that the scalps had been peeled from the skulls—a classic expression of war, of one group's domination of another.

These are not isolated findings regarding the early Anasazi. Across the Colorado Plateau, there is evidence of massacres at this time. In southeastern Utah alone, two other caves have revealed group carnage: In one, a deposit of severed arms and legs was unearthed. And painted on the cave wall above another mass grave is a pictograph of early-Basketmaker origin, which experts believe portrays the flayed skin from a human head.

Worldwide, archaeologists have noted that similar cultures-in-transition have seemed, at the very least, to live defensively—in response to a perception of invading hostilities. LeBlanc theorizes that this was most likely caused by a change in subsistence strategies, that people were "repositioning themselves" in reference to the shift in values placed on resources.[5] In such a context, one would expect acts of aggression to be minimal and incidental—skirmishes during raids to gain a few extra food stores or other goods. But in the case of the early Anasazi, a few cists of corn would hardly have solved the problem. As population expanded and people spread out to stake claims on new plots of land, they found that the best real estate had already been claimed, that additional productive soil, water sources, and game were hard to come by. Many groups, it is theorized, were forced to settle in marginal locations—places that could not sustain them. The only way to make up the difference in resources was to ambush another settlement, wipe out its residents, and take over the turf.

During this time, there was also what one archaeological writer has called "the darker side of Basketmaker spiritualism."[6] Nonviolent burials became relatively elaborate. In one cave, the men were buried with their dogs, the women laid to rest in loosely hanging aprons and necklaces made from snail and abalone. In many caves, both sexes were interred with yucca sandals—often a new pair. Such details are typically viewed as a sign of cultural advancement, as if a heightened appreciation for aesthetics had appeared alongside an increase in the standard of living. This would explain the time taken to indulge in such elaborate funereal efforts, and the sending of luxury items to the grave. But here's the curious stuff: Concealment became important enough that soft, seamless bags were used to enshroud the flexed bodies of the dead. Baskets were inverted over skulls. What's more, human scalps decorated some of the remains like jewelry—suggesting that the violence committed to obtain them was, to those adorned, a glorified event that would score them points in the next realm. So one is left wondering if all this attention to the dead and to the rituals performed on their behalf actually point to a life that had diminished so much in quality that its participants were looking to the afterworld as escape. Perhaps too they saw the spirit world as a place of reward, a place where they would live well for having endured the terrestrial plane—for all the endless labor, the constant vigilance, the pervasive violence, the stifling immobility; for the unwavering want for water, meat, sex, rest, peace. In the face of all that, what a promise death might have held.

VERNA HAS BEEN laid out in the pine box without embalming fluid. Her long gray hair has been washed, combed, and plaited to perfection; her long Quaker-style skirt is crisp and arranged in neat folds. But her face is untouched.

I was raised in a culture that conducts public viewings of all its deceased. On the Blaisdell side of the family—as in any Mormon brood—anyone who passed away was filled with fluid, caked with cosmetics, and then displayed in the casket the night before the funeral. The line to approach the casket was an endless strand of friends, relatives, and other members of the ward. And though the sight was not ever bothersome, the number of people who actually touched or kissed the body always unnerved me. Early on, I made it a policy never to approach the deceased. I feared that if I got too close someone would push me down, force my lips onto a cool, waxy cheek. Then, I was certain, my dead relative would bound to life just long enough to sit up and pull me into the casket—where I would suffocate in formaldehyde-scented silk and lace. Fortunately, my mother shared my aversion, and my father was never present at a

Mormon viewing. This meant I escaped most of the more intimate paying of respects, except for the time my grandmother caught me circling the periphery like a satellite and marched me into line.

And then there was my father's body. Paige and I had gone to the mortuary to collect his personal belongings and to sign the consent to cremate his remains. I hadn't anticipated seeing him then, but the mortician had asked, and suddenly I was walking through a mauve polyester curtain into a small, linoleum-lined room. There came the first words of the poem I would write that night, would then read aloud with my sister at the service. As introduction, I explained to the crowd that it was titled "Marrow" because, in the right company, my father loved to crack open bird bones and suck out the insides—this from a man who insisted that my sister and I use a fork to eat both fried chicken and bacon. When I said that, the audience sat stiff and blinking—most of them couldn't imagine the gentleman they knew from the opera, or from the business community, committing such barbarism. My knees buckled in horror, but Paige grabbed my hand and squeezed it.

"We have to be strong now," she whispered.

The tip of the slender branch flexed so hard it almost broke.

I am feathers. I am tree roots. I am stone.

These are what I turned to in the face of death, when I most needed some kind of mooring. I can't say that anything else was of comfort.

I had studied his face. There had been no effort to apply postmortem maquillage. I sought the familiar landmarks, but gone was the purple, bulbous mass that had been my father's nose in more recent years. In its place was a butte of refined pink skin that met without flaw a smooth and supple topography. For a moment, I was certain that it was all a mistake, that the body before me looked nothing like him. But there was the pockmark on the side of his

nose. Caterpillars of salt-and-pepper eyebrows. The narrow side-
burns he wore even when they were unfashionable. Without disappointment and alcohol to make him haggard, he was extraordinarily
handsome.

A swoosh of the curtain, and then my sister was standing at my
side. At first we put our hands on one another's arms, fearing to
touch him. At last we fingered the blanket that covered him from
the shoulders down. Beneath our tips came the crinkle of Saran
Wrap. It was an awful sound, and I considered the irony that my father, a man of wool and down and animal hides, was full of a syn-
thetic material designed specifically to enhance domestic living—a
product used to prolong the life of leftovers. Instead, I thought, his
chest cavity should have been rubbed with garlic, then stuffed with
fresh bundles of sage. And I could hear him telling me how important it was to know what it is that you eat. To know how and where
it lives, how it breeds—to know its habits and wanderings. And then
to know it as flesh in your hands, to pull from the carcass those vital
organs, to roll them in your palm and consider their wondrous, life-
pulsing functions before you fried them up for gravy.

Still, I could not directly touch his skin. Perhaps it was too many
distasteful Mormon viewings in my youth, or perhaps it was the per-
sistence of my father's lifelong intangibility. Or maybe it was simply
my own fear of such an intimate loss. All I know is that when I left
that small, sunless room, after I signed the form that would fire the
oven, I walked out into the light on South Temple to find the Angel
Moroni looming in the sky above and a gnawing lack of finality. I
didn't know then how that sensation would grind me down, threaten
to wash me away—long after I had declared that I had made peace
with his death. And for years I would be blind to its transference
onto Herb—would misunderstand his flood of energy as the source
of my attrition. And here I am, blaming his transience for my own
sense of impermanence, and unable to admit how I grip him too
hard, how I nearly sever his basic functions in the process. And

when he projects back at me that tyranny, I can only see the wild animal who takes me by the throat. He doesn't squeeze, just holds his fingers there, and hurls at me the most hateful words he can conjure. When he finally breaks his hold, he spins about the room like a madman, and still I can't see how he is attempting to re-create the momentum I have squelched. Instead, I cower. I weep. These only add to his sense of oppression. And after each sparring, we spend days trying to undo the damage, but really the wounds never heal. By the time we are standing under the pine tree in Harmon's yard, paying our respects to his wife, there is a deep festering in each of us—a decomposition that, if we dared to admit it, smells way too far gone.

ONLY DAYS BEFORE the funeral at Lila Canyon, a letter to the editor was published in the *San Juan Record* comparing our SUWA to the Taliban.[7] The attack feels personal, and, combined with the escalation in ORV incursions and energy development, makes Herb and me feel more at odds than ever with the community. Racine is the only person to defend us publicly, telling the author of the letter that we may be misguided in our efforts but we're by no means terrorists. When I stop by for tea, she recounts this to me, and I thank her. She winks and says of course, we're her favorite enemies. Then I stop by Jessica's house to complain. She stares into space, as if she's peering into another dimension. When she speaks, it is unclear whether she is referring to the townfolk or to me:

"How sad to be that full of hatred and fear."

"FIGHTING BETWEEN MEMBERS of the same species," writes Paul Shepard, "is very different from the killing of prey by predator, and psychopathological fighting is very different from normal conflict."[8] Some violence is acceptable, he seems to suggest, for cultures that use myth and ritual—even organized spectacles of isolated violence and scapegoating—can heal conflicts, assuage group neuroses, and safeguard cultural norms. I think here of my great-great-great-grandfather Egan, how his peers excused his shooting of the man who slept with his wife. This rather showy instance of bloodshed not only restored his marriage to some semblance of order, but also reinforced for his people the one-sided rules of Mormon polygamy. But if a group is threatened by *disintegrating forces*—for example, Shepard lists "acute deprivation, alien invasion, and unusual climatic events"—things can get messy.[9] I think here of John D. Lee, one of Egan's colleagues, who at Mountain Meadows led a group of Mormons and Paiute to ambush a wagon train of 130 non-Mormon, California-bound emigrants known as the Fancher Party. After a standoff that lasted nearly a week, Lee eventually tricked the emigrants into a surrender, at which point the men, women, and older children were brutally slaughtered. Following the carnage, the wagons were plundered, the horses and cattle driven off. The dead bodies were stripped of clothes, piled high, and then hastily covered with dirt—only to be scavenged by wolves. Later, the emigrants' bloodstained clothes would be worn shamelessly by Mormons in towns adjacent to the massacre site, and their livestock would be seen corralled in the same locales. The message was loud and clear: *We will be wronged no longer. Enter Deseret at your own risk.*

Such an overt and extreme show of force was uncharacteristic of the Saints, but at that point in their budding history, a great deal of insult had already been heaped upon injury: Here they had finally reached the promised land—at last escaping the persecution they had suffered at the hands of the Gentiles—and then the United States goes and annexes the whole place from Mexico. Next thing, gold is discovered in California, and the people they had hoped to be rid of invade the territory in droves, trying to get to the mines. Then, in a pre-election effort to distract a deeply divided nation from the gnawing issue of slavery, President Buchanan sends in the

U.S. Army to unseat Brigham Young and put a stop to polygamy. At the same time, the Saints were pretty hungry—for Deseret farming was failing miserably in the face of drought and cricket plagues, and other, more indigenous resources had been largely used up. To top it all off, the Saints had just received word that one of their most beloved apostles, Parley P. Pratt, had been murdered. Unfortunately for the Fancher train, Pratt had met his demise in the same part of Arkansas from which the emigrants had originated.

Shepard believes that widespread warfare would be largely prevented by returning to our more mobile hunting roots, by reinhabiting a more vibrant and less anxious way of life. He points to a sadistic indigenous people in New Guinea, a group that inhabits a tract of wilderness without outside contact. Distant observers mistake their behavior as "celebrated primitiveness," but Shepard points out that their homeland is shrinking, and no longer supports large mammals. He blames their rampant aggressions on the oppression of their hunting psyches and physiologies, and concludes that "yam-harvesting is no more a suitable occupation for them than supermarket shopping is for a man in Detroit."[10] Their acts of violence he says, have come to be "dominated by ferocious sorcery cults whose grisly fantasies serve less as a safety valve than as perpetual machines of fear and hate."[11]

I TURN AWAY from the casket and look at Herb. I cannot get my head around what is happening to us. Now he too, at times, is the enemy—and I am certain he would say the same about me. This new sense of adversity is baffling and sad.

Still, there is some deep underpinning of both love and lust, and so we keep trying. And as we stand beneath a sky that is once again officially void of aircraft, I begin to wonder if we would be better off selling the house, burning our possessions, and taking off into the desert. Common sense tells me that we have evolved too far beyond that world, destroyed too much of it, to reinhabit it. And there are, of course, too many people. But I am desperate enough to imagine that maybe, just maybe, at least Herb and I could pull off some micro-version of prehistory—that our only problem is that we simply haven't gone native enough.

WE DRIFT BACK from the casket so others may approach. In the meantime, several men have perched a small electric organ upon an open ironing board, while a group of boys has connected the instrument to a long series of orange extension cords that snake up the hill to the house. The Seventh-day Adventist minister has arrived from Dove Creek, where our neighbors worship every Saturday. The church organist has come too. I feel a self-consciousness about being a newcomer among people who are such an integral part of one another's lives, about being at such an intimate gathering. To help assuage the feeling, I look around for Howard, but his mother died only hours before, and I suspect that he wouldn't have had time to return from California. Everyone else I have met is deep in conversation, as is Herb, so I wander up the hill to the greenhouse, and seek refuge from the wind.

Inside, the air is warm and more moist than any that has coated my lungs in a long while. I circle the fig tree to the most direct sunlight and bask in intensified rays filtered through the transparent ceiling. Leaning up against the bark is a shotgun. I am certain it is the gun whose report I occasionally hear scaring a bear out of the orchard or a coyote from the chicken coop. There is a peculiar distinction between this gun and those that I have known: this one was used solely to protect food, never to procure it—for Seventh-day Adventists are strict vegetarians. But I grew up knowing guns only as useful tools—as the means by which we acquired the majority of our meat. Until there came a camping trip with another family, some other Gentiles from our neigborhood. In the middle of the night, on the shores of the Green River, below its headwaters in Wyoming, a man crept into camp and entered our friends' tent with a knife. We heard the father trying to reason with the man while his wife and kids whimpered into their pillows. I remember watching, wide-eyed and motionless in my sleeping bag, as my father put on his boots and withdrew a revolver from his duffel bag. It was dark, but I could see how swiftly the off-white of my father's Duofold moved across the tent, could hear him load the gun as he slipped out into the night. It didn't matter that he had been drinking—at that moment, my father's voice and hand were stern and steady. The intruder protested only once, then allowed my father to escort him from camp. I remember the feeling of safety, knowing that my father would guard the perimeter until morning. And I remember the sense of awe and near horror when I realized that bullets were for more than bringing down a good dinner.

I approach the gun. My breath quickens, and my heart races. I reach out tentatively, stroke the barrel. Its cool metal makes clear that my relationship to guns, perhaps to violence in general, has changed. What I mean is this: Now in my consciousness is my father's final earthly act. And knowing that I could actually kill Herb. I mean really kill him. Once, while climbing Notch Peak, in the Great Basin, I came upon a good-size spear point, perfectly chiseled. I was fuming about something—who knows what. Without thought, I raised the point back over my head and brought it down on his breastbone—deliberately, and with force. He clutched his chest and doubled over, gasping. His sternum was bruised for days.

The next day, he kept looking at me with bewilderment. I tried to apologize, but instead got rather academic. I explained how, as far back as the early Basketmaker period, food-getting implements were also used as battle armaments. I described the atlatl, how it had hurled a spear throughout Archaic times only to be replaced by the bow and arrow, not only because they could hunt smaller, quicker game, but also because they proved superior for shooting at other humans, especially when aiming uphill at a defensive site. I told him how what looks like a digging stick from that time was also the earliest form of a shield, used to bat away flying spear points, and how there was an oak club, fashioned in concert with a snare made of human hair. The club was used to drive small mammals and birds to the ends of box canyons, where they were caught in the snares and bludgeoned. On occasion, that same hunting club was used to smash human skulls—like those found in Cave 7's mass grave.

I don't know why I said all that, but his response was that I was not like other women, that I must truly love him.

"And I am certain," he said, tenderly rubbing his chest and wincing on the intake of breath, "that I will eventually die by your hand." It was perverse, but his eyes were wide and alive when he said it.

I WALK TO the doorway of the greenhouse and look down the hill. It looks as if the service is about to begin. I am thinking about Herb, about the physical volatility between us. An outside observer would surely label us as the classic domestic-violence case, but I am not sure that the stereotype applies. Even if I resort to cowering and crying, it is only because I don't know what else to do. In other words, we behave the way we do because we have no role models for such passion and emotion, no context that allows for our way of being.

Again the thought of the desert comes, and the urge to retreat into its deepest corners. Perhaps there we could find the right way to express ourselves. Or perhaps we need to stop going the rounds with one another and redirect all that enmity at the trucks that are rolling across the land at that very moment. And now there are reinforcements: fifty-thousand-pound thumper trucks have been hauled in and lined up like genetically modified soldiers. Side by side they march, across three-hundred-year-old soil crusts, across trees, across animal burrows, across ancient relics. Intermittently, they raise themselves up onto enormous steel pads and vibrate with all their mass, sending shock waves deep into the red earth. The tremors they cause tell the companies where the oil is. The drills, the roads, the sludge ponds will follow.

I start down the hill, looking ahead at the people who have gathered: Seventh-day Adventists from all over the Four Corners. A few gray-haired Sundowner bikers—part of a group who parked their Harleys out here after roaring into town twenty years ago. There is the county's criminal-defense attorney, a woman who represents mostly down-and-out non-Mormons when the jury is stacked with people who go to church together every Sunday. For her efforts, she gets paid mostly in donkeys, hay, fence repairs, and spare automobile parts. But the people whose presence I most notice are those who are absent: There doesn't appear to be a single Mormon in the group. Nor are the two neighbors who have not spoken to Herb or me since we moved in present.

And there is this: as I weave my way to Herb's side, there isn't one dirty look, or a single cold shoulder cast our way.

And so, when the minister leads us in prayer, I am actually able to bow my head, and I can't wait to give thanks for this feeling of spaciousness—this feeling of just being myself amid a group of people. Still, I am out of practice. Through squinted eyes I stare at the circle of legs and feet. Cowboy boots. Motorcycle boots. And lots of black patent-leather church shoes, dusted with fine red dirt, topped with pairs of pantyhose stuck with pernicious clumps of jumping cactus.

The organist's fingers strike several chords, and the gathering launches into "Amazing Grace." I turn my face from the ground to the sky. I squeeze Herb's hand as the group's voices float into the silent blue canopy above. He squeezes back, and suddenly there is a tethering. There, with the lion man and the eclectic, eccentric folks of the Lila Canyon hamlet, I gain a faint sense of what it means to belong to both a place and a people.

I once was lost but now am found . . .

How odd that I would feel this way with a man I am ready to murder, with folks I hardly know—but I'm going with it.

JUST AS WE WERE leaving the house to come help bury Verna, the radio was broadcasting a national address by the secretary of defense. He was detailing the precision of the sophisticated weapons deployed for the initial attack on Afghanistan, and declaring the mission a success. He had added that there was of course going to be *collateral damage*. It took me a minute to comprehend that he was referring to the country's civilians.

The disintegrating forces:

Acute deprivation. We are starved for space and sustenance. For security and sovereignty.

Alien invasion. So many encroachments. And Paul Shepard asks, "How are we to become native to this land?"[12]

Unusual climatic events. Drought. Thumper trucks. And when the desert is drained, with what will we embalm it?

To the victors go the spoils. There are those on the defensive, who think we're capable of committing terror in the community, against the oil industry. If only they understood that we're more inclined to take one another's scalps.

Later, I will wish we had. It would have been preferable to breaking one another's hearts.

⇥ 11 ⇤

Dwelling

SHE INSISTED ON *civility, even though the house was nothing but a cold and barren hovel made of mud. And she remained poised, even when the rains turned relentless and the roof, almost rafterless, threatened to implode like a fallen chocolate cake on Elder Kimball's visiting head. The apostle had made it a point to call on her often, whenever her husband was away on Church business, and so there he was, sitting on one of the few pieces of furniture, when the ceiling began to heave and groan. But Tamson, she kept right on asking after Kimball's health, kept on pouring tea into chipped bone-china cups and apologizing for the lack of pastries to accompany it. She kept right on, even as Kimball leapt from his seat, even as he bolted out the front door, even as he shouted over his shoulder to get out while she still could. It was only when the ceiling started to sag that Tamson set down the teapot, gamely gathered her skirts, and stepped up onto the recently vacated chair. And, high on her toes in the center of the room, teetering precariously but with unquestionable grace, she plunged a table knife deeply into the sodden roof, and a fine, controlled stream of water cascaded down her face and arms.*

The incision was deep, and it relieved the mounting pressure immedi-

ately. Still, she took no time to congratulate herself for a disaster averted, for there was the mess the leak left on the floor. Most folks would think that moving a pool of rain from a surface made only of dirt and sawdust was hardly worth the effort, but Tamson was adamant. She got right down off the chair and began to sweep, summoning her boys to help. After all, one never knew who might come to call.

With a crude broom made from bunches of rabbitbrush, she pushed the mud out the front door. On the threshold, pausing for a brief moment to catch her breath, she looked out across the fort, across the 422 earth mounds like her own. Beyond those repetitive rows, beyond the endless outer wall of the fort, there was nothing but another wall, this one built of dull gray clouds. Only 875 acres of a single community crop, winter wheat, provided any variation in the view.

She had not been prepared for such monotony. Despite talk of a seriously prolonged drought, it had rained mercilessly since her arrival, and so she had not yet seen the way the Wasatch Range rose up from the desert floor in staggering surges of purple, or the way the sun blazed across the marsh grass that embraced the shining inland sea. No, all she had seen so far was the compound around her—a place that had forgone quality and good taste in exchange for quantity and haste, an expansive, unimaginative enterprise designed to accommodate the flood of faithful that would soon be crossing the continent in droves. Howard Egan had escorted her and the boys to the Utah fort one year after he had first set foot in Deseret. And no sooner had he unloaded their wagon than he was off again, headed back east to retrieve his second wife. Had he stuck around, Tamson would have asked him to point out the vistas he had so compellingly described upon his return to Winter Quarters in the fall of 1847—images that had left her breathless and brimming with anticipation.

Her life now: She often sat—either in prayer or taking a turn in watch over the wheat, which couldn't possibly survive another cricket raid. Other times, she was just beyond the compound wall, hunched over and scrounging the alkaline soil for roots and anything remotely green— while her boys scratched the brush for jackrabbits, even lizards. They'd *learned to take anything edible, anything at all to stretch out the meager supply of flour and cornmeal. The rest of the time, Tamson had her boys peeling bark off the fort's fence posts, to fuel the kitchen fire. It was hard to believe, but in just one year the trees on the valley floor had been used up for the outer fort and the stockyards, and the men had quickly become too consumed with Church affairs to get out into the foothills for more timber. It was why the houses had been built with hardly any frame to speak of. It was why Tamson's roof was made mostly of earth and straw.*

Still, the brethren considered life in this city of Saints to be a step up from life on the wagon trail, and certainly an improvement over living among Gentiles in any condition. And so they did their best to keep the place neat and civilized. Tamson, being a stickler for decorum, gladly kept up appearances—and in fact did so better than most. But the truth was, she had quite preferred the journey to the destination. Crossing the plains, then the Rockies, she had been absorbed by the landscape, not set apart from it. She had marveled at how it informed and enlivened her every step.

And there had been many steps. She had walked most of the way, getting up in the wagon only when the team needed real driving. In fact, when her husband had gone ahead on his mount to scout for Indians, or to assist another family, it was she who singlehandedly brought three yokes of cattle and a wagon full of children through many of the rough spots. Others still talked about how it was Tamson who managed the Echo Canyon stream-crossing twenty-seven times without mishap, and how, more than any other driver, she avoided the stumps and rocks that sometimes hung up a wagon for hours.[1]

Also, her husband was a terrific tracker and marksman. Big game was more scarce than when he had made the trek the year before, but, unlike so many other continental crossers, the Egans and those fortunate enough to accompany their outfit always went to bed with bellies full of fresh meat and gravy. More than anything, though, traveling together as a family meant that, no matter where on the wagon train he was needed during the day, Howard Egan returned to Tamson each night. Together they would feast, then pray. Later, after the boys had climbed under the wagon box to a pile of furs and wool blankets, with the moon soaking through the stretched canvas tarp above, Egan would consume her in the same way the land did—and their combined effect made her more certain than ever that she was standing in the grace of God. And no matter how far away her husband rode during the day, no matter how many miles she trudged behind, she had the peace of knowing they moved in tandem. Along the same trajectory, in unison, they marched to the drums of heaven.

So, if she had to share her husband with other women, so be it.

But then she had arrived in Deseret, and the shift in atmosphere and living conditions made it hard for her not to consider that perhaps the Heavenly Father had suddenly forsaken her. She had to endure not only the overwhelming sense of confinement, but also the nagging deprivation—of both aesthetics and nutrition—like none she had ever experienced. And Egan had been elsewhere almost the entire time she had been in the Salt Lake Valley. Soon he would return with Nancy, who would live in a structure exactly like Tamson's. She knew that it would be prudent to join forces with the second wife, that their combined efforts would produce more food and fuel for both households. Besides, a jealous woman was such an uncomely thing to behold. Yes, she would give Nancy a warm welcome; she only hoped her home wouldn't be on the same street. She couldn't bear to see Howard enter it in the evening—not to exit until morning. In such monotonous hovels, with so little to distinguish between the two wives, she couldn't help thinking how interchangeable the two beds would become. Meat and scenery she could survive without, if she had to. And a home—especially one this shabby—she'd gladly forgo. Even God's blessing she could do without, if it came right down to it. But to lose the man she loved was a fate worse than perdition.

As she stood staring out at the homogeneous housing, the monoculture quivering in the wind, a man sent by Kimball arrived with a large pine post, easily stout enough to support her ceiling. Had Egan been around, he would have seen his wife stand there, posture-perfect and ankle-deep in mud, and politely but firmly refuse that precious gift of cut timber. Had he not spread himself so thinly between Church duties and coupling with other women, he might have heard her say, with her speech and manner a model of finest comportment, that she would not have such a thing, thank you very much, "set up in the middle of her parlor."²And in 1849, had he not galloped off to seek California gold, his obligation to Kimball after Brigham Young counseled that each of the Church leaders should send someone in a search for gold "for their own advantage . . . owing to the large amount of time spent by them in counciling [sic] for the public,"³ Tamson might not have forgotten the feel of those bones in her bed, the taste of the meat he brought to her table. But the waiting was long, and the forgetting came—despite her hunger for a good meal, despite God's commandments, despite the Church's and the community's inevitable condemnation. It was survival, really, the only way she could cope with the madness of monotony and one-sided monogamy. And so, one day, when her old friend James Monroe appeared at the door, when he took off his hat and asked her how she was faring in Deseret, she took him in.

All the way in.

EARLY SUMMER COMES, with the realization that winter and spring have passed with hardly a day spent not working. Next to a calendar inked over with foundation deadlines, I sit at the computer and craft proposal after proposal, trying to obtain grant money to support our group's mounting efforts. Herb is working harder than ever. At his office in town, he scribbles an endless string of legal briefs, imploring the federal courts to stop the worst of the development. The challenges are ridiculed by the locals—despite Herb's pointing out that the SUWA challenges less than 1 percent of approved oil and gas permits.⁴ And between the filing of appeals, he's out in the desert, running from one site to the next, monitoring what has become a continual influx of mineral-location and -extraction equipment. Many nights, he throws down his sleeping bag next to oil-rigs-in-the-making, or a set of thumper trucks, only to be awakened at first light by the terrible rumble of massive machinery roaring to life. He complains that his bones and teeth ache from the constant shimmying of sand, that he can't sleep for the shudder of sandstone. He shrugs it off: he'll bounce back, he says, just as soon as he can stop the bastards. But the desert, he is certain, will never be the same.

On the nights when he actually comes home, it is often past midnight. By then the cabin is dark. And in the loft above, he can hear the click of my fingers across a keyboard lit by nothing more than the glow of the monitor. Before, he would chastise me for running the computer after sunset—night use drains our solar power. But the cause has hit such a feverish pitch, and so he is willing to go without power—go without everything, if need be.

"We are warriors," he declares. "We'll do whatever it takes!" He even thumps his chest when he says it.

Indeed, the effort feels valiant and righteous, and we are both heady with the notion. As a result, a new solidarity forms between us. It makes the days almost bearable, and the battles between us finally cease.

We begin to travel together again. I go with him to Salt Lake City, to watch him argue a proceeding meant to stop a coal mine proposed for a place called Willow Canyon. En route, he takes me to visit the proposed mine site, a caramel-colored parting in the sandstone escarpment at the west end of the Book Cliffs, between the towns of Price and Green River. The enclave is whiskered with rare marshlands and hanging gardens fed by sparkling seeps. Songbirds thrum among the sudden foliage, and mountain-lion tracks—large prints followed by two tiny sets—are etched in the damp sand. The mine, if approved, would wrench open the cliffs' gentle folds. Trucks would constantly rumble back and forth to the highway, spiriting away the deepest, darkest parts of the canyon. And in the process of removing the coal, the water sources would be drained bone-dry—if the aquifer wasn't collapsed entirely.

Standing at the site, Herb tells me that the rancher who runs his cattle there had called his office in a panic. The man knew that losing the water and the grasses that depended on it would make the allotment nearly worthless for grazing; Herb asked him to sign on to the lawsuit to stop the mine, but the rancher refused.

"That's like getting into bed with the devil," he had said. "If you can't fix it without my name on it, then I'd just as soon sell off my herd."

Herb had told the guy to suit himself, he'd do battle without him.

AFTER THE COURT APPEARANCE in Salt Lake, we take a hike up the ridgeline above my childhood home. From a backpack, Herb produces a bottle of my favorite wine and two glasses. Taking care not to spill my glass, I fall back on a bed of yarrow and blue-bells, watch aspens finger the sky. Herb leans over me, slips a silver-banded garnet on my finger, and asks me to marry him. The red stone, and the carefully premeditated proposition, make me hyperventilate. Herb sits me up, has me breathe into the wine's paper sack to catch my breath. With my head halfway immersed in brown paper, I nod yes. And I am thinking, I can do this, I can follow him anywhere. I can live off the pieces that aren't already dedicated. If inserting myself into his kaleidoscope of duties and desires is what I must do to keep our lives on the same course, then so be it.

I begin to cut corners at work and forgo writing poems, just to be with him. I lose contact with the few friends I have made in Monticello—save Jessica, who keeps calling, who says she is there for me when I come up for air. When I finally make time for her, I explain my change in lifestyle. Her children whirl around us like dust devils, but she listens carefully. Then she narrows her wide green eyes at me and smiles that knowing smile I have come to anticipate.

"You do whatever you have to do to make it work with your

man," she says. "In the end, no matter how hard you work, no matter what you do with your time, there won't be much else that matters."

For the rest of June, Herb and I travel across the Utah portion of the Colorado Plateau, wandering through a number of places that are proposed for both wilderness designation and fossil-fuel development. Together we cross mesas and sagebrush prairies, then delve into canyons. Each day, we walk so far we can barely drag ourselves into the tent at night. And despite any professional points the arrangement has cost me, despite the way the rest of my life has slipped away, I am blissfully happy with the scenery and companionship this life affords. And I feel good. My muscles have grown strong again, and my eyes are once more bright. The nagging ache in my back and shoulders—an occupational hazard—has all but disappeared.

BY JULY, I learn that I am pregnant. I envision slowing my pace some, but I never imagined how such a natural condition would halt me quite literally in my tracks. Soon, I am too sick to travel, too sick even to raise my head from the pillow. Herb, on the other hand, is suddenly possessed by a maniacal nesting instinct that competes strenuously with his workload. He stays at the office even later during the week, but on the weekends he scrambles to put on a new metal roof that requires no fewer than eight thousand screws and, with scraps from various unfinished projects, slaps up a makeshift bedroom off the west end. The cabin goes from rustic to haphazard—a work-in-progress that lacks in details. Insulation and drywall never make it into the bedroom, and rain gutters remain absent from the new roof. I suggest that we attend to these things before we get into other projects, but already he has ordered tile for the floor, and French doors to a new deck that runs the entire length of the south side. So frantic is he that he forgets to eat or drink water, and he tosses off my pregnancy cravings and complaints by asking how the pioneer women managed without lime-flavored Popsicles and heartburn medication. But he says he can empathize: thanks to a weak inner ear, he gets nauseous every time he drives his car. And before the sawdust has settled, before any of the things he has begun are completed, he's driving off in the Volkswagen Bug to do field-work. From my reclining position in the loft, I see him waving farewell. Alongside his outstretched arm, a half-stuffed sleeping bag flaps wildly out the open window.

I lie there in bed and watch the small egg of a car disappear down our road, until there is nothing but quiet. And the silence I have always loved is suddenly unbearable. I will myself from the pillow and stumble downstairs, out into the yard. Something is coming unhinged, and there is no way to step back from it, to consider if it is hormonally induced.

Black and red. The colors of rage. The colors of the finest prehistoric pottery that the Anasazi had to offer. It appeared along with the fancy Chacoan-style stone palaces just before the culture vanished—both signals that life, for the ancients, had gotten too elaborate for their own good.

Black and red. The colors of oil, and coal, draining from the blushing desert's deepest veins.

WHEN THINGS SETTLE, I can no longer face the land's bold, raw mass. Nor can I face the house—its empty and unfinished state. Sky reeling, stomach lurching, I sprint for the south side, to the heavy, cellar-style doors that lead into the earthen basement. I stand for a moment on the threshold, hovering half in darkness, half in light. Then I plunge inside, with the desert bearing down on me, breathing down my neck its heat and light and brash colors.

I close the doors behind me, and the relief is exquisite. Fumbling for the small fluorescent light that hangs above the power inverter and a row of twenty-six golf-cart batteries, I flip its switch to illuminate an old chaise longue tucked back against the cistern. I set it up, go back to extinguish the light, then paw my way back to the chair and stretch out. My eyes adjust with the aid of a small hole used to drain water from the truck into the cistern, and eventually I can just make out the walls. When we bought the house, the old man who built it had described the backward process—how he had first erected the post-and-beam structure, then, only after it was complete, gone underneath with a garden hose and soaked the hard dirt until he could chip away at it with a shovel. Over the course of a year, he and Robert's eldest son, who worked for two dollars an hour, dug the entire basement by hand. Crude as the space is, it's actually very functional. As in a cave, the temperature remains so constant that we never have to worry about pipes freezing in winter. And on a day like today, the space is unusually cool and refreshing.

In a land of extremes, this kind of subterranean shelter is ideal, which is why pit houses—the underground lodges that preceded the more notorious Anasazi stone houses—were the preference of the Basketmakers. On average, the first of the semi-permanent prehistoric abodes were excavated to a depth of four to six feet beneath the earth's surface, by means of rock chisels and scrapers. Beams cut from piñon and juniper trunks were laid across the top of the pit, then covered with dense brush and soil. Sometimes interior posts were added for extra support. More trees were used to make ladders, which were often inserted through a hole in the roof to gain entrance.

In prehistoric terms, this period of architecture was relatively wood-intensive and probably stands as one reason that Basketmaker ruins are usually located near dense piñon-juniper forests. But the Basketmakers didn't just use the forest for the trees: once they hauled away the timber, they burned and cleared the understory, and used the bare but relatively fertile soil to grow squash and corn. Later, they added beans—sometime between A.D. 500 and 700. The preparation of legumes also added to wood consumption: to be made edible, they required considerable cooking and preparation. Crude pottery was already being made, and pots placed over an open fire soon replaced the previous method of cooking, in which hot stones were placed in pitch-coated baskets. The ceramic vessels could withstand more heat than the previously used cookware, and in turn, this allowed the early Anasazi to dry and store beans so they could be cooked at a later time without any real nutritional loss. And because food could now be cooked at a full boil, people were getting more from their corn staple. Before, when corn was consumed in a raw state, only half the carbohydrates were metabolized. With squash, the beans and corn satisfied the people as a complete source of protein—something that had been in short supply since the era of big hunting ended. And as the Basketmaker kitchen became more sufficiently stockpiled and nutritionally adequate, there was even less of a need to roam a broad area in search of supplementary wild foods.[5]

IN MY NAUSEATED, overheated state, I can greatly appreciate a life lived largely below ground, a never-ending menu of simple, starchy foods. And each day that Herb is gone, I descend to the basement with a bottle of water, a loaf of bread, and a bag of potato chips. There I sprawl for hours in the dull, dark void. I know I am supposed to be walking, and eating lots of fresh greens and protein, but just the thought of these actions makes me vomit spontaneously. And so I don't think of anything. I simply stare at the shadowy walls. I love how the scrape marks from the old man's shovel have left indentations—how the walls look almost galvanized in the narrow beam of sunlight that streams through the cistern hole. And with a dearth of light, I can not only bear the redness, I actually find it delicious. I have heard of pregnant women craving dirt—actually eating it—and, indeed, it takes everything I have not to lick the walls. Upstairs, the cell phone rings. Outside, the dogs bark when one of the neighbors stops by to check for signs of life. I respond to none of it. Eventually, I take to reading books—by headlamp.

The subject of choice is the Basketmakers of San Juan County. I read that their pit houses were dug more deeply as the culture grew increasingly stationary. Along with agriculture, it appears that the advent of these more profound and more permanent homes spawned a more dogmatic sense of ceremonial life, as if the increase in intro-spection was commensurate with the depth of the pit houses—the sum effect being more time spent underground, devoid of sensory stimulus. In other words, a spiritual life began to be sought at the expense of a sensual one. All this at a time when beans added to their culinary repertoire the one amino acid that meat had previously offered their bodies—a development that made it easier to forget their most visceral yearnings, and the former life that had sated them.

I read too about fetal development. One day, I open a book by a woman biologist who uses quantum physics and its emphasis on matter-as-energy to describe how the human body is nothing more than "vibrations existing in a sea of vibration."[6] These vibrations, she explains, can be *coherent* or *incoherent*; bodies have "receptors that transform these vibrations into the touchable, seeable, hearable, sen-sations we think of as matter and the physical world."[7] She describes how vibrational coherency enables the mind/body system to make sense from the intricate patterns of space, weight, texture, form, color, and even language. Conversely, incoherency—unnatural vibra-tions that assault the body—hinders the function and development of both the heart and the brain.

That night, when I am above ground and Herb returns home, I tell him what I have learned, and announce that I do not want any ultrasound tests performed on the baby—that I fear the barrage of waves may do harm. He says that's just fine, it's not the baby he's worried about anyway. He takes my shoulder square in his hands, tries to ferret me out. He asks if everything's okay. Running his fingers over my scrawny arms, he says I look half starved. He looks at the wood planks stacked with food, and turns back to me, perplexed.

I decide not to tell him about my unbearable urge to claw red clumps of dirt from the basement walls and shove them in my mouth. Instead, I tell him I need more protein. He points to the cans of beans, the super-size jar of peanut butter.

Even though I have no stomach for it, I next say, "What I need is meat." It isn't exactly a lie—I know it's what my body needs to keep up with its new task of building something like a hundred thousand new nerve endings per minute. But what I really mean is that I want Herb to acquire our dinner, and be home at a reasonable hour to grill it up for me. He reads between the lines, and flares. Can't I see how much he does for me? How he is doing the best he can? How beautiful the house will be when it is finished? And when he starts to walk away, to fire up the saw to cut one last board for the new room's ceiling before dark, I call after him, tell him I am no bride-to-be. Rather, I feel like a mere mistress among his many competing commitments. Even the profound hurt on his face doesn't stop my next words:

"I haven't forgotten what I need. Had there been anyone who had come along, any warm body at all to this godforsaken place in which I am stranded, I would have gobbled them down."

All the way down.

THE FOLLOWING WEEKEND Herb spends at home, and he doesn't so much as lift a hammer. Instead, he packs the car with dogs and beach towels, then drives me to a long, thin finger of Lake Powell that crawls right up to the southern edge of Highway 95. It is a place we have often stopped en route to other destinations, a convenient place to let the dogs drink and swim. In the warmer months, we jump in with them, hoping it is far enough away from the main channel to avoid serious sewage contamination. I survive the drive with my head between my legs, fighting the persistent urge to release the morning's waffles across the car floor. It is only after the car has come to a stop that I look up, and before my head is above the dashboard, I know something isn't right—Herb and the dogs are unusually silent. And as I reach the windshield, I see what's wrong— there isn't a drop of water in sight.

Rather, there is a sea of slickrock, a thousand crevices scrawled across it. Each fissure is so narrow that its rims nearly touch—like pursed lips. As they move away from us, the crevices widen and deepen, eventually joining one another to form larger canyon systems. We walk between them, peer down. Beneath the rims, the sandstone walls are blandly uniform—the former spectrum of browns, oranges, pinks, and crimsons faded to the dull, lifeless gray-white of temple granite. Even the sandy bottom is void of color, and studded with rusty cans, sandals, and fishing lures.

Herb asks if I want to walk, to see if we can reach the new shoreline. Despite my desire to float in the water, to have it cool the hot, greasy film of quease, I beg him to take me home, out of the heat and light and away from that relentless rock. The sight of it hurts more than ever—for now I see it as a thin red veneer that roofs an anemic underworld.

Herb sighs, and gets back in the car. I sit down on the slickrock and cry. And, for once this summer, it is not out of self-pity—or at least not obviously so. This time, I am lamenting the Colorado River, and its incarceration behind a massive and monotonous slab of concrete. It's hard to believe for even a minute that the river forgot its pulsing course through Glen Canyon, the way its currents rushed wildly through a steep, narrow chasm only to spread out languidly when the walls opened up again. What a gorgeous, vigorous life. What a constant, kinetic caress.

And now the drought. The lake's recession may be the reservoir's demise—for some scientists claim that the water level will soon fall below the turbines. Some say it will also be the Colorado River's death knell—that it will never recover from this oppressive and inert state. Driving home, I share these thoughts with Herb, and we agree that the rapid evaporation that is taking place is really the most masterful of jailbreaks. Right out from under our noses, the Rio Colorado is escaping. Particle by particle, it offers itself up to a parched and greedy sky.

It should be the most powerful of metaphors—enough to make us question all the changes in our conjoined life, especially the way it has slowed and settled us. But I am of Mormon stock: we get married, we settle, and on the promised land we stick it out in a sort of suffering way. And Herb is a Catholic boy: no matter how freewheeling he appears, some inherent sense of guilt drives him mercilessly toward social convention. And so the cabin will be upgraded to a rather comfortable house—coupled with an uncomfortable increase in the mortgage payment. The wedding invitations will go out by next week, and the baby is due in March. To pay for these life enhancements, we will both take on more work.

Before we reach Lila Canyon, we have decided to exchange our vows on the banks of the San Juan River. It is a free-flowing stretch, one we had often floated—before we got too busy.

The irony of this decision evaporates too quickly, up and away into the atmosphere, out of our grasp.

IN EARLY SEPTEMBER, two weeks before the wedding, second-trimester bliss sets in, and I can hardly remember the summer's unpleasantness. The only *aide mémoire* of those dark months is the sudden appearance of an extra twenty-five pounds—shocking, but also a relief after my body's initial weight loss. The only sensation that lingers is my inability to tolerate the heat, so I pack the car and head north. Besides, I would be needing a larger wedding dress than the one I had bought.

Impulsively, I skip Salt Lake City's department stores, and continue on to Malad. My mother had said that my grandfather feels bad that he isn't up for the drive to attend the wedding, and when I surprise him with my visit, we agree that this is time better spent together anyway. I have brought a fresh cut of lamb—his favorite dish—and we make a long and leisurely lunch of it at his kitchen table. Afterward, I drive him into town to see my grandmother, who has been in the nursing home for several years now. Like my grandma Ada's, her last years have been clouded by Alzheimer's, and she has needed full-time residential care. When we enter the home, my grandmother is standing in the hall, her once-imposing frame diminished to little more than a shadow. In her arms she rocks a baby doll. When we approach, she stares blankly at me, then turns to my grandfather. Her eyes narrow and her mouth hardens.

"Dale, I see you've been out with the hussies again. Is this your new girlfriend?"

Her eyes are blazing accusations, and my grandfather's jaw trembles. We both try to smile, and ask about her baby. The distraction works. We follow her down the hall to her room, so she can change the baby's diaper. We walk just behind her, and my grandfather points to the monitoring device she wears.

"She keeps getting out of it," he says. "Keeps escaping . . . and they find her wandering the streets. Fortunately, someone always sees her and calls it in before she gets too far."

I can imagine my grandmother standing out on Main Street, her nightgown flapping around her shins, her bare feet filthy.

"She'll say to them that she's just trying to get home." His voice splinters like the wood of a toppling tree. "At least some days she remembers she has such a place."

Back at the ranch, my grandfather leaves his boots and hat in the back hallway and shuffles to the living-room window. He can hardly see it for the macular degeneration that has consumed his eyes, but still he stares out at the view: A modest patch of grass in the front yard, followed by the irrigation ditch and the country road, then the fence line on the other side of the pavement. After that, there is a field, lined by sunflowers and dotted with fresh bales of hay. The far end of the pasture is framed by the Bannocks, a small range of mountains that rise suddenly from the valley floor, as they do so often in the Great Basin. Everything is green, yellow, gray. Not a drop of red anywhere.

"It is as beautiful as ever," I say, walking up next to him.

He nods, pleased that I have noticed.

"A long time ago, I promised your grandmother that I would never let anything obstruct this view. A lot of developers are going to want that field, to put in a subdivision for the folks who are looking to get out of Salt Lake and Pocatello. You've seen all the others they've gotten their hands on—the way they subdivide and then plop those stupid new manufactured homes down. Would do me a world of good financially, to go that way. But I made Lorraine a promise, and I intend to keep it; I'll sell off everything else before I let go of this."

I asked him what was his best memory of this place, and he told of riding off for a cattle drive; he'd be out for days in the elements, with rain filling up his boots and the scent of crushed sagebrush coming up from beneath the thunder of hooves. As he spoke, his face lost twenty years, and his cloudy eyes burned bright and clear.

"Then I'd load the horses and drive home. I'd pull up to the house, and your grandma would be standin' there in the front yard, arms crossed, scanning the horizon for any sign of me. She'd look so pretty and concerned. And every time I'd walk up, achin' for having missed her, she'd just scowl and give me the cold shoulder for a few days."

He sighs. "It must have been hard on her, to be here alone, looking after everything—especially when the kids were little. Sometimes I think maybe my absences drove her to this crazy, awful forgettin'."

———————

THE NEXT DAY, Herb meets up with me in Salt Lake. He declares the house completed, boasts that he has even cleaned up the scraps and put away the tools. I know that his ideas of *completion* and *clean* are suspect, but still I am awed by his Herculean efforts. And in my new and improved state, gratitude and devotion are easier to come by. Together we go to our first prenatal exam, and squeeze one another's hands tightly as the midwife puts a stethoscope to my already protruding belly. When she hears no heartbeat, she says not to worry, it's so early. She recommends an ultrasound, to which we halfheartedly consent. It confirms that the fetus has died in utero.

It is advised that I be put under general anesthesia, so a doctor can eliminate the tissue. But we are dumbstruck by the news, and unable to take such swift action. We decide to return home and wait to see what my body does on its own. We also decide to go ahead with the ceremony, for—despite the obstacles—the loss has made us more determined than ever to stick it out together. I spend a few days roaming the slopes of the Abajo Mountains, basking in the calm shade of evergreens. I meditate on this latest death, and envision again and again my body holding on until after our wedding day. When I return, Herb asks what I did. I try to describe my thought process. I can't quite bring myself to call it prayer, but I feel a certain new serenity.

THE MORNING OF the autumn equinox flares across the San Juan Mountains in southwestern Colorado, then spills over the Colorado Plateau into the town of Bluff. I steal from my room at the Recapture Lodge down to the water's edge. The river's rippled skin catches near-horizontal beams of early light and tosses them onto the backs of two blue herons. Side by side, the birds are stalking fish in the still water above a side eddy, just downstream. I remove my sandals and walk out into the current. It pushes gently against my legs. I dig my feet into the sandy bottom and brace myself against the opposing force.

I am standing like that when the herons heave their bodies into the sky. Their wings flap like heavy canvas as they skim the top of my head and fly upriver, into the rising sun, against the morning breeze. Backlit like that, they look like pterodactyls. Then angels. Things both ancient and otherworldly.

Perhaps this is a new beginning for us. Perhaps we can learn to dwell in the desert with greater ease, to inhabit it in a way that doesn't rumble with adversity. Just weeks before, I had explained this to an anthropologist friend, had offered up my full theory of how a return to the hunter-gatherer lifestyle might bring us into better harmony with one another, and with the land. Perhaps, I said glibly, the whole world would be better off if we just went native.

My friend had thrown back his head and laughed. Then he looked at me with condescension, as if my notions were too naive too bear.

Amy, you can't go back.

Eventually, the sunball eclipses the birds in flight, and I wade back to shore. I kneel in the sand and consider those words. My heart resides in this desert, with this man I am about to marry, precisely because of those notions. Besides, they beat the hell out of the alternatives:

Ada. Her eyesight gone, and with it the ability to make art. Alzheimer's promptly set in.

Grandma Blaisdell. She looked out that window for her husband until bitterness made him almost unrecognizable.

My father. He drank to forget the hopelessness that eventually possessed him. It is the same hopelessness I see in the anthropologist who scoffs at me, on afternoons when he phones intoxicated and flings harsh words at those who love him.

Yes, the battles, the losses, they take their toll. Every day is a struggle, for the desert, for my lover, for a place to dwell as if I were an integral part of things. And the effort has shaken me—left me teetering precariously.

The thunder of Herb's voice. The rumble of ORVs and thumper trucks. The pound of the judge's gavel as it ensures the demise of my homeland.

Black on red. Passion and fury are close cousins, and hard to bear. But the alternative is apathy—a white on white, a monochromatic scheme where spirituality is bleached of both sense and sensibility.

With that last thought, I turn back to the lodge, to go don a suprisingly large wedding gown—whose fabric is every color imaginable.

JESSICA ARRIVES at nine o'clock to help me dress. Her face is flushed, and her stomach pokes her dress out just enough to remind me that she is as pregnant as I had expected to be on my wedding day. There is a bittersweet moment when I realize that our babies will not be growing up together, but Jessica's attentions help to usher away the feeling. Soon she has me dressed in an opalescent silk gown and cowboy boots, and my hair swept up among tiny red rosebuds. She touches up my lipstick and hugs me goodbye as I step carefully into a small handmade canoe draped with garlands of paper flowers and autumn-kissed tamarisk. Paddling downstream toward the wedding site, I can hear bagpipes bouncing off the canyon walls. The San Juan carries me around the bend just in time for me to see Herb approaching the site on horseback. He too wears cowboy boots, along with a Scottish kilt and a cowboy hat. A crowd of people fill the north bank, on which friends have strewn with dried flowers and prayer flags. The south bank, the Navajo side, is vacant—save the two ravens that heckle us from a dead snag on the shore. I wonder if the two birds are the same ones that egged us on four years ago, during our naked mud fight in the San Rafael Swell's Muddy Creek, and I decide they are there to remind us what we have, what lies beneath all else that has happened.

STANDING BEFORE the crowd is a Ute Indian elder in a fringed buckskin suit and a headdress made of raptor feathers and colorful beads. He plays his flute, then waves a bundle of burning sage throughout the site as he chants a wedding blessing. It is not lost on me that the only Indian to attend our wedding is the one whose presence we have paid for—after I denied Nora my trees, she had never called again. And though we will invite this elder to attend the evening festivities back at Lila Canyon, he will not show up until the next morning—and then it will be with all of his brothers, sisters, and cousins in tow. They will be laughing and staggering, in search of more booze after an all-night binge. He will look nothing like the way he did the day before.

The canoe floats up next to the wedding party, and I take in the array of faces. There are friends and family from all over the country—from places as far away as Thailand and France. And there are many of our San Juan County neighbors—among them old-time Mormons and BLM bureaucrats. And it is in this vast mix of people that a point is driven home: the folks in the closest proximity to me are the folks whose ways feel the most foreign. For, one by one—save Jessica—any blossoming friendship has been stymied by Herb's and my protests of public-land use. Even those who agreed with us privately arrived eventually at a moment when they felt it was too risky to be viewed as allies of ours, or, at the very least, they were turned off by the rancor that surrounded the public debates of which we were a part.

And yet here they all are, as they have been here all week, helping Herb and me prepare for this day, helping us to juggle our joy with a newfound sense of grief. And as I step out of the boat, a rounder, heavier version of me than I have ever been, I feel again the makings of community. Or perhaps this is the very definition of community—and perhaps I have missed this all-too-elemental idea all along. And so I finally see: To truly inhabit a place is to learn to dwell with the differences that threaten to divide it. Otherwise, one beckons monotony.

The Ute man chants, and the bagpipes wail. Jessica wipes my brow and lifts the hem of my dress so I don't trip on a piece of driftwood. And there stands Herb, looking at me with that fat-cat grin, like he wants to devour me. I turn inward, thank my body for holding on, and ask the small spark of life that had briefly grown in there to come again when our lives aren't reverberating with such unrest. And then I turn outward, feel the sun on my cheeks, and smell the scented smoke hovering in the air.

Herb takes my hand. The slender bones of his fingers, the copper-penny freckles across the backs of his hands: my attention to them is almost obsessive, and it elevates and elates both cells and neurons.

I can't go back, for the way has been forgotten. But there is the hope that this marriage can push us ahead, toward something that recalls what we once knew.

≒ 12 ≒

Flight

I AM STANDING shoeless in our front yard, wearing a short pink dress with thin straps. Late-September sun nudges my bare shoulders and legs. In my arms is a baby girl with the most exotic eyes—large, the color of water-stained slate. They stare straight into the blue of mine. Her tiny hands clutch, almost fiercely, at the dress fabric.

Then the *click-clock* of hooves on the cobbled dirt road. The exasperated snort of a horse. The intense gaze ruptures as I turn to see who approaches. And there is my father, sitting atop a wooden cart, guiding the reins of a harnessed buckskin. He waves, and even from this distance, I can see the brightness in his eyes, the brilliance of his smile.

He pulls into the driveway and jumps out. His body is spry, and he looks younger, more vibrant, than he has in many years. He pats the horse's pale-blond forehead and steps around to greet us. I recognize his typical weekend attire: A lightweight gentleman's flannel—the kind with suede patches on the elbows. Pressed jeans and leather field boots. And a broad-brimmed felt hat, a ragged pheasant feather stuck in its band.

We stand, boot to toe. He never once looks at my attire, or the amount of skin it reveals. Instead, he seeks my eyes.

It's time, Amos.

I look down at my baby. Then back to my father's outstretched arms. A brutal moment of understanding is upon me, the piercing realization of why he has come.

I will take good care of her. A whole lot better than I did you.

For the first time, I truly believe my father. And when I hand her over, she doesn't cry. She takes one last look at me, and then fixates on him. He holds her tenderly. For the rest of my life, I will gorge on this memory.

The horse nickers as he tucks his granddaughter into the seat beside him. And then he turns to me one final time. Through the tears I can barely see his body, let alone his face. But I hear the metronome of hooves and the creak of the wagon, as they retreat down our road. And as my eyes dry, I am pretty sure he waves before they disappear over the last knoll in sight.

WHEN I AWAKE from this dream, my face is still wet. Herb is on his side, eyes wide, staring at me.

"It's time," I echo my father's words. My husband nods silently.

We drive back up to Salt Lake City, and obtain a prescription for a drug that is used to induce labor in cases like mine—where the fetus dies but the body, for some reason, does not expel it. We drive to the stateside condominium my mother and stepfather had recently purchased, where we wait for the contractions to begin. Even at the last minute, the midwife and others had asked if I was certain I wanted to go this route, had reminded me that surgery would be far less messy and painful. I had nodded emphatically, while Herb squeezed my hand in support. He understood how I needed to be both witness to and participant in this brief cycle of life and death.

That said, I do not know what to expect. Before my father ended his life, my experience with death had been mostly limited to the animals we ate. And of all the fish, birds, and ungulates that were cleaned on our patio and cooked in our home, the only three that gave me pause were the ducks my father acquired from Liberty Park. The city had drained the lake at the center of the park, leaving the resident waterfowl homeless. The domestic brands—those with clipped wings and no survival instincts—were offered as pets to any citizen willing to cart them away.

It was a Saturday afternoon in spring when my father brought them home—a white one and a pair of mallards. He brought them into the house in a cardboard box, which he set sideways on the kitchen floor. The three creatures tottered out and readily ate Cheerios from my palm; they even stood patiently while I tied baby bonnets around their sleek heads. I christened them each with a name, then, from the box and an old baby blanket, I fashioned them a proper nest. The ducks settled into it while I went downstairs to the family room for piano practice and an hour of television.

When I emerged for dinner, I sat down to find two roasted carcasses on a platter in the middle of the table. I looked to the corner of the kitchen, saw that the ducks' nest was empty. I fled the table, shrieking. I didn't speak to my father for a week, and I didn't eat any animal flesh for nearly a month.

WHEN THE TREMORS BEGIN, I crouch on the floor of my mother's guest bathroom. My body heaves, and there is blood, lots of it. Herb is right there, kneeling in red viscosity. He leans into the pain and breathes with me. When my body finally releases the beginnings of our child, he scoops them up, wraps them in a piece of fabric left from the hem of my wedding dress. Not once does he flinch.

Back at Lila Canyon, he fashions a box for the remains, digs a hole beneath a grove of piñons on the northwest corner of the property. I stare down into the dark, black space framed by damp cayenne-colored earth. Then I look up and out, between the tree boughs. The backdrop is my most beloved view in the world: Cedar Mesa, and the Abajos. The middle ground is Harmon's house, and the ponderosa under which Verna is buried. The foreground is the ancient hunting camp just outside the grove. Though Herb has made his mark on almost every other square inch of the property, this site remains as we found it—a circle of worn, charcoal-licked stones that encase a scattering of flint chips and ceramic sherds.

Whether we feared the disturbance of spirits or relics is hard to say. All I know is, choosing to dig in the site's proximity was not a decision made casually. But in the end, we had acknowledged the place as one of scenic serenity. It is also a place that the dogs gave wide berth—a place they are certain not to disturb—and this fact alone overrides any sense of archaeological propriety. On top of the grave we pile the most colorful rocks we can find, and the wilted red roses from my wedding bouquet. The setting is like a needle, threading together the disjointed pieces that now define my understanding of death:

Dead coyote nestled beneath a piñon tree.

Roasted fowl on a silver platter.

Verna's body in a pine box.

My father's body on a stainless-steel gurney.

As we kneel there, the world around us delivers: Hard pellets of gray rain come down, beating brush and evergreen until the scent of sage and sap rises up like incense. The wind moves through the trees, muttering incantations, and the sky curves over us—an apse of cosmic proportions. And later, when the dogs take greater pains than ever to circumvent the area—even on the heels of a jackrabbit—I will finally begin to believe wholeheartedly that there really is some other territory where spirits who have taken flight from their physical bodies ultimately reside. And I will begin to believe that perhaps, someday, I'd like to go to that place. And for a brief moment, I even wonder what I might do in this life to guarantee my passage.

FOUR MONTHS LATER, Herb and I fly to the Southern Hemisphere. The trip is an official three-month sabbatical from work, and much needed. In equatorial South America, we first travel to a wildlife refuge high in the Andes of Ecuador, where we volunteer on a ranch that is converting its livestock operation back to traditional alpaca—whose hooves are light on the soil, and whose wool turns an impressive profit. Next we enter the Amazon jungle of Peru, where we paddle a dugout canoe through a relic arm of the Madre de Dios River. And, finally, the Inca Trail, where we hike through a string of ancient ruins all the way to Machu Picchu.

We have chosen to travel during the rainy season, and so each leg of the trip is completed mostly in knee-high Wellingtons and raincoats—not Gore-Tex, but the serious, rubberized kind. Much of our travel involves wading through deep mud, and sometimes even hacking at dense tangles of flora with machetes. We pass through villages full of Incan descendants, where we find that the Quechua Indians' language, customs, and dress are still very much alive—far more so than those of the southern-Utah tribes. In one setting, a jungle man cures Herb's dysentery by brewing the leaf of a common plant that grows right outside of the hut in which we are staying. In another village, we are invited to join an all-night festival that centers on the cutting of a single tree. And in Cuzco, we drink and dance alongside a procession that features a woman wearing a mask with a large penis for a nose.

Everything—the wet, lush green, the rich native traditions, the playful and lusty celebrations—bespeaks Deseret's antithesis. And yet, one day when the rain finally stops and we bare our feet to a few rare rays of sun in an effort to dry out the jungle rot that plagues them, and Herb asks me if I miss home, I nod—immediately and emphatically.

"Wouldn't it be cool, though," he says, holding his foot up so I can see how leprous it looks, "if we could flit back and forth between the two places—spending half the year in southern Utah and the other half down here?"

To live the life of migrating birds hardly sounds far-fetched at this point. On these exotic travels, I had expected to play the role of tourist, or spectator, and have found that it feels no different from how I feel at home. And so to Herb's second question I nod again—say yes, I could move back and forth between the two continents. And for the first time ever, I consider how much good it might do me to live far away from a place so dry.

And I am not just referring to the climate.

AFTER TWO MONTHS, Herb and I part ways in Lima. For the last four weeks of our sabbatical, he has chosen Costa Rica, to try surfing. I am trying to attend to my own life again, and have decided to return home for a quiet month of writing. After a red-eye flight to Salt Lake and a quick nap at my sister's house, I head south.

In Monticello, I pick up the dogs from the dog-sitter and make a stop at Blue Mountain Foods before continuing on 191. And as I turn onto the road above Lila Canyon, the first thing I see is a Texaco truck full of survey equipment. I turn right around and drive into town to Herb's office, from which I send him an e-mail. The next day, his reply confirms my worst fears. Not only may the petroleum companies have oil and gas leases out on the BLM land behind us, but they may also own subsurface rights for resources beneath the private properties that border it—as if the world below can be separated from the one above.

"I hate to tell you this," he writes, "but you just might wake up one morning to see a rig set up in the yard. And you won't be able to do a damn thing about it."

I try to stick to a writing schedule, but I can't stop thinking about the truck. The dogs and I begin a daily patrol of the neighborhood, scouting for more industry vehicles. We wander every dirt road, public and private, seeking signs of passage. At night I go into town and get on the Internet, where I read about places like Wyoming's Powder River Basin, where over 75 percent of the forty thousand leases projected for development in the next decade lie beneath private properties.[1] Landowners have stood by in horror as corporations come onto their land and proceed to build roads, wells, power lines, pipelines, wastewater discharge pits, and compressor stations that sound "like the engine of a 747 revving up for takeoff."[2] The large amounts of water required to produce natural gas from underground coal seams—a process that can consume one hundred gallons per minute for two years running—have drained domestic and stock wells alike—and many of the wells that continue to produce are now contaminated.[3] However impossible such an intrusion onto someone's land may seem, it is perfectly legal under existing law.

FOUR FEET OF SNOW interrupts the onset of spring, and the accumulation seems to have deterred any additional industrial traffic on our mesa. For good measure, I continue the patrols on skis. My only unusual finding is a single set of men's bootprints, which completely circles our property. The gait of them seems to break every now and then, and turn in toward the house. Each time the prints do this, it is at a point where the person wearing them would have had a direct line of sight into our windows.

For all its glass, this house has no curtains. We didn't see a need for them in such a private setting, but now I wish I had brought along those I left hanging in the rented blue house. When the sun goes down, I call in the dogs and lock the doors. And if I arrive home after dark, I practically fly from my truck to the front door, key poised, ready to unlock the deadbolt as fast as is humanly possible.

HERB RETURNS home from Costa Rica early, claiming he missed me too much. I suspect that he merely wanted to get back to work, that he cannot bear to miss out on all the latest action. But he doesn't even stop by the office to check the phone, or look at mail. Instead, he asks where I'd like to go. I tell him to take me to Fremont country.

From 95, we cross the Colorado River, and drive back roads into the more remote section of Canyonlands National Park. In between the main canyons carved by the Colorado and the Dirty Devil, there are rolling, bare-boned plateaus and an endless maze of side canyons. This is no-man's-land—where Butch Cassidy and the Wild Bunch hid out following big bank heists. And in prehistoric terms, it's a kind of borderland—a region where the northernmost Anasazi mingled with the most southern of their northern neighbors, a people who occupied the Great Basin province on the west side of the state as well as much of northern and central Utah. They inhabited the Colorado Plateau all the way to the Colorado River and sometimes just beyond—sometimes seeping into the north and west portions of what is now San Juan County.

Alongside the Basketmaker-era Anasazi, the Fremont Indians cultivated squash, corn, and beans—although they did not develop the same dependence on domestic cultigens as their neighbors did. Instead, the Fremont remained more faithful to the gathering of wild foods, and continued to hunt mountain sheep, bison, deer, small mammals, and birds. And they fought. Evidence of warfare is found throughout Fremont ruins, just as it is in those of the Basketmakers. For example, Fremont rock art shows many figures carrying large shields—and in some cases the figures' torsos themselves are shieldlike, as if self-defense was literally an embodied way of life.

We are somewhere above the confluence of the Green River and the Colorado. I marvel at what a formidable boundary that conjoined waterway is—and at the fact that prehistoric people somehow crossed it. Knowing the Basketmakers' propensity for violence, having seen the battle shields that dominate local Fremont art panels, I can imagine either bank serving as a battlefield between the two cultures. Perhaps the Basketmakers looked across the water and saw in the Fremont nothing but primitive pagans who needed to get with the new program of farming and religion. Perhaps they found a way to traverse the river for the express purpose of civilizing their neighbors. And perhaps the shields in Fremont art reflect that culture's drastic effort to stave off encroachment. It's possible, for, even that long ago, there seems to have been a compulsion to subdue the savages. There is the obvious reason for this timeless and universal trend: The more sophisticated a group became, the more it needed additional territory and resources, and part of its evolution was to acquire the means to obtain such things. Because the tried-and-true ambush/annihilation strategy could get dangerously messy, colonization and religious conversion became more fashionable methods for profit and dominance. If the lowlifes resisted, the enlightened could march on a few encampments, flex their well-armed muscles by spilling some token blood, and get everyone back in line. It made sense: Growing food and acquiring other staple resources was, just as it is now, hard work. Especially in a land of extremes. And so, if you could rope someone else into doing it, all the better.

Some say that the taming of the savage—along with the wild landscape he inhabited—was driven by deeper, darker motivations. Paul Shepard suggests one could only survive the early life of agriculture—with all its exhausting, anxiety-ridden drudgery—if one were to adapt psychologically. Like a prisoner of war, he would do incredible mental gymnastics in which he would come to embrace the paralysis and monotony of his life. In this convolution was a clutching at conformity, a desperate and hostile rejection of anything outside that increasingly concrete existence. And so anything and anyone that did not fit into his myopic little mastering of the world was to be viewed as a threat. Untamed land and nonfarming people became the projections of his fear and deprivations—repressed in an effort to maintain control in a lifestyle and religion that offered very little. And then those things also become targets for his subsequent aggression.[4]

Of course, it is just as likely that the two groups fraternized in a more friendly way—that the battles depicted were the exception. Because, for all their differences, the Fremont and the Anasazi were actually enough alike to have shared strikingly similar rock art styles. Like those of the Basketmakers, the Fremont art panels are dominated by trapezoidal anthropomorphs—"heroic and elaborate" in design, and often wearing ornate headgear.[5] There are likenesses in torso decoration, and in the attention to necklaces, hairbobs, and armbands. Such common themes, says rock-art aficionado Polly Schaafsma, indicate a parallel in ideologies.[6] There are even a few places in southeastern Utah—namely, near the Abajo and La Sal Mountains—where art panels demonstrate a merging of the two cultures: Typically, San Juan Basketmaker anthropomorphs were designed with crescents for headdresses, but in the Abajo–La Sal–style art, these figures sprout horns from the sides of their heads—a Fremont signature.

But why the seemingly anomalous integration? And why did it occur only on the borderlands? Is it possible that, as the Basketmakers continued to shift more toward agriculture and the religious practices that accompanied it, a few renegades resisted the trend and stuck with their previous hunting and gathering ways? In keeping with Utah parlances, we could refer to such mainstream dropouts as "Jack Basketmakers." Perhaps the Jacks weren't too readily accepted by their own kind, and so they drifted to the edges of San Juan Anasazi turf, where they found like-minded community among a few Fremont. Perhaps they established outposts there, where they wouldn't be too closely scrutinized for continuing to live a little more on the wild side of things, foraging more than farming, and more ecstatic than ecclesiastic.

Not that mainstream Basketmaker communities weren't without their own growing pains. Throughout the San Juan country, they seemed to be fluttering back and forth between two realms of religiosity. On the one hand, anthropomorphic art persisted—even though the figures were diminishing in size and importance relative to the rest of the symbols. On the other hand, alongside the shrinking anthropomorphs, small stick figures of humans engaged in ordinary activities were becoming more prominent—which led at least one reputable archaeologist to surmise that there was cultural movement toward a more secular life. Schaafsma challenges this, pointing to the simultaneously growing significance of birds, which also have been globally associated with shamans and their ability to assume an altered state in order to visit other worlds. Noteworthy, she says, are the frequent representations of the duck, which she points out is "at home in the sky, on and even under water," and therefore is a "natural model for mobility in several realms."[7]

And herein lies a possible explanation for the pervasive warfare of the Basketmaker era: sparring between spiritualities. There was the old way, in which a trained elite of holy men took wing from their bodies and traveled to other worlds—where they gathered wisdom and guidance from ancient ancestors and other deities with connections to animals, water, and other gifts from the earth. Then there was the emergent way, which seemed to plug any warm body into its priesthood—bodies that were incapable of transcendence, bodies that had to stay put and wait for communiqués from a single omnipotent deity who, for the first time in human history, may have overshadowed the horned masters of flight. In those times of change, it must have been confusing to know what to believe, to know to whom or what one should supplicate. And for a few, the idea of turning over sacred power from a specialized spiritual guide to a bunch of couch-potato priests must have been terrifying. It would be like living in a town where the sheriff deputizes men who don't know intimately the laws of justice, who barely know how to fire a gun.

It would have been like growing up Mormon.

AFTER A DAY of wandering the back roads on the west side of the Colorado, Herb and I drop back down to Highway 95. There we meet up with our friend Steve, one of southern Utah's premier canyoneers. More than perhaps any contemporary, he knows the most remote and unusual corners of southern Utah, and he has agreed to spend the last eight days of our sabbatical with us, hiking two remote canyons in the vicinity.

He leads us into the kind of unmarred scenery that I rarely see in redrock country anymore—not since the advent of serious off-road vehicles. As we pick our way along the wash bottom of the first canyon, I comment on this to Steve, who replies that the area isn't as untouched as it looks. He points to an obscure ruin high on the cliff face above us, and tells that several years ago he rappelled onto the ledge, where he saw a superb array of intact relics—including decorated pots without a chip on them. Abiding by his rigid sense of ethics, he touched nothing and left no trace of his passage. A year later, skid marks on the canyon rim above the ruin led to the grim realization that a helicopter had landed professional pot-hunters, who in no time at all had lowered themselves into the site and scoured it of its artifacts.

Steve's story plays out in my head like a scene from a James Bond film, where the villains have all the latest technology and a direct line to the international black market. But they aren't the only ones to have absconded with the desert's antiquity. In *The History of San Juan County*, historian Robert McPherson hints at a long tradition of local looters. He is gracious in his description of their sense of entitlement, but one gets the gist of their convictions when he notes that federal efforts to thwart such activities have resulted in the locals' calling for the county to secede from the nation.[8]

Part of the justification for removing relics from public lands is that the stuff gets removed anyway—either by visiting thieves or by institution-sponsored digs. The reasoning is that even the professional excavations fail to *preserve* anything—once the artifacts are removed from their desert context, they lose much of their ability to offer any further understanding of ancient culture. What's more, the official expeditions often take stuff just for the sake of acquisition, and in many minds, that is no better than taking it for personal profit.

Consider, for example, the Princess. She was exhumed by Richard Wetherill, the man who discovered the Basketmaker culture, on his second Grand Gulch expedition, in 1897. At Green Mask Spring, beneath a hauntingly intriguing pictograph of two white anthropomorphs with red circles on their breasts, the cowboy found three enormous baskets. The first two covered exquisite blankets—one made of turkey and bluebird feathers, the other speckled with those of an exotic canary. The third basket was drawn down over the head of a perfectly mummified woman whose skin had been painted from head to toe. Like a western tanager, she had a red face and a yellow body.

Given the splendor of her burial, the corpse of this female was deemed Wetherill's most spectacular find. Accordingly, he took great pains to extract, package, and ship her eastward. She began the trip as a donation to the American Museum of Natural History, but through a series of questionable dealings, she was bounced from there to a storage unit in Philadelphia, and then back to the deepest corner of New York's Museum of the American Indian, where, as the author Dave Roberts discovered after four months of rebuffed efforts to see the famous Wetherill mummy, even "professional researchers" such as himself were for some reason denied permission to view her.[9]

There was a time when Basketmaker sites were replete with fascinating objects—things that, with enough time and enough inquiring eyes upon them, would have explained volumes about the people who crafted them. Within this context, bird feathers are especially provocative: Robes and blankets made of turkey feathers—like those buried with the Princess—were typically buried in a manner suggesting that such garments were prized possessions, even sacred and ceremonial in purpose. This understanding, coupled with examinations of prehistoric trash heaps and fossilized human waste that were distinctly turkey-free, indicates that the birds were never eaten. Add this to the rock-art panels depicting villages under attack, in which people are fleeing with nothing but turkeys in their arms, and one becomes certain that the birds were held in a regard far above that devoted to today's barnyard breed. Had enough evidence been left undisturbed in sites where it could be linked to other clues, a clear picture of the bird's significance might have eventually crystallized.

Other Basketmaker ruins have revealed the vivid feathers of exotic birds—even the scarlet and blue of macaws—meaning there was trade with people as far away as the Southern Hemisphere. The feathers beg interesting questions, for their appearance in redrock country must have been accompanied by seductive stories of climates more mild and fertile—the makings of an easier life. The same picture would have been painted by the coastal people with whom the Anasazi traded for abalone shells. So, knowing what was out there, why did the Anasazi stay rooted in country as unforgiving as the Colorado Plateau? Was it as simple as a deep love of landscape? Or was the decision spiritually inspired? Or could they have gotten so tired, so immobile, that they couldn't fathom the journey?

Had the feathers remained *in situ*, such questions might have also been answered.

DESPITE THIS new information about the canyon's plundering, our route still feels pristine. There is an unraveling as we travel farther into the belly of redrock country, a sense of one world separating from another. We wander in and out of deep, voluptuous narrows, sometimes using the opposing forces of our limbs to straddle the space between the walls in places where the canyon floor falls away into a dark, echoing oblivion. Where the walls open up into a stream channel, there are broad banks of thigh-high grasses, a stunning spectrum of gold, green, and blue against the red soil. Above them, on the rich varnish of the more open cliff faces, float varying styles of horned beings—Archaic, Basketmaker, Fremont. At one point, we stumble beneath a steep overhang where glittering drops of springwater land on a palette of mud marred by nothing more than the feet of mice. The water accumulates to form a thin silver sheen; each new drop that strikes it resonates through the grotto like a perfectly rung bell.

It is the most heavenly place I have ever seen.

SEVERAL DAYS LATER, we scramble up through a weakness in the canyon wall. Topping out, we are nearly flattened by the vastness of the mesa on which we stand, and by the expanse of sky that gawks over our heads. Our group circumvents a large thronelike formation; in its shadow we look for an old trail, along which Steve's cache lies. From it food and fuel supplies are refreshed; then we head off toward the rim of the canyon on the mesa's far side. By the time we reach our descent into its depths, my legs are exhausted, but ahead there are long rappels, and crossings through deep, shadowy pools of water. The swims are accomplished only with the aid of a sleeping pad, inflated to float one's backpack across the water's surface. One arm guides the precariously perched pack; the other arm dog-paddles rapidly, in a race to beat the hypothermia that lurks in such wet and sunless recesses of the desert. One swim is especially long, and as I thrash toward the other side with chattering teeth, Herb and Steve cheer me on. The vigorous effort and excitement prompt a chilly self-admission of how sedentary my life has become, how such adventures now leave me sore for days. And the effortless camaraderie reminds me how lonely my days have gotten. But, for now, I feel deliriously alive again. Indeed, I remember why Ada migrated south every spring and fall. I can understand why the Anasazi remained, despite the allure of easier-going places. And I can't believe that for even one moment I considered living elsewhere.

THAT NIGHT, I spread my sleeping bag in coral-colored sand, still warm from the few hours of sun that hit the canyon bottom at midday. As I collapse into the down baffles, I whisper to Herb that San Juan County would be more bearable if only we could get out into places like this more often. I say that even Lila Canyon just isn't far enough out there, that nothing but the desert's most remote pockets will do.

Herb is quiet, and so I turn to him, propping myself on an elbow. I tickle his face with a leaf that has fallen from the grizzled cottonwood that leans over our beds. In the last gasp of light, I see his eyes roll up beneath his eyelids, then close. Whether he is succumbing to fatigue or frustration is hard to say.

"I think we need to get you back among people," he mumbles through a half-yawn. "Not further out on the edge of things."

But I am not listening. I am exhilarated, and have chosen to take advantage of this crisp moment to try to explain something difficult. I scoot in close to Herb, and tell him how, one night when we still lived in town, I had been walking in the woodlands beyond the golf course when a new insight had struck: just two months before my father killed himself, I had published a story in a national magazine, a personal piece that cast my father in less-than-favorable light. Why I hadn't realized before then just how little time stood between that publication date and the night of his suicide was beyond me. Dusk and an overwhelming sense of culpability had crept in. And as I stood there, trying to digest it all, a single Canada goose had buzzed my head; his shrill honk and great wings had nearly floored me.

"You know what that means, don't you?" I ask.

Contrary to popular belief, Canada geese are not strangers to the desert, so this fact is insignificant. What I am getting to is that this particular fowl flies in skeins—or at least with a mate—and is not typically seen alone. More important—in the case I am building—is that they are first cousins to the duck. And I go on to explain how, ever since that night, I have had this overwhelming feeling that an imprint of my father remains, as if he is hovering somewhere in my peripheral vision.

"It's as if he's not at rest, you know?" I nudge Herb, to make certain he's not sleeping through this. And then I tell him how the dream after our wedding has only served to intensify the sensation. And then I really go out on a limb. I tell him about the boot tracks around the house, tell him about my growing suspicion that they belong not to an intruder but to my father—for that's how physical, how material, his presence feels.

"Maybe he's trying to communicate with me—you know, to settle all of our unfinished business."

There was a time when Herb would have heard this and considered even my wildest theory. But three years is a long time in which to keep reeling someone back into reality.

"Marie Ogden, move over," he mumbles as he rolls on his side, back toward me.

For this last remark, I throw a handful of sand on him. There is no better way to tell me how crazy I have become than to compare me to the religious maverick who in 1933 led a small group of followers to Dry Valley, just north of Monticello, to establish the Home of Truth. The location, which sat on a rim just above the lower portion of Canyonlands, was deemed "the axis of the earth" by Marie's personal typewriter, which came to life and provided its owner with daily announcements from God. Eventually, when one of her followers died of cancer, Marie declared that she would also receive divine messages through the woman's corpse. Three times a day, Marie saw that the body was washed and fed—even as the rest of her brethren came close to starvation for lack of financial means with which to purchase food. When local authorities investigated, the corpse was found to be perfectly preserved—thanks to all the saltwater baths—and this left the county with no legal grounds to demand a proper burial. For a long time, Marie continued to converse with the dead woman; all the while, through the *San Juan Record*—which Ogden had purchased—she unabashedly described the revelations received through the rituals enacted upon it.

"Hey," I finally say to Herb's back, "I am just trying to make sense of everything. There's no framework, you know. And I just can't get settled in my own skin."

But my husband is a man who is at home wherever he is. And from his canyon bed of sand, he is already snoring.

JUST WEEKS AFTER we return from our canyoneering trip, Herb receives notice that an ORV event has been proposed on the mesa between the two canyons we had just explored. He responds immediately with a flurry of written protests, his main objection being that the area is included in a bill before Congress, to be considered for wilderness designation. To send a long strand of vehicles onto the mesa, he argues, will invalidate the land's qualifying wilderness characteristics.

We'd seen how these events go. The spring Jeep Safari in Moab had started out as a benign mom-and-pop gathering, where old Jeeps crept along backcountry roads on a sort of extended Sunday drive. Now hundreds of monster rigs would tear through previously inaccessible country—and we'd watch as they winched themselves with trees, as they'd lose patience and take detours across delicate soils and blooming cactus. Sometimes they'd toss out their garbage. Sometimes they'd puncture their oil pans and look the other way while the fluid drained into the only water source for miles. After a few annual events, the places where the vehicles had gone were unrecognizable.

For the San Juan event, Herb and I both appeal to friends at the local BLM office. People with whom we had paddled the San Juan. With whom we had barbecued burgers and drunk beer. With whom we had celebrated our wedding. There's no doubt that in their hearts they agree with us, especially given that there are plenty of other scenic trails that the riders could use. But we find that none of the staff has explored the place in question. After all, it's hard to get that far into the backcountry when you are tied to a desk, buried in bureaucracy. And without that intimate knowledge of what's at stake, the place remains a mere idea.

In good faith, Herb invites the new BLM field-office supervisor to our home for dinner. Patrick is from the Midwest, and still has a wife and daughter there. Several things become readily apparent: He has taken this position temporarily—a mere step on the agency's career ladder, whose top rung guarantees a good retirement pension. And he has absolutely no connection to redrock country—he doesn't even know the lay of the land in his charge. After a few glasses of wine and a bowl of my beef stew, he says all the things we had hoped to hear: The locals are a bunch of backwoods yahoos who don't grasp what the ramifications are for drawing such public attention to their backyard. God meant for a man to use his legs—either on the ground or by straddling a horse—and there's no dignity in putzing along on such a slow and squatty little machine.

By the time Patrick and Herb bond over their Catholic upbringings and clink glasses of single-malt scotch, he goes as far as to say that the good ol' boys of San Juan County aren't going to tell him what to do, that under his watch any place that qualifies as wilderness will be left alone. Later, when the man refuses our couch and stumbles out to his car, Herb turns to me with an almost childish expression of delight and says he knew it was only a matter of time before someone with some clout saw the light.

JUST DAYS LATER, Patrick approves the event—including the route we have contested. He won't return Herb's phone calls, and avoids me on Main Street. The local BLM staff defends his decision; they have justified it by saying that increased organized ORV use will allow for better monitoring of the activity. I send an open letter to Patrick, begging him to act on the desert's behalf. He never replies, not even after he relocates back to his family a few months later, nor do our agency friends who also received copies. In fact, they mostly stop calling altogether.

As for the rest of Monticello, they are less offended by our protests than they have been on past issues. This time, they just laugh at us. Indeed, in all our efforts to get along, the only thing that has changed is that they no longer see us as a threat. We are no longer equated with terrorists, but instead with something as mildly irritating as mosquitoes. Smug remarks are made to our faces, and before we can reply, people turn and walk away, shaking their heads and chuckling. Though she spares me, even my friend Racine can't help gloating in Herb's face over this one.

The community's response only fuels Herb's convictions. Just barely has he finished reading the BLM's decision when he is on the phone to the Salt Lake office, planning to mount a second ambush on the event plans. He rants to the media, and researches options for legal recourse. And he looks to me for a *Go get 'em, honey*, but all I feel is relief, and it washes over me in all-consuming waves. My rationale goes like this: if we are no longer threatening, then we are no longer in danger of being aggrieved. It means I can stop locking the doors. Let the dogs run freely again. Forget about curtains. Somewhere deep down I know my reaction is cowardly and lame, but I no longer care. I am worn down—not just from my own losses and loneliness, but from fear, and the rancor of the battle itself. To the Southern Utah Wilderness Alliance, I write a letter of resignation. And when Herb comes home that night, I tell him that, no matter how things shake out, the fight has gone out of me. Then I tell him I need to get the hell out of this godforsaken place.

THAT NIGHT, another dream: I am on the ranch in Malad, standing in the corral farthest from my grandparents' house. There is a hulking red bull in the corner—one I encountered there in real life when I was seven years old, when I tried to convince my cousins that we should stage a bullfight. At the time, there were straw bales in the middle of the corral, and I figured we could easily scramble up on them if the bull charged. The other kids didn't think it was a good idea, so I got in there by myself. In cut-off jeans and sneakers, my scrawny body faced off with the enormous beast. I called him names. I waved at him my red sweatshirt—the closest thing I could find to a red cape. The bull became sufficiently infuriated, and with spittle flying and head down he charged me—horns aimed at my retreating backside like dark shiny missiles. But he was slow and lumbering, and I escaped with ease. Still, it was thrilling, to feel him bearing down on me. And to inspire that kind of rage in him had made me feel deliciously powerful.

Now the bull stampedes my unconscious, and the dust flies. This time, I know I won't outrun him. When he catches me, the goring is swift but deep. I lie sprawled in red soil, a thousand castles of it collapsed beneath my body. Black blood spills from the rented earth, but from my own wounds spurt a hundred ducks. Necks thrust forward, bills punching at the air, they heave their bodies into the sky.

They have passengers: My father. My unborn daughter. Indians wrapped in turkey robes.

And there I am, several versions astride several birds: One with a basket over her head, her identity completely hidden from view. One smiling, too eagerly, her long, modest dress whipping her legs. Another with a big round shield for a torso, her fist raised in the air. And then there is the naked one—arms raised in imitation of the flapping wings beneath them, circles of mud painted on her breasts.

The flock lifts off, falls into formation. It veers not north or south, but eastward. I have no idea where we are headed. My father is astride the lead duck, and he looks like he is geared up for an adventurous journey. He looks back at me, smiles, and waves me on. I smile back weakly, then look down, for one last glimpse. Pawing at the receding desert below, snorting hotly, I see the black-horned creature. Whether he's a devil or a deity is hard to say.

But he bellows victoriously.

PART IV

⊰ PUEBLO ⊱

Kiva

THE YELLOW GRADER SAT *in the middle of the turnoff like a sleeping tiger. Its transmission in park, the engine purred. Not far away, the driver rested under a juniper tree, his lunch of fat-free yogurt and carrot sticks spread before him. He didn't mind the unexpected break in his routine—in fact, he welcomed it after scraping away so much dirt. Not that he didn't love the work—he derived a deep satisfaction from making a clean, flat swath where only two rough and ragged tire tracks had been. Now just about anyone could get out here, in any vehicle, and actually enjoy the drive. Yes, the man took pride in that, in being a part of San Juan County's mission to make the desert accessible to all.*

What he did mind was the four men standing in front of his machine. When he turned down this spur and lowered the blade, they had stepped out in front of him, arms folded across their chests. Two had long, ratted hair and beards. One was indecent—sporting slick running shorts and not much else. The fourth was an old man in a felt hat and jeans—a man who had rowed people down Glen Canyon before it was flooded, a man who for decades had been leading, and still led, good old-fashioned horse-

pack trips into this country. The county man recognized him from a variety of public meetings—had, along with the county commissioners and all their attending constituents, rolled his eyes when the old man expressed concerns about the hazardous waste being trucked in and stockpiled at White Mesa, about the water wasted on the golf course, about the increasing inability of his saddled patrons to find quiet and solitude in the backcountry.

When they first stepped out, the men had regarded him—smiled, even. He had returned a nod, then radioed his supervisor. The call went through clearly, and then there was nothing to do but stretch out with his lunch beneath the shade of the juniper and scratch his back on the tattered bark. From his resting spot, he regarded the men—all from Moab with the exception of the old man, who lived just outside of that sinful city but within San Juan boundaries. No matter that he had run a ranch there for over two decades, that he had lived in Green River before that. As far as the driver was concerned, he too was an outsider.

None of the men present minded the wait. Harts Point was as beautiful as it gets—a sagebrush-studded, slickrock-stained prominence suspended between the rise of the Abajos and the implosion of the Canyonlands. Indeed, the breathtaking scenery was precisely why they were all here in the first place—and the county had claimed a historic right-of-way as justification for opening it up. But these other guys—these scruffy-looking half-critters that stood between the grader and the point's end—they just wanted to lock it up like some kind of gated community for the privileged few. He envisioned the task of getting his wife and kids out here on foot, the prodding and cajoling it would take to get them even twenty yards away from the car. He did this as he patted his soft belly, never admitting what a feat it would be for him too.

"Damned elitists," he muttered. He knew in this instance that God would forgive the poor language.

Soon the press arrived. Then the manager for the Monticello BLM field office, and his only on-duty federal law-enforcement officer for nearly two million acres of land. And finally the San Juan County sheriff arrived, followed by an entourage of deputies in white four-wheel-drive Blazers.

The sheriff nodded knowingly to the driver, shook hands with the BLM boss and a few of the more sympathetic journalists. Then he approached the four men in front of the grader. To them he didn't so much as tip his hat.

"This is a legitimate county activity, boys. You'll need to move."

Cameras flashed. Pens scratched paper. The four men stood stock still. Finally, one pointed at the road-grader.

"The agency has served the county a notice of trespass—which confirms this road-grading is illegal."

Everyone looked at the head bureaucrat. Tentatively, he nodded. It wasn't often he took a stand against the locals. But he had orders from above that told him this time was different. At the moment, the agency couldn't afford another lawsuit from the greens, and, besides, the feds had to draw the line—before the Utah counties got it in their heads that they could take over public lands entirely. Of course, it was an election year, and the White House was looking for all the kudos it could glean from a nation that largely supported additional land protection in the West. In more ways than one, Utah was the reddest state there was—and all those shades of red made it the obvious place to sacrifice votes in exchange for a few new designations.

But national politics were hardly front and center in the BLM manager's mind. He knew that enforcement of this violation meant his kids would get hell in school the next day. Good thing he had applied for a transfer—and to another state altogether.

"Uh, yes, that's right. This morning it was hand-delivered to the county attorney." He turned to the press to explain his position better. "It was issued because the county ignored our first order to cease-and-desist unauthorized roadwork on federal lands."

The sheriff got on his radio. Spoke for a moment, then signed off.

"The attorney hasn't seen any such order."

A cell phone rang. The man in nylon running shorts seemed surprised. Perhaps he hadn't yet seen the new communications tower on Abajo Peak, the way it brazenly needled the sky like a church steeple, the way it made communication in this proposed wilderness area a breeze. Hesitantly, he pulled the device from a small waist pack—the only other item to adorn his person—and said hello. After he hung up, he whispered to one of the long-hairs. The two of them stepped away from the bulldozer—as per the order phoned in from the environmental group for whom they worked. The sheriff grinned.

The other long-hair remained. He looked out across Canyonlands, then down to his feet, at the soft, yielding soil. His eye traced the pinprick tracks of a darkling beetle. The serpentine imprint of a midget faded rattlesnake. He may have looked like an uncivilized good-for-nothing, but actually he was an independent biologist with a mile-long list of credentials. For one thing, he knew every inch of this desert and the mountains that rose up out of it. And he knew what had already been lost—knew how the desert was on its way to becoming a sterile, senseless void. He looked up at the row of uniforms.

"Arrest me, then."

The old man moved next to him.

"You'll have to cuff me too."

The sheriff grabbed the old man by the arm and dragged him out of the way. The old man objected, but the cop ignored him. He failed to treat the old man as a venerable elder, as someone who knew this country better than he and all of his posse put together. Meanwhile, four deputies surrounded the biologist, who stood alone in front of the machine. He was the smallest of the four, tiny and wiry, like an elf. At first, he resisted. Then, as they overpowered him, he simply let his body go slack. His lack of defiance caught the officers unaware—and they went down too. Pressed flat beneath their collective weight, the elf man tasted the sweet red earth in his mouth.

Quickly the deputies recovered themselves. They wiped their sweaty brows. Dusted dirt from their uniforms. Reached for handcuffs. One barked Miranda at his prisoner, while another demanded his name.

The detainee looked up and smiled. "Clark Kent," he replied.

FROM THE BACKSEAT *of the sheriff's Blazer, the elf man observed the scene. There were a few scuff marks, but no bloodshed. In all of Deseret's history, with the exception of that unfortunate incident at Mountain Meadows, there had hardly ever been any violence. But the elf man was beginning to think that maybe, just maybe, there should be. A good brawl seemed better than this war of words, documents, and legal proceedings—for they made the land seem almost beside the point. Besides, what both sides really wanted was to beat the living shit out of one another—and that wouldn't change even if a wilderness bill was signed into law.*

But the press was there, and in this never-ending battle over the desert, public opinion was everything. Hence the civil demeanor of the county employees. Hence the unexpected phone call to the man in shorts— which had ordered the two SUWA staff to step away, had told them that paid environmentalists can't afford to break the law.

But beneath the surface, blood boiled. It was 1996. By executive order, President Clinton had just declared the Grand Staircase–Escalante National Monument. It wasn't wilderness protection, but it was the next-closest thing—and even though the Hole-in-the-Rock route would be largely preserved within the boundaries of the new designation, San Juan County had joined other rural Utah counties in suing the president; the Farm Bureau called it a "federal land grab of the worst kind."[1] Across Deseret, dummies of the United States' chief executive officer had been hung in effigy. Black balloons had been released into the sky.

As the deputies set off with their prisoner for the county jail in Monticello, the elf man craned his neck as best he could, to gain one last glimpse of Harts Point before the road-grader dissected it. And as the machine roared to life, his face confessed something that could only be described as reverence, his lips fluttered in a way that could only be likened to prayer.

The deputies looked back too. Their faces conveyed a similar venera-tion, but the elf man could see that they weren't looking at the big picture in the glass, at the way the snow-scrubbed mountains spilled blue into the scarlet stone lands below. Instead, their eyes were trained on the road-grader. And as the blade flayed open the desert, the biologist watched the deputies' faces grow flush, their lips purse and murmur breathlessly.

He could only characterize what he was seeing as a state of exaltation. And at that moment, he saw the blade through the eyes of his enemies. For them, it was not even remotely a tool of desecration, but instead a kind of holy hand, parting an impassable red ocean so that others might tread across the promised land, on their way to redemption, in safety and ease. And after the harrowing journeys their forebears had made to get here, these guys felt they had every right.

So, he thought, the distinction lies not so much in where we find the sacred, but in how we access it. His only question was, could the grace of place be felt if one had used forced entry?

He looked once more at the deputies, who were revering the road that unfolded like a wake behind the grader. They remained flushed and breathless. Then again, he thought, their altered state might just be the lingering effects of exertion . . . for wrestling me up from the ground is probably the most action these big ol' boys have had in a long time.

WHEN AUTUMN COMES AGAIN, the San Juan ORV event takes place on Cedar Mesa despite Herb's efforts. Herb goes to monitor impacts, but at this point, there is little more he can do. He sinks into listlessness and irritation, and it is only when our friend Danny returns from his scorching summer job of surveying desert tortoises in the Mojave and begs us to get out with him that Herb perks up. We agree to escort Danny to Harts Point, which our friend hasn't been able to bring himself to see since the day he was arrested there in '96. Now he is ready to examine how the place has fared with the new road. Herb and I load the dogs and packs in our truck and follow our friend's ancient Subaru toward the turnoff. Perhaps it is Danny's complete devotion to the moment, or perhaps it is that he cannot bear to see how well traveled Harts Point has become, but along the way he detours us to an adjoining draw. We readily agree to the change in plans, for the meandering ravine—which has also been proposed for wilderness designation—has been officially closed to vehicles. Surely it will make for a better hike.

Before we even begin our descent, the tracks of dirt bikes appear—five, maybe six sets of wheels. They are easy to count, for the tracks are abreast—spread out across the desert like an unraveled braid. We follow them into the ravine, through flattened grasses and collapsed stream banks. Herb and Danny pull out a camera and notepad to document the location. Without a word, I turn around and leave the draw. Danny starts to call to me, but Herb quiets him.

"Let her go. These days she usually just goes back to the truck and sleeps."

THE NEXT WEEK, Herb and I drive east, into Colorado, to a small, sleepy cow town at the base of the San Juan Mountains. The town is a stone's throw from the Colorado Plateau, and from the pastured mesa on which it sits, I can see easily the details of its closest edge—a crimson anticline that gives way to the sweep of Paradox Valley, framed by the Canyonlands Basin and both the La Sal and Abajo ranges. We spend the day visiting Jessica and her family, who had loaded their furniture into a moving van and relocated here earlier that summer. I had known the move was coming—every time we spent the morning on her porch, sipping tea, as her children careened across the yard, Jessica would point to where the sun had emerged between fourteen-thousand-foot peaks, to where the jagged skyline of the San Juan Mountains sawed away at the sky.

"Now, there's a place you can raise your kids," she would say. "Close to the desert, but just beyond reach of its heat."

It is good to see my friend, whose departure from San Juan County has solidified my sense of isolation. And I like where she lives—another small, sweet town with big skies and views. That evening, after we bid Jessica and her family farewell, we stop by the local saloon for a burger, and find that the cowboys at the bar seem not to care that we aren't locals. They don't even look twice at Herb's ponytail—in fact, they tip their hats cordially. One man who still wears his spurs after a day's work buys us a round of whiskey even after he hears what we do for a living. That this gesture occurs so close to the heart of former Deseret is almost astonishing, and the idea of being so near to the promised land and still so free of its grasp begins to enthrall me. I tell Herb that I want to stay the night—that in the morning I'd like to see what's for sale. Since my husband is a man of speculation and vision, looking at real estate is one of his favorite pastimes. He readily agrees.

Even later that night, we creep back to Jessica's new house, where we quietly unroll sleeping bags on the porch. As Herb's breath capitulates into snores, I lie awake and wonder how it is that for months Jessica has begged me to visit, and that I have found every excuse not to come. When she had finally asked outright why I hadn't been to see her new house and life, I had said that every time I head off somewhere I end up turning around, that I seem to be in a perpetual state of retreat.

"What is it that you fear?" she had asked.

There was no answer to her question that I could articulate. She reminded me then of her shamanic training, and gently offered to make a journey into the spirit world on my behalf. But once she found my guides, she said, she would need something specific to ask them.

I had considered this. I concluded I had nothing to lose—no beliefs that competed with or contradicted what she had to offer. The question sprang from my lips without premeditation:

I want to know if I am meant to become a mother.

A FEW WEEKS LATER, Jessica phoned me. Her voice sounded strange, like that of someone with jet lag who hasn't yet caught up to the current time. She said that she was exhausted, that she had to work hard in the shamanic realm to find those with whom she had to speak. But as she described diving into a pool and descending so deep she thought she would drown, I listened halfheartedly. The idea of living within a culture informed by the visions of shamans was romantic—something that, in theory anyway, sat better with me than the religious experience into which I had been born. But whether shamans could actually journey to another world and consult with spirits who watched the human race fumble from afar, was not something I had ever taken seriously—especially when I applied it to contemporary people with white skin. Indeed, if I imagined such a thing, all I could think of were wealthy urbanites paying obscene amounts of money to be led into the desert by some self-proclaimed guru to spend a weekend ingesting peyote and beating drums until they could say they had encountered their primal selves. Whenever I saw advertisements for these commercial forays, I couldn't help thinking of my grandpa Blaisdell, who always said that if a man really wanted to know what he was made of he had to feed himself and his family, straight off the land—through at least a decade of droughts, fires, pests, and predators.

With the phone cradled between my ear and my shoulder, I examined my nails while Jessica continued. I still wasn't convinced that what she had to say would have any bearing.

"When I looked up toward the surface, it was as if the world above had vanished. Something told me that the only way I would ever breathe again was to go deeper. My lungs burned, and my head felt like it would explode, but at that point I really had no choice. And then, all of a sudden, I broke through, into a small, shadowy cavern. There was a woman sitting on a rock. I climbed up next to her and sat. When I looked down at myself, I had become a young girl. 'You are Amy,' the woman said, 'at ten years of age.'

"She said that something had happened then, something that completely inundated your trust in people. There were guides who tried to comfort you, she explained, who tried to salvage what they could of your innocence and faith. But you were a lost cause. You would have nothing to do with anything that even remotely resembled a human—let alone something divine. In fact, you could barely breathe around others, would start gasping for air whenever you entered the chapel in which you were expected to pray."

I was ten when my parents split up. My mother went to work, and my father began to fade from our lives. Later that year, when the man my mother was dating began to punch holes in the walls of our home, when he eventually turned his fists on us, my father was already so insubstantial that he had been unable to act on behalf of his daughters. Through all this, I had suffered from severe asthma. But Jessica had known none of this.

"You ran off, flung yourself into the rocks, the trees, the wind. The guides had to ask the natural world to offer you refuge until the day came when they could once again summon your attention. They told me to tell you that the time has come, that the alienation you feel is caused not by any outside factor but by the restraint of your own breath and spirit.

"And this last thing that I have to say is not from them, but is plain earthly advice from me—as your friend and a mother of three. Bearing a child will catapult you into a new realm, a realm into which you have been trying to muscle your way. But be forewarned—you are not prepared for what you seek, and when you find it, you will not have the luxury of retreating at will. In the wild world, you indeed found hallowed ground, but kneeling on it has failed to infuse you with anything soulful. In this sense, you are no better off than those you criticize."

For weeks, I had lain awake at night, sorting through Jessica's words. And for some reason, they prompted me to contact Ellen Meloy, a nature writer living in Bluff, whose most recent book had been a finalist for the Pulitzer Prize. She had invited me for a visit, and when I arrived, she was standing outside, her gaze trained on a ridge above the San Juan River. The wind had been relentless, but we defied it by hiking to the very top of the ridge and sitting so our faces took its brunt. Ellen had pulled from her pack a thermos of hot tea—a blend of Chinese herbs whose name I didn't quite catch. We had taken turns sipping from the thermos cap and squinting out at the desert below, down at the last leg of the Hole-in-the-Rock route. She said how funny it was that, in a place like this, we hadn't sought one another's company before now. I nodded, and went on to say how strange it was too that there had been no local publicity regarding the acclaim her book had received. She told me then that the Monticello book club had been scheduled to read it just weeks earlier and had invited her to join them afterward for a discussion. But when she arrived at the Monticello Public Library, not a single book-club member was present. The librarian had apologized for getting her to come all that way, but said that folks had decided to boycott the book because in its pages she had described a redrock tower as "phallic."

We had laughed then about there being room for only one phallus in the desert sky—and it stood atop a pointed building, with a shining gold tip in the shape of a wind instrument. Then I had asked her what kept her going in the face of such communal misunderstanding. She replied that when she wasn't writing she painted—and that the combination of pecking words and mixing colors balanced the times she floated the San Juan with her husband, who worked as a BLM river ranger. And then I asked her if it was enough—if those things not only staved off loneliness, isolation, deprivation, and heartache, but actually fulfilled her.

Beauty and passion. What else is there?

Her response had reminded me of Ada. And, lying there on Jessica's porch, redrock country in almost spitting distance, I wonder why I am not more like Ellen and my grandmother, why these two aspects of life are not enough. Or perhaps they are, and I don't yet realize how they elude me. My greatest fear now is that, with the fight gone out of me, I will succumb to some mind-numbing apathy. As I drift off, a vague sense of horror accompanies my last thoughts: despite all the gorgeous moments I have had in the desert, the landscape of my desires has failed to provide me with what I have sought.

Likewise for the man of my dreams. And as I lie there watching him sleep, I wonder about this bond that holds us—even when we antagonize one another so. When any other thing in my life has disappointed or betrayed, I have simply walked away.

BY NOON the next day, Herb and I are standing on a grassy five-acre parcel—the front half of which looks out at the dramatic San Juan Range. Before sloping away to a creek bottom edged with narrow-leaf cottonwoods and willows, the back half looks out at the red spread of the Colorado Plateau. All around us are privately owned pastures, heavily irrigated with the substantial snowmelt off the high country above—mountains that get far more snow than the La Sals or Abajos. The pastures are loaded with cows, less harried-looking than the bovines of redrock country. Herb doesn't even blink as he makes the offer. If he is pained by how it will tear him from his work, his son, and Lila Canyon, he doesn't show it. At the time, I am so desperate to leave that I don't realize what he is giving up, and that he is doing this entirely for me. When I ask him what we will do for a home, and how we will make a living, he brushes off the questions. He's already pointing to the building site, describing with great flair which window will capture what view.

"Have faith, my dear. That's the one thing you sorely lack."

Faith. After all that has come to pass, I still shudder at the word.

DRIVING BACK toward Utah, I don't even notice Herb's quietness. I am too busy thinking about the fact that there isn't a single Mormon church in the county—and that the closest temple is back in Monticello. This would be the farthest I have ever lived from such a building.

"Remember when we took the temple tour?" I ask.

Stirred from his thoughts, Herb nods slowly.

We had entered the newly renovated Monticello temple not long after the wedding and the miscarriage—and only three hours before the church would forever close its doors to the public and rededicate the building to sacred rituals. It was a blustery Saturday, and Herb wanted to see how a Mormon place of worship compared with the Catholic churches he had known. He didn't believe me when I said that they were bland as could be, that he would not be moved on any level. He had responded that he was a spiritual guy, and that all churches managed to evoke something in him.

We had waited with the crowds in an outbuilding. At the front of the room, a television broadcast a video about the spread of Mormon temples throughout the world. When they called the tour group to which we had been assigned, we were led to the temple's foyer, where we donned the white booties I remembered from the tour I took as a child. Then we followed our tour guide inside.

"How many of you are already members of the Church?"

The Church. It was the first question he asked. In response, I had raised my hand, then looked at Herb. It was true that my name was still on their books, that I had not been excommunicated. But Herb hadn't noticed my declaration of affiliation. He was caught up in the moment, eyes shining with some kind of eager reverence. I stared at my husband in disbelief.

"The Monticello temple was the first small temple ever built. But this renovation has tripled its size. We needed the space for more baptisms, more weddings. That's a testament to the strength of the faith of the brethren in this region." The tour guide's voice faltered with pride, and he dabbed his watering eyes with a handkerchief. With his wife bringing up the rear, a rather heavyset woman whom he had introduced only as his eternal companion, we were ushered past the recommend desk—the checkpoint where it would be determined, once the temple was in full swing again, whether you had the proper credentials to enter. Passing by the desk had sparked a certain thrill in me—and that old familiar thought bubbled up in my consciousness.

Cover. I'm in.

The rooms were white, with gold and beige accents, but fairly nondescript. The wall and floor coverings, as well as the furniture, looked like something you'd find in a Holiday Inn business suite. There was hardly an iconic image anywhere. Nothing appeared to have been created by the hand of a craftsman, to have been added to heighten the aesthetic element. We wandered through several rooms and hallways, each one banal beyond belief. The brightness in Herb's face faded a bit.

He whispered, "I thought it would be more, you know, *temple-like.*"

Standing there, I couldn't help thinking about the underground chambers in which the Puebloan-era Anasazi conducted their religious activities, and how they had remained surprisingly plain—even as their living quarters, pottery, and rock art became much more elaborate and their religious practices grew in complexity. Most often, Puebloan kivas were built on sites where earlier Basketmaker pit houses had been, and typically they were round, with a three-foot-high bench encircling the interior. The bench supported pilasters of an equal height, which in turn held up a cribbed roof. A log ladder provided entry and exit. The dirt floor was dented with a fire pit and a *sipapu*, a small hole used by spirits to emerge from other worlds below. It is as if they improved upon the Basketmaker kiva, made the interior more comfortable and functional, because they were spending more time within its walls.

Beyond these basic common features, most kivas held few adornments. In fact, throughout the course of the Puebloan era, they only underwent two distinct changes. First, they grew larger, to include what are known as *great kivas*. Second, these expanded centers of social and religious activity came to be located along a truly extraordinary network of roads. Used to connect small outliers with the larger settlements that had cropped up throughout the Four Corners region, these roads were used as trade routes. At that point in Four Corners prehistory, spiking populations of sedentary people and the correlating dependence on agriculture would have made the trading of food a necessity, to prevent local bouts of starvation or malnutrition. In other words, if a certain crop fared well in one area, its growers could trade the surplus with another group who lacked it—in exchange for something they possessed in excess.

It is along the trade routes' most likely points of rendezvous that great kivas appear. Anthropologist Stephen Plog points out that, at this time, blood-related tribes were growing into multi-clan villages. Within those more loosely bound communities, certain groups—say, those who had the best soil and water sources—had more control over food production and distribution. The imbalance between haves and have-nots would have created social tension, and conflict. And so it was no longer enough that each family practiced its own tribe's rituals within the privacy of its own sacred space. Instead, religion was becoming more standardized, more formalized. The gathering of larger, more widespread groups became the mechanism by which to establish a more widespread group identity, which in turn ensured a broader sense of cohesion and cooperation.[2]

What's interesting is that it all happened by way of routes that were by no means mere footpaths through the desert. Rather, they were totally cleared swaths between fifteen and forty feet wide—seemingly overdone, given that the ancients lacked beasts of burden or any mechanized means of transport. And the roads were cut in straight lines, no matter what obstacles the immediate topography imposed. These curious characteristics have led some researchers to conclude not only that Anasazi roads must have served as trade routes, but that they must, like the great kivas that sprung up alongside them, have held religious significance too.

Reflecting on kivas and roads leads in turn to parallel thoughts about the early Saints, who on April 6, 1853, laid the first cornerstone of the main temple in Salt Lake City. By that point, Deseret had been firmly established, and outlying Mormon settlements had cropped up across the Western landscape. The temple would serve as the brethren's linchpin, an epicenter for both culture and spirit. Indeed, thousands of "very happy people" came "from many miles" to witness the beginning of construction.[3]

Howard Egan's son included his recollections of this event in the published version of his father's diary, and describes how he and other boys stood on a dirt mound to get a good view of things. But he also remembers that they graded the road in front of the temple in a fashion that would come to characterize the streets in all Mormon towns—arrow-straight, clean, and wide. The junior Egan recalled that they "cut down a very large oak tree that was standing in the middle of where they wanted the road," and how sorry he was that they could not have detoured around it—especially since there was only one more tree as large in all the city.[4] He had reflected on how, each year, when the tree had been loaded with acorns, he had climbed up into its limbs to gather them. His last remark in the entry is this: "I can't see now why such landmarks should not have been preserved."[5]

OUR TOUR GROUP entered the third room of the temple, and suddenly, after all that paleness, we were standing before three large murals. Spanning across three walls, the paintings conveyed the sweeping views of southeastern Utah better than any representation I have ever seen. They avoided the predictability of red and instead broadcast the dark colors of the quintessential storms that brewed around the Abajo peaks. The brooding sky sprawled across the Canyonlands on one side, Cedar Mesa on the other, washing the desert in its contusional colors. Everything—the sandstone, the sagebrush, and the piñon-and-juniper stands—it all leapt from the canvas in terrifying shades of blue, violet, and gray. And there was form, thousands and thousands of square miles of corporal topography: Erect pillars. The slits of canyons. Nippled buttes and voluptuous, yielding hills.

The effect was both sensuous and awesome. I wanted to fall to my knees. Instead, I looked around. Other than my husband, not a single person on the tour was looking at the murals. They were taking direction from our guide, who ushered them into seats that looked like standard-issue banquet chairs in a convention center. I waited until the last minute, noticing that not a single road had been painted into the desert, that the artist had chosen to portray it in a pure, untouched state. Finally, the guide's wife touched my elbow and pointed to a vacant seat, where I sat and waited for the guide to mention the art, to tell us something about the artist, but he never even pointed to the work. He talked about how there had been some misunderstanding about Mormons' not being Christians, some accusations made about how they had supplanted the Holy Bible with the Book of Mormon and Doctrine and Covenants. He wanted to clarify that Mormons did believe in a Heavenly Father, and in Jesus Christ, His Son—just like other Christians. A non-Mormon, a woman with bleached hair and a tattooed trail of rosebuds on the bare ankle that peeked from beneath the hem of her pant, raised her hand and asked why they didn't revere Mary in the manner that other churches did. Our tour guide glanced quickly at his wife, who nodded knowingly, then replied that the Heavenly Mother was so special that God had said we must never, ever talk about her—that He held her on a pedestal where she was never to be seen or spoken to, for fear that her purity would be sullied.

I could see the woman blink with surprise at his explanation, but the man was already on to other subjects.

"I have traveled all over the world," he said. "And I have seen members of the faith in the darnedest places. You can spot them easily, because they are trying to live with such goodness."

I picked dog hair and cactus quills from my wool sweater. The act helped me feel more visible, more substantial. Then the brother pointed to the chandelier hanging in the center of the room. It too looked like something from a hotel or a banquet hall.

"The current prophet, President Hinckley, was here for only a few minutes when he saw this hanging."

He paused then, and dropped his voice to a whisper. His eyes were shining with tears again. Herb looked a bit choked up himself.

"He said to us, 'There are crystals missing.' Can you believe that? He could tell." The brother's voice broke as he shook his head with incredulity.

WE HAVE JUST CROSSED the Utah state line, at the northeastern corner of San Juan County, when I ask Herb about the tour.

"What about it?" he asks.

I confess how unnerving it had been to watch him be so swept away by the whole thing. That he had looked, for part of the tour at least, like if they had offered to dunk him then and there, he would have gone right under. Later, I remind him, he had said as much. Had said too that it didn't really matter in which house you worshipped God, just that you did. Had said that he thought joining the Church would help us integrate into the county.

"Yeah, so?"

"You do things, big things, on impulse. After all, it's how we got together. And now you have bought this property and are ready to move to another state without a second thought. I am beginning to wonder if you have anything that tethers you, or if I should brace myself for the situations that will make you forget this marriage."

It sounds harsher than I had meant for it to sound, and Herb bristles.

"So I live in the moment. It beats the hell out of living in the past, like you do. And if you're not mired there, you're tossing all of its disappointments into the future and dwelling on the certain doom it will bring—like you're doing right now, like you do with everything in your life. It's like you've created this beautiful space, this beautiful place of refuge, but you won't emerge. It's like you've *become* the desert itself—not the beautiful, sensual reality of it, but the awful emptiness. I try and I try to enter this place to which you have gone, but there's nothing desirable about wresting my way in."

His face is red. His eyes are blazing.

"And after all we have been through, I would think you'd now know that there are a few things on which I do not waver."

We drive the rest of the way in silence. I feel the wind blow through my empty expanse, and I shiver. I know that the exchange is the kind that will grind down a relationship, the kind that shifts the shape of things to come.

⇥ 14 ⇤

Vessel

THE WINDOW OF *the old farmhouse was smudged with the smoke of a thousand stove fires. But if she pulled a chair under the window and climbed up, if she brushed back her golden curls and pressed her small, pale pearl of a nose against the pane, she just managed to observe their approach. Every morning she waited there, to pinpoint them while they were still mere specks at the end of the Malad Valley. By the time they spilled into the foreground of the Blaisdell ranch, they took on the appearance of bright, exotic birds. They were a spectacle to behold: The way their long, swift strides made their patchwork skirts flash red, purple, turquoise. The way those silver beads and polished stones glittered from wrists, necks, ears. And their hair. It was as black and shiny as anything she'd ever seen, like rippled moonlight on night water.*

It was the eyes that she sought, eyes she knew would be far darker than her own. Not once did she catch even a glimpse, though. These women's faces were shadowed under wide felt brims that shielded not only the blazing high-desert sun, but everything else around.

They passed every morning, this procession of brown-skinned

women—on their way to work in the potato and corn fields of the surrounding farms. And they passed again every evening, returning to their
families on the reservation—miles away. From her perspective, behind
the glass, they were mesmerizing in every aspect. And to know that it was
their darkness—that which marked them as the sinful, cast-off Tribe of
Israel known as the Lamanites—that made them significant to her. For it
was her job to help redeem them, to render them white and delightsome.
And when Christ returned, the Indians would show thanks for their salvation by doing away with the nonbelievers. She knew that, above all
others, they were the people to save, so in turn they would employ their
fierce ways to subdue sinners. Then and only then would the Savior again
walk the earth.

And that's why she wanted to see their eyes. She wanted to see what it
would be like to look into the soul of a savage.

But one morning, there was a scolding because she dropped the eggs
just collected from the coop, and the young girl sassed back. That afternoon, when the women passed by, her mother pointed to them and told her
daughter unequivocally that she was going to give her away to the Indians. For a long time afterward, she repeated the threat, until the little girl
began to believe it. Soon she was having nightmares, and a rash of anxiety broke out all over.

For a fair and devoted daughter of Deseret, there could be no harsher
lesson, no graver understanding of her destiny and expendable worth: To
live knowing that her own mother would pass her out the window. That
she would place her in sin-stained hands. That she would have her look up
into a face that for millennia had failed to reflect the grace of God, and
forever fear for her own salvation.

THE MOONLESS NIGHT DANGLES from the January sky like a
plum, an orb of ripe purple skin illuminated by crystalline pinpricks
of starlight. There is no snow, for the drought has pressed on. Inside,

the stove fire died hours ago, and the cabin has lost all residual warmth. Herb and I crouch at the bedroom window, shivering with cold and the sound of gunfire.

I am pregnant again—just barely, and perhaps against better judgment, for we remain far from what we have been to one another. It's not that we think that having a baby will fix things, it's that we believe our situation to be temporary. For, in the better moments, there is still a deep, maddening love. And just over the border, in our soon-to-be town of residence, we had felt an entirely different aura. We are banking on things getting better after the move, after Herb's workload lessens, after I bounce back from a string of losses. And so here we are, staring out into the darkness, trying to determine from which direction the shots are coming. And I can tell Herb is think-ing my own thoughts: thank goodness we're planning to leave be-cause this is no place to raise a kid.

A car suddenly races up the road, away from Robert's house. Downstairs, the dogs yip frantically and scratch at the door. In a place like Lila Canyon, you get to know the sound of each neigh-bor's vehicle—and this is not one we or the canines know. I pick up the cell phone, dial the neighbors. Robert answers immediately. He doesn't sound too sleepy. I ask him if everything's okay.

"Oh yeah," he says. "It's just that we got a lady from our church here with her kids—guess her husband's been beatin' on them. Cops over in Dove Creek served him a restraining order, but the guy didn't take it too well. We were hiding her here until he cooled down. But he found us out—drove clear over from Colorado in the middle of the night. He wouldn't leave, so I finally fired a few shots from the porch to scare him off. I'm on my way out to the main road now. I'll sit watch out there the rest of the night, in case he tries to come back. Sure sorry to have disturbed you."

It is then that we look at each other, and suddenly we are back to standing on seamless ground. Again we are moving in tandem: instincts kick in, senses prick, hearts pound. On this we agree: we'd leave right now if we could.

This response is not because we are gun-shy, or even because a volatile man may be lurking around the neighborhood while any official form of law enforcement seems to be missing from the mix. Indeed, it is no fault of our neighbors, who are doing an honorable thing—in fact, it has nothing to do with them at all. Rather, it is because the whole scenario epitomizes the vast sense of desolation and estrangement that seems to hang over San Juan County—making it a breeding ground for rancor. Of course, I feel this particular brand of malaise anywhere in Deseret, but here it has managed to encase my nerve endings in some barbed and febrile sheath. It is the same feeling, I see now, that has kept my husband overly occupied and even on the run.

WHEN FIRST LIGHT LURKS on the horizon, I am still sitting on the edge of the bed. Herb rolls onto his elbow and tells me that he's been trying to find a way to break something to me, to tell me that, for this last year before we move to Colorado, he is going to close down the Monticello office. He's needed back in Moab, he says, to work in a more central location with the rest of the southern-Utah team. I can't say that I am surprised by the news. It will take everything the group has to respond to the Department of Interior's sudden announcement to open up for fossil-fuel development some of the BLM's most pristine and scenic lands—lands that not only have been proposed by citizens for protection, but have actually been identified by the agency itself as having wilderness characteristics worth safeguarding. In the past, such lands had generally been off limits to development—for there is considerable public policy requiring the agency to keep them in their *de facto* state of wildness until Congress can determine whether they are worthy of official, permanent protection. But, then again, the nation's executive branch has never possessed so many glaring ties to the oil-and-gas industry. The decision had, overnight, effectively released millions of acres from their protected status.

"I'll be working a lot of hours, and gone a lot of nights. I was hoping I could talk you into coming with me somehow, but I kept putting it off, fearing you'd say no. But you'll come now, won't you?"

I stare out the window. He knows that I would have us get out of Utah altogether, that we would live in his hand-me-down pull-along trailer alongside the new house as it's being built. He knows that only that kind of drastic distance will get me to leave this place— that any option in between the two, anywhere else in Deseret, won't change things as much as they need changing.

"I can't turn my back on this, not now—not when things are this bad. And it will be so good for you, to live near more like-minded people, to have a bookstore and organic vegetables." He has a point. Moab does offer things that the rest of rural Utah does not. I turn to steal a glance—only to see his eyes dart frantically about the room, like he's grasping for the one tantalizing thing to convince.

"I know it will be hard for you. That you will miss this house. But I swear, we can come back and spend every weekend here until . . ."

The baby comes. I turn back to the window. That promising shade of newly born pink has just grazed the peaks of the Abajos. I watch it draw down the mountain, infusing the hope of a new day. Herb glosses over mention of the pregnancy by saying that he's already figured out where we can stay, a place that will be really comfortable for me. He goes on to list all the things we will do when we return here for the weekends, all the ways we're going to make the most of our last days in the desert. But I am nodding in agreement. It's probably the best we can do for the year ahead. And since there's no need for additional persuasion, I raise my hand to wave his words away.

The gesture weighs heavily. It is the white flag of the battlefield, my signal of defeat. For, despite my husband's good intentions, I know we won't be returning to Lila Canyon—save the day we load the furniture and hand the keys over to someone else—not even for a single afternoon. And so at last I admit: in this remote corner of my beloved homeland, in the place that I sought salvation, I failed to find what I was looking for.

Perhaps the Mormons are right. It seems we were not meant to seek heaven on earth.

THE VERY NEXT DAY, we load the truck with two large duffel bags and the dogs and head toward Moab. Just before we hit the outskirts of the big tourist town, at the very northern tip of San Juan County, we turn off into the foothills of the La Sal Mountains and wind our way toward a small valley cut by the persistent flow of Pack Creek. In less than twenty-four hours, we have enacted Herb's idea, and arranged to stay at some friends' vacant vacation home just down the road from the historic Pack Creek Ranch. The ranch, with its refurbished cabins, is now more of a getaway destination and is owned and operated by Jane and Ken Sleight. Ken is the famous old Glen Canyon River guide whom San Juan County officials have continued to refuse to take seriously—the man who stood in front of the bulldozer with our friend Danny. As we approach the lower end of the ranch, we see Ken bent over, tightening up a fence line. He glances up, and when we wave, his face beams with recognition. Ken has taken a real liking to Herb, who was present at a county meeting when Ken had stood up to say that he was there once again to express concern about the hazardous waste being stockpiled in the open at the edge of the White Mesa Reservation—but that this time he had come as a citizen who had been diagnosed with cancer. When the county commissioners responded with more eye-rolling and snide remarks, Herb had interjected strenuously, and told the men that they were the rudest bunch he had ever known. Ken—who was the basis for Edward Abbey's Seldom Seen Smith in *The Mon-*

key Wrench Gang—was not a man who needed defending. But he still appreciated having at least one person in the room who insisted on maintaining a certain level of courtesy.

"Would you look at that," Herb exclaims. "We are getting a downright warm welcome in a San Juan County neighborhood!"

We wave back to the old man, turn up a gravel drive just across from his pastures. The drive winds through sagebrush and stands of piñon-juniper—a familiar landscape—but the home we walk into is far different from our place. This one is a finely appointed second home, belonging to Utah friends doing a career stint on the East Coast. We had used the house before, and knew that our friends were having trouble keeping out the local mice and pack rats, so, when we called and offered to declare war on the infringing rodents in exchange for a year of squatting privileges, they readily agreed.

"I had forgotten what a sweet place this is," Herb says. He is practically skipping from one furnishing to another, admiring the fine Southwestern décor. Then he starts pointing out the amenities.

"Baby, just think how much easier your life's gonna be—with running water, central heat—and then an air conditioner for this summer. There's even a dishwasher and laundry room—and a hot tub on the deck. And check this out—we've got satellite TV! I'm telling you, we're moving up in the world . . . Hey, do you know how to work this thing?"

He grins madly as he tries to figure out the remote controls for the dish and screen, but they prove to be beyond either of our technological comprehension and he tosses them aside. Then, suddenly, he's out the door, to reconvene with his colleagues at the Moab SUWA office.

VERY QUICKLY this pregnancy proves to be even worse than the last one. My husband returns home each night to the same scene he left in the morning: Bedraggled wife is sprawled on couch in certain pair of baggy black sweats and gray T-shirt. Having mastered the remote controls, said wife stares mindlessly at back-to-back reruns of *Law and Order*. A mound of plastic Popsicle wrappers rises up from the floor and threatens to obstruct the screen. So ill am I that I barely turn to look at him, let alone speak—except to tell him I haven't been able to take on any contract-writing work, or do anything else, for that matter. I can't help being resentful. He's out in beautiful places, doing fieldwork with friends, while I am prostrate. He is baffled—he was certain that the change of scene would do wonders for me.

Then, one day, he strides in and announces that he intends to have the entire house built before the baby comes.

I stare in disbelief.

"I have to," he says. "The only way I can qualify for a construction loan and mortgage is if I do it while I have this job—especially if it looks like you might be out of the workforce for a while. I checked into it—they'll give me the money, but the structure must be completed within twelve months."

"But you're busier than ever with work. You are already spread so thin . . ."

"It's now or never, honey. I just gotta make it happen." He sounds like he's straight off the big screen—a regular Hollywood superhero.

For my husband's imminent undertaking I feel not so much as gratitude or delight—and for our interim accommodations there's not even a sense of relief at the promotion in lifestyle it has brought. Instead, there is a hefty ambivalence—and it competes with, complicates, the other fears and frustrations at hand. The design we have conjured on paper is only eight hundred square feet, but it has in-floor heat. A large sunken bathtub, with jets. The refrigerator has an ice maker; the master bedroom, a skylight. There will be a washer and dryer, and a city water line feeding them. By American standards, these things aren't exactly luxuries, but for us they mean a mortgage five times the one we have for Lila Canyon. And to pay for and maintain it, we'll have to work more—leaving less time to enjoy what we have acquired. All this in a new locale where we don't yet have jobs. Indeed, in spite of everything we had intended, our life is gaining both a complex mass and velocity.

Too much too fast. It's like standing in a canyon when the flash flood hits. But that seems to be the way it goes in redrock country. In A.D. 900, the early Puebloan Anasazi underwent a process of rapid-fire growth that eradicated the last aspects of the simple life. It was mostly an increase in both precipitation and population that forced the issue: Cotton, a water-intensive crop, was suddenly a viable option for clothing all the new bodies. At the same time, more food was needed to feed all the new mouths. For both purposes, the Anasazi needed more territory—and so, in a very short period, groups spread out to occupy every canyon and mesa in the region. "At no previous time," wrote the historian Robert McPherson, "had there been as many people spread over so much of the land."[1]

In each new locale, farming intensified. Intricate irrigation systems were constructed from notched stones, and wider areas of woodland were slashed and burned for more crops. Bigger, more secure granaries were built high on the cliffs, and to access them, mind-boggling hand- and footholds were gouged into the sandstone.

But the upscaling didn't stop there. Shelters suddenly emerged as real dwellings—large and elaborate in design. They were framed with *jacal*—woven saplings packed with mud. Around this framework, where stones had once been crudely stacked, rock was carefully masoned, creating a far more permanent structure. Throughout the San Juan country, many of these dwellings were multi-roomed, multi-storied homes—not on the grand scale of those that sprang up at what is now Navajo National Monument in northern Arizona, or Mesa Verde National Park in southwestern Colorado, but there was a notable increase in size, workmanship, and attention to detail. By the middle of the Puebloan period, life in the San Juan region was arguably faster-paced, more intense, and far more elaborate than in any culture before or since.

Herb and I, with the fast track we were on, would have fit right in.

We square off in the living room, and suddenly our tandem momentum comes to a screeching halt. At this moment I hate him more than ever. I wouldn't see until later that it wasn't manic ambition that drove his fast and furious plan, it was his desperation to get me out of Deseret. All I could grasp then was that he would be gone more than ever, that I would spend the pregnancy alone. Of course, the repetition of history confirms: Howard Egan unloading Tamson in Salt Lake and heading out again. My grandma Blaisdell scanning the horizon, looking for my grandfather's horse. My pregnant mother standing on the porch, calling out to my father as he takes off to fish.

With six generations rolling up behind me, I hit him with a freight train of brutal words. And had I not been so blinded by rage, I would have seen the size of the wound inflicted. I would have seen, for the first time, my incorrigible lion man in retreat.

HERB IS WORKING like mad during the week, then, on Friday evenings, driving straight to our new property—where he stays until late Sunday night. My resentment toward him ripens, for he doesn't even have time to deal with the pack rats that have penetrated the drywall and set up shop in the baseboards beneath the kitchen cupboards. I can't get off the couch, except to get another green Popsicle from the fridge—the only thing that quells my roiling stomach, and then for only about three brief minutes at a clip. I lie there and listen to the scrape of yucca leaves and juniper branches as the rodents drag them in from outside.

Finally, I pick up the phone and call a young couple who live in

a schoolbus outside Moab, climbers who were known to take on sea-
sonal odd jobs to support their full-time occupation of scaling desert
towers—a lifestyle that involved many nights of camping at the base
of a backcountry rock formation, interspersed with long days spent
on ropes—hundreds of feet off the ground—in search of the most
aesthetic line of ascent. Word has it that they are working more this
year, to pay for a piece of state land they bought at auction. When
they come to the house to give a bid on rodent eradication, I find
that I quite like them—and that I have grown almost desperate for
company to which I can really relate. Kiley is a striking and stat-
uesque woman, full of grit and fiercely stubborn. Johnny is a warm
and handsomely understated man, equally determined. After we
agree on a price, they tell me about the place they live: It is a 160-
acre section of state-owned land which they had watched for years,
saving and waiting for the day the Utah Trust Lands put it up on the
auction block. When it was posted, they managed to outbid a man
who wanted the place for an ORV park. He approached them later
and tried to get them to sell off at least the corner then being used
by four-wheel-drive vehicles to access adjoining public land. They
said thanks but no, and he got a bit hostile. The next weekend, when
they went out to walk the property, there were fresh tire tracks
through it—a lot of them. Although the public record showed clear
title without public easement, apparently the off-road community
thought otherwise.

The couple responded by fencing off the route and posting *No
Trespassing* signs, only to return the next weekend and find their
work torn down. There were more tire tracks; from an old juniper
tree hung a noose and a hand-painted sign that read *Tree Huggers
Die.* John and Kiley put up a second fence. It too was promptly dis-
mantled—this time, by a San Juan County sheriff's deputy. They arrived just as he was leaving; he told them that the jeep trail across
their property was a legal public right-of-way and that if they ob-
structed it again he'd arrest them.

Rights-of-way on public lands have often been declared by rural counties, but private-property rights in the West have always been considered inviolate; this access issue thus represents a whole new level of entitlement. When I say as much, Johnny replies, "This is the new West. We're not talking horses and cows. We're talking about go-anywhere, do-anywhere machines. To them, no ground is sacred."

AT LAST I SUCCUMB to taking an anti-nausea medication, which provides all-too-brief periods of time off the couch. It's after the first dose that I finally muster the ability to put on my shoes for a walk down the driveway. At the bottom, I stop and weigh whether I dare go farther. The dogs, elated to be out at last, beg shamelessly—and so I push on, following the down-valley fence line of the ranch. Then I keep walking, toward the north end of the valley, where a small wash cuts into the bordering mesa. Slowly I stumble into the wash, stopping every ten steps or so to fend off simultaneous urges to faint and heave.

The La Sals are a laccolithic range—sisters to the volcanic plugs that created the Abajos, and nearly as arid, especially when compared with the mountain ranges above our new Colorado property. The La Sal foothills, in which this valley and adjoining washes sit, aren't much lower than Monticello, and so the high-desert transition vegetation and fauna are almost identical. Only the soil and rock differ: here at Pack Creek, the earth's crust has a more yellowish tinge, with a texture that is grittier, less refined. So it is surprising to walk over and lean my body into the steep south-facing wall of the wash and find it cohesive to the point of tackiness. It nearly suctions my skin.

Natural clay. The Anasazi collected it from deposits alongside arroyos and at the base of embankments such as this one. The raw material was ground with a mano and a metate, then cleaned and worked like dough. Ropes of the dense, cohesive earth were rolled between palms; urns, pots, bowls, and cups were formed by coiling the ropes and stacking them on top of one another in various lengths to form the desired shape of vessel. The vessel was made watertight by pinching the stacked coils together and then scraping them smooth. At this point, decorative paint was sometimes applied with brushes made from the chewed tips of yucca leaves. The pieces were then set to dry next to a pile of burning brush or animal dung—after which they were fired in a shallow, rock-lined pit.

Of all the excavated Anasazi corpses, only female skeletons have been found buried with potting tools. Apparently, among the ancients—as it is with contemporary Puebloan Indian cultures like the Hopi and the Zuni—pottery-making was strictly the labor of women. To say "a woman's work is never done" was in this case fitting, for the rapid heating and cooling that the utilitarian pottery endured in the Puebloan Anasazi kitchen ensured its short lifespan and made pottery production an ongoing task for females. Studying one excavated Puebloan site, archaeologists calculated that, in twenty-five years of single-family occupation, the inhabitants had tossed into the trash heap approximately 480 vessels.[2]

The clay's dank mineral smell is distinctly tantalizing. This time around, I know there is both a term and a reason for my craving of soils; *pica* is Latin for "magpie," a bird that will eat nearly anything, and it is believed to indicate certain mineral deficiencies in the body. Mouth watering, I scratch a clump of raw clay from the embankment and roll it between my palms. The mass would indeed require a great deal of attention before it would result in a beautiful piece of pottery. It's hard to imagine how expendable those pots were, and how many a woman would have produced over the course of her life to replace those that were broken.

I stay leaning into the sun-soaked wall and absorb its warmth. It has been a dry winter, but a long and cold one. I am certain that the houseplants I left behind at Lila Canyon are frozen solid, but Herb's had no time to go rescue them. At that very moment, he is in Colorado—marking the foundation site for the excavator who plans to scrape a pad the minute the snow melts. I, of course, have been busy on the couch.

It is strange how disconnected I am from the home-building process. But, then again, I am fairly detached from the production taking place inside my own body. Every time I turn my attention to it, the horrific malaise flares up and brings me, literally, to my knees. So I have found it easier to avoid the whole thing with any readily available distraction. Even now, my mind gladly escapes into ancient Puebloan times, and I envision the women kneeling right here, gathering clay: Digging. Grinding. Kneading. Rolling. And then, finally, coaxing the earth into form.

And, given the rate at which middle and late period Anasazi women were having babies, they were no doubt here in some prenatal or postpartum condition. It's curious to imagine these women, on the ground, their lives defined as much by the vessels they were creating as the vessels they had become. Theirs was a time characterized by a proliferation of art, in which "design elaboration [was] rampant,"[3] and pottery especially blossomed, in terms of color, design complexity, and form. This was an unusual, albeit brief, time in Anasazi history—marked by the simultaneous occurrence of long, intense work weeks and heightened artistic expression.

And I wonder, did they find pleasure and stature in their roles—working long hours of domestic drudgery but still creating life and art? As difficult as it is to discern any slice of prehistoric life on the Colorado Plateau, it is especially hard to know what it was like for these women of the middle-Puebloan period. For all the pottery, there is very little imagery depicting the female side of Puebloan Anasazi life. There are the limited and expected images of women with babies in their bellies, or of women giving birth, but they have a mundane quality about them. They are totally unlike the humpbacked, flute-playing god of fertility named Kokopelli, who first emerged in Basketmaker imagery but by the mid-Puebloan phase came to wield an oversize, erect penis. And for all the renditions of the virile Kokopelli, those of his female counterpart, Kokopelli Mana—who in modern Puebloan tradition is both playful seductress and fertile mother—are rare.[4] Both images were a departure from the previous Basketmaker anthropomorphs, which were far more androgynous, and the shift suggests that men alone had come to do business with the gods, that they had moved into a realm of power and privilege that was unavailable to women.

It makes sense: By A.D. 1000, agrarian living had completely replaced the old ways, and men's and women's worlds had been sharply divided. Only men were participating in kiva ceremonies, so one can assume that a male-centered ethos was forming, one that largely defined social and religious matters as well as politics and the economy. So perhaps Kokopelli was actually an expression of the emerging concerns with lineage, property, and crop productivity—social constructs that described a new kind of man. Indeed, such a drastic departure from man-as-hunter would have necessitated a symbol both exaggerated and rigid in form. And maybe at this point bloodline, ownership, and crop success became so male-identified that femaleness only served to confuse the new paradigm of progeny and property. Perhaps, then, Kokopelli Mana was kept in check so as not to threaten the new ways. Perhaps her presence and power had to be downplayed, just as Kokopelli's would have been amplified.

And I can't help wondering if women of the period had been stripped of spiritual significance and status altogether. For if they could not see themselves in the image of the new gods-in-the-image-of-man, if they were not privy to some sort of divine inspiration, then even the most powerful of creative pursuits, even childbearing and pottery-making, might have lacked honor and purpose. That kind of barrenness in the soul would have plagued Puebloan Anasazi women, afflicting them with the worst effects of sedentism and agrarian living. Indeed, it was during this time period that women's life spans in particular were brutally short.[5]

Of course, as with any social science, we really don't know. But history does repeat, and among the Mormons, the same trend seems to have occurred. Polygamy aside, there was a time when the roles of Mormon men and women were not so divided. Their on-the-run frontier lifestyle was largely one of foraging—and it required from the sexes a certain kind of unity, that their roles be cooperative rather than distinctive. That unity was what made it possible for Utah to become one of the first suffragist states in the Union—if only so Deseret could wield some political clout. It was what allowed Howard Egan to ride ahead and know that his wife could handle both shotgun and wagon just fine.

Spiritually, women's roles at the time were not so discernible from men's either. They too could conduct many of the blessings and healings that priests provided, and they were acknowledged as holding some powers of prophecy. Not ironically, it was during this early period in Church history that the Heavenly Mother was visible and accessible to the brethren. One of the founding prophet's polygamous wives, a poet named Eliza Snow, wrote her into a hymn. And Joseph Smith himself consoled a woman who grieved the death of her mother by saying that not only would she see her biological mother again, but she would also "meet and become acquainted with [her] eternal Mother . . ."[6] In 1910, the Latter-day Saints' own newspaper ran an article titled "Our Mother in Heaven," which stated, "The heart of man craves this faith and has from time immemorial demanded the deification of woman."[7] In the two decades that followed, Church apostles would refer to the Mother in Heaven as one who stood next to the Father, "in all her glory, a glory like unto his companion," and as a "glorified, exalted, ennobled Mother."[8]

But the spiritual lives and status of women would change after the Saints made their exodus out west—once they made the desert bloom like a rose, and its indigenous people white and delightsome. Simultaneously, the Heavenly Mother receded into the shadows. It was then, as the Saints settled, that the lives of men and women divided and mutated like cells, that the powers and privileges of women seemed to vanish. Soon they had no ability to offer blessings, or to receive revelations. By the 1970s—a time when the rest of the country was embracing both feminism and the civil-rights movement—the leader of the Mormon Church had reduced the Heavenly Mother to the mere description of "restrained," a role model of "modesty."[9] And as late as the last decade of the twentieth century, First Counselor and soon-to-be President/Prophet Gordon B. Hinckley was advising regional Church representatives to "counsel priesthood leaders to be on the alert" for people praying to the Mother in Heaven and "to make correction [that is] firm and without equivocation."[10] At the same time, Church leaders announced that, "in light of the instruction we have received from the Lord Himself, [it is] inappropriate for anyone in the Church to pray to our Mother in Heaven."[11]

By the turn of the millennium, one survey revealed that most Latter-day Saints believed that any discourse about the Heavenly Mother—let alone praying directly to her—was forbidden.[12] Indeed, enough people had been excommunicated from the Church on her behalf that it seemed a major offense; Mormon scholars were disciplined for merely pointing out the Heavenly Mother's significance in early Church history. But the severity of the transgression can only really be understood by comparing it with another pursuit for which Church authorities have also articulated explicit disapproval: When then President Spencer W. Kimball spoke out frankly against hunting in 1978, no one was disciplined for going anyway.[13] In fact, my childhood recollection of the opening day of deer season was that nearly no Mormon boys were present in the classroom.

LEANING AGAINST the embankment, clay in hand, I press the organic matter to my cheek. When I peel it away, there is an impression of the bone's contour. I sigh. In my mental detour through history and culture, I have come full-circle to face my own dilemma.

Wilderness warrior. Mate. Mother. My upbringing occurred without one powerful—let alone sacred—archetype for that which I embody. In Mormon theology and iconography, there was nothing close to a Valkyrie—in Norse mythology, a female deity with powerful soldier traits who raised slain heroes from the battlefield and delivered them to divinity. Even the Virgin Mary is all but absent. No wonder that I turned from God to geography. That I quit my job and can't carry a child. There has not been available a single archetypal image in which to reflect upon my purpose, worth, or potential.

And what of the women in my life? How could they have been mentors when they were as spiritually alienated as I? Ada's ecstatic experience through art may have rivaled that of the shamans, but when all was said and done, she was still a daughter of Deseret. And after all the years in which she had been barred from the men's club to which my grandfather and father belonged—an elite establishment that stood in the shadow of the Salt Lake Temple—she was practically giddy with gratitude the day they allowed the wives to enter through the service door. Later, when they hung her artwork in one of the club's private dining rooms, she was flattered to no end, in an obsequious sort of way.

And my grandma Blaisdell. It's no wonder she told my mother she would be handed off to the Lamanites. For she understood how little she had to offer her daughter. She understood that, among the deserts of Deseret, the terrain of womanhood could be a wasteland, that desertion is very much the territory of the feminine. From within my grandmother's own spiritual void, domesticity was drudgery, and there was no way to claim maternity as holy ground.

It comes down to this: There is the One—that which is supreme. And then there is the Other—which, if born into the right body, is embraced by the One as the Beloved. But if we are born into any other body, made in any other image, we are Coyote—that which is forsaken.

And so my mother, sister, and I were born not from the divine but, rather, from the canine. My father too, for Deseret's banishment of the Heavenly Mother affects everyone, male or female. Some learn to survive; they lope around the periphery until they bend their hearts and minds to accept the lopsided paradigm. Others find a new religion, or new cause, to counter. Some go mad. Others migrate out. And some simply end their lives.

But the problem doesn't stop there. To disavow the feminine is to reject also the maleness that corresponds. I see it now: This is the chain of reactions that so fully sabotaged my childhood relationship with God. And my knee-jerk rebellion ensured that I wouldn't see beyond the black and white—that I would fail to develop as an alternative my own intimate idea of a higher power. From there, I would fail to belong to any group of people for any lasting period of time. Because, ultimately, I would fail to belong to myself.

You're either with us or you're against us. My entrée into womanhood marked the time when my father pulled back in near repulsion. It was a time when I rejected him too—not because of his drinking, but because we had moved into separate realms. From there, separation degraded to polarization. And then any fumbling attempts at affection or connection—ill-timed and drunken as they were—could only be perceived as molestations.

And now, with my lion man. The reason we have spiraled down to bouts of near violence and estrangement has very little to do with his antics. No, the reason we have come to opposite ends is far more primal, more original, than anything he could have ever inspired on his own. Indeed, the paradigm was in place long before we ever met.

It's almost instinctual, the way we organize our thoughts into juxtaposing concepts. There is the civil world, with its clearly delineated road map, which will deliver us from suffering to eternal happiness. And there are the desert wilds, where anything can happen. Where the only thing that marks the way is redrock and ruins. Where the only certainties are beauty and destruction.

And even as all this bears down on me, I can feel the familiar internal scoff: I don't need God. I don't need a people. I can make and tend my own fire.

Still, there is the ghostly shiver of something severed.

The Saints sing hosannas. The lost tribe howls in the wilderness. I am torn between complex vocalizations.

I once was found but now am lost . . .

This exodus turned excavation has unearthed an empty, cracked vessel.

Expendable, I am.

I STAY LIKE THAT for hours, staring at the microcosmic world of clay and wash-bottom stones. When I finally look up, the sun has dropped behind the Moab Rim. The dogs are curled together to fend off a frosty night air that has crept up. Shivering, I turn and look out to where the mouth of the wash opens into a wider world: The sagebrush floor of Pack Creek Valley. The La Sals, singed with last light. And the weight of Deseret's history bears down on me, impresses what is at stake. Of course I lost the first baby. Of course my marriage is in jeopardy. And how could the people of San Juan County accept me, my point of view, when I had never really claimed what lay within those internal boundaries?

You can't go back. But I can move forward in a different way. I can revisit this notion of something larger than myself, something that breaks down these dark and doomed dualities. I can still salvage my marriage. I can still defend the desert. And if this baby will just hang on, I can learn to be a mother.

JOHN AND KILEY SPEND several weeks tearing out insulation and rodent nests—even pulling out rat carcasses. It is a nasty job, but not once do they so much as grimace. I grow to depend greatly on their company, and to yearn for the simplicity with which they live. When they invite Herb and me out to witness the annual Jeep Safari event that will invade their property, I readily agree—for I want to see their land and their life, and support them in their struggle.

Fortunately, when the day comes, I feel relatively well. It is Easter morning, and Herb has returned from Colorado early, so we can spend the day together. The sound of a viable heartbeat has left us trying our best, although our separations have left us treating each other with annoying formality.

We drive over to a mesa just south of Pack Creek, where John and Kiley's land is located. Trucks and trailers clog the turnoff, and soon we find that we can't get anywhere near the entrance to their property. We park and walk to their southwest boundary, where we come upon a line of forty ORVs. John and Kiley stand at the front of the line, talking to the lead driver, while the rest of the convoy rev their engines impatiently. The newly tied noose swings in the breeze just behind them.

It is like a scene from *Mad Max*. The vehicles look like dune buggies on steroids—with tires almost as tall as I stand. The air is greasy and putrid with smoke, and the noise of the monstrous motors is numbing. It is only ten o'clock in the morning, but music is blaring from stereos, and beer cans are being tossed from coolers into the hands of passengers.

Front and center in this spectacle, I spot a woman almost twice as far along as I. She wears a tight neon-pink tank top and cut-off shorts, and she is perched up on the side of a rock crawler. Her skin is so tan it's almost orange, and when she throws back her head and laughs, the sound is shrill enough to compete with the engines. Her large orange belly jiggles and glistens with suntan oil.

Shivering, I zip the front of my sweatshirt. Spring has graced the desert, but it's not yet that warm out. Then I look up and down the line at the rest of the women. Most are passengers, and many are dressed similarly to the pregnant woman. Not that I have a problem with baring skin, or wearing bright apparel, but somehow the tableau reminds me of garish hood ornaments. The men are curious too. In size, they are mostly hefty—puffed up like their vehicles. They are dressed in bright, scant, and sporty summer attire—the last thing one should wear when venturing into the harsh and exposed backcountry of the desert. They race their engines and crane their necks to see what's happening up front. Everyone looks wound up, a bit agitated.

And it occurs to me: These people are not the hardworking, mild-mannered, modest, and polite version of Mormons that I grew up with, nor are they like San Juan County old-timers. These are hybrids—the new West to which Johnny refers. They may or may not go to church, but they lack my father's genteelness, and they definitely don't ride horses or run cows. They are extreme recreationists—the same type who are wealthy enough to own the big powerful boats and high-powered personal watercraft that now dominate Lake Powell. And, more than any rancher, they hate environmentalists.

I can't help thinking that they embody what may be the Last Days in Deseret—not in a Christ-returns kind of way, but in terms of what the landscape can withstand. I think back to middle-Puebloan times, when life was moving at a fast clip and getting increasingly complex. Things seemed pretty abundant. After all, good soil could be tilled, good rain was coming down, and ruins would reveal little evidence of the endemic warfare that plagues a stressed culture. But this time in prehistory is fleeting, a mere blip. So what seems like stability was probably a time of decadence and gluttony—substitutions for a once-meaningful life. Though art and design were prolific, the exaggeration of Kokopelli, the scantiness of Kokopelli Mana, and other imagery easily lead to the conclusion that things were horribly out of balance, that things were being held together by a one-sided and dogmatic set of ideologies. Case in point: despite decentralization, despite an evolution in lifestyle similar to that of their southern neighbors, and despite increased communication with a much broader world, the pottery of the mid-period Puebloan Anasazi remained remarkably homogeneous throughout the region. This conformity, combined with the new phallic/farming iconography, could easily be chalked up to reflections of what San Juan historian Gary Topping calls "an intensely group-centered ethos."[14] From this perspective, it seems clear that in mid-Puebloan life, for all the new advancements and luxuries, there was a need for an unyielding cultural and religious identity—one that would keep things from falling into chaos. And, sure enough, as soon as the rains dried up, as soon as life got just one step more arduous, this carefully, elaborately constructed culture of excess toppled into fanaticism and violence.

EVERY NOW AND THEN the riders cast glances at us—and I can see that they have made a judgment because we are on foot. Or perhaps it's the way we dress—or they have already aligned us with John and Kiley. Whatever it is, we are not-one-of-them, and they show it in a way that far surpasses any look I've ever gotten from an old-school Mormon.

You people. Despite all my recent glimmerings about the way we enter into adversity, I too have an opinion—a very bleak one, which I cannot help. Disgust and bile rise up in my throat. And here it is again—the rage of Otherness that has threatened to doom my personal life has also rendered me ineffective as an advocate for wilderness protection, as an advocate for anything at all.

I look back at the pregnant woman. She and her husband are bickering. Up front, voices rise as Johnny and Kiley show the temporary restraining order issued by a judge—closing the route for the weekend until its legitimacy can be determined.

Herb touches my arm. "Let's go. The noise and fumes must be killing you." I appreciate that he's put my well-being before the conflict, and nod. We back away as the ORVs forge ahead, heading north across the property, across the foothills of the La Sals, toward Pack Creek. Over the course of our route, we only ever cross one dirt road, but it is amazing how far we must go before the smoke and din fade.

THE NEXT DAY, Kiley calls, and she is nearly hysterical.

"They ran over Johnny. Today they lined up to drive a closed route on BLM land next to ours, and when he stepped up to point out to the lead driver an agency-issued sign reading THIS IS NOT A TRAIL, the guy gunned it and nailed him. Ran right over Johnny's leg."

I motion for Herb to get on the other phone. Kiley continues.

"I called 911 and said there had been a vehicular assault and that a man was down. When the San Juan County deputy showed up, he just laughed. Told Johnny it served him right for stepping in front of a vehicle. Then he cited him for disorderly conduct! And our friend Bud ran toward the rock crawler as it hit Johnny— he was arrested for aggravated assault because he had a tool in his hand!"

Kiley is crying now. "You know, when we went before the judge to ask for the restraining order, he started off the hearing by saying that we should know he owned an off-road vehicle."

I'm thinking how surprised I am that a San Juan County judge issued a temporary closure at all. But in the end, we will see clearly whose side he was on, and then Johnny and Kiley will have to complicate their sweet, simple world by taking the issue to the Utah Supreme Court.

HERB'S AND MY LIFE will get increasingly complicated as well. Two years after I have the baby, near psychosis and worsening health will send me to a number of medical professionals, and we will finally discover that my body had stopped producing hormones almost entirely. Two-and-a-half years after I give birth, the doctors will look back at my health history, at the miscarriage and the difficult second pregnancy, and be certain that I had been in a hormone-deficient state for some time—at least since my father's death. But for some reason, bringing my soon-to-be child to term will take the hormones entirely off-line: Progesterone. Estrogen. Testosterone. DHEA. All those magical cellular secretions that excite, invigorate, stimulate all other bodily systems. The very building blocks that, in proper proportions, make us male and female. That make us passionate and rapturous and full of life.

There will finally come a day when I understand how this biological crisis was perfectly synchronized with one of a more psychic nature—and how together they disrupted everything: sexual and reproductive function, brain function, adrenal output, insulin production, metabolism, emotional stability, and sleep cycles. I lost so much weight that not a single curve remained on me. Eventually, my teeth began to crumble from my mouth.

One doctor will say that she is seeing the cease of hormone function in women who have experienced prolonged duress and deprivation in their lives. She will say that she's been seeing the problem with alarming frequency—that one doesn't have to suffer abuse to have it happen. She has mused that perhaps it is the stressful, sometimes meaningless times we are living in.

Whatever the reason, these women are out of balance, she says, not female in the way that nature intended. Some of these women display an estrogen dominance that exaggerates the qualities that are stereotypically female; they are weepy, frail, and passive to the point of being victims at every turn. Others may be testosterone-dominant; they will demonstrate increased aggression, irritability, and other more typically masculine traits. And others, like myself, are so depleted all the way around that they are reduced to mere ghosts—androgynous, vaporous beings not unlike the Basketmaker anthropomorphs.

Perhaps it has been some unconscious attempt to find my way back to something more soulful. But in the end, I will learn, biology still governs a great deal. In my body, a psychic calamity had articulated itself perfectly. And forever I will wonder if the ambivalence about my sex and its relationship to all things masculine was what ceased this vital physiological function. At the very least, I know, it made for lack of maternal bliss and a drastic departure from my spouse.

I CAN BARELY HEAR what Kiley is saying, for the growl and whine of engines in the background. That's why I ask her to repeat what she says next—I need to be sure I heard her correctly the first time:

"And you know what the kicker is? Hours go by—we drag Johnny out from under the vehicle, we deal with the crowd and then the sheriff—and then we finally realize . . ."

She laughs wildly, like a raven.

". . . that the big macho-lookin' guy driving the lead vehicle—the asshole who raised his fist and then ran over Johnny—was actually a woman."

⇥ 15 ⇤

Abandonment

EARLY-MORNING CLOUDS OBSCURE the horizon, and the sky breaks and scatters yellow-gray, like a string of old pearls. The desert has been drained of color, and there is little distinction between land and atmosphere. But I don't need to look out the window to know the loss of definition. I need only to think of where Herb has gone for the weekend, to reflect on the hollowness in his voice when he called the night before. And when he enters the house that evening, I ask how the trip was. I ask how our acquaintance, with whom he stayed the night to save on hotel expenses, is doing. I don't ask why he didn't camp, like he usually does.

It was fine. She is fine.

For the first time ever, he avoids my gaze—avoids even looking at our seven-month-old daughter. Head down, he skirts me like a clump of greasewood and goes to the kitchen sink, where he washes his hands for the longest time. Ruby is asleep in my arms, folds of my shirt clasped tightly in her fists. It's been like this since her birth: she hangs on day and night, refusing even momentary separation. It's as if she is already aware of what she is born into.

———

A WEEK LATER, the world is still vague—and for mid-April, un-seasonably cold and windy. It is Herb's birthday. Johnny and Kiley arrive in the afternoon to help with preparations for a party I had planned over a month ago—while I was still operating under the be-lief that I could recover whatever had been lost, that I could restore what lay in near ruin. With our two friends there, I present Herb with a new climbing rope. I had meant it to be a symbol of partner-ship, a gesture of my willingness to be tethered together on a lifeline. And I had intended for it to convey my eagerness to venture out to-gether again, to return to a way of life in which we had thrived.

The gift, the party—they were part of an overall salvage effort spawned by the epiphanies of early pregnancy. Until the day I gave birth, I had remained very ill—mostly bedridden. But after that day in the clay, I had realized what was at stake. Sweat pants were traded for sun dresses; I even painted my toenails. On better days, I drove to town and surprised Herb with picnic lunches. On the most man-ageable weekends, I followed him to our new home and sat in the shade of a piñon while he pounded nails. I even got myself aboard a friend's boat on Lake Powell, and within the cloistered walls of Cathedral in the Desert, I had floated alongside my husband.

But any progress I made in my soul-searching, any healing that took place in my marriage, was set back when I went into labor a month early. It was the same night my grandma Blaisdell finally died. The next day, my grandfather would say that Ruby was extra special to him because he imagined the two—great-grandmother and great-granddaughter—having met as they passed between worlds. Indeed, there were thirty-six hours between the time my water broke and the moment when Ruby emerged. For the duration, my grand-mother could have given her an earful. And it would explain why, the moment Ruby finally entered the world, she grabbed on to me and refused to be handed off for any reason at all.

Right away she needed extra care, which kept us in Salt Lake City for weeks. We finally returned to southern Utah, only to have her develop a serious respiratory illness that had me rushing northward again. Herb was triangulating madly between Salt Lake, his job in Moab, and the new house—which had been flung far off schedule. Subcontractors had fallen away like dominoes, and the bank's financial penalties for failing to meet construction deadlines were looming.

Everything was in chaos. Still, I continued to try—despite a blue-lipped baby who never slept, despite her refusal of a bottle and constant, deafening demands for my breast. At five o'clock each morning, she finally let go of me for one precise and inexplicable hour. If Herb was home, this was when I would creep into the spare bedroom, where he had begun to sleep, and give him what little I could. But he took the feebleness of my efforts as disdainful rejection. And soon the fissure between us was a canyon, vast and endlessly deep.

AND AS I STAND THERE and watch Herb unwrap his gift, we are yet unaware of my physical condition, of the overall toll the changes have taken. All week long, since his return from that ill-fated night, I have tried to figure out how it has come to this—how such a deep, passionate love could falter so. But I have said nothing. Done nothing. I am too exhausted to face what has happened. And by now Herb is in an entirely different reality—totally detached from me except in his duty to help with our child. I realize this when he removes the ribbon and paper from his gift, when what I had intended to express with it does not register with my husband in any way: He lifts up the rope, blinks eyes that are as bloodshot as my own. Then he looks not at me but at Johnny.

"Cool, man. Now we can go have some fun together."

It is then that I conclude that any personal revelations I have had about my contributions to the demise of our bond—any subsequent efforts to make amends—were too little, too late.

THAT NIGHT, I retreat into the back room so I don't have to watch Herb fawn over a petite young woman he has befriended in recent weeks, or see him gulp shots of alcohol in the ravenous way he once kissed me. Even down the hallway, I can hear him knocking over furniture, breaking glass. He swears loudly, and everyone laughs. But by early morning, he is heaving into the toilet. When he can finally pull his head out of the bowl, he crawls across the carpet on his hands and knees, to the edge of the bed, where he asks forgiveness. It's five o'clock in the morning, Ruby's one restful hour. I am grateful that she allows me to feign sleep.

IN A MATTER OF DAYS, Utah becomes officially uninhabitable. Herb has yet another month to go with his job, and we still haven't moved our belongings out of Lila Canyon. But he doesn't try to stop me from leaving for Colorado. He takes the last of his sick days and vacation time to put the finishing touches on the house, so the building inspector will issue a certificate of occupancy. Johnny and he are still on site, putting away tools, when Kiley and I load her vehicle and mine, when I close the door to the Pack Creek house and drive away. He's not there to see how easily I leave it all behind.

We time the drive to coincide with Ruby's nap schedule. Still, she protests mightily about not being in my arms—refusing to fall asleep until we near the state line. It's a back road we are on, one that sees little traffic, and so it's easy to miss the weather-beaten, paint-chipped sign that says *Welcome to Colorful Colorado*. Still, the crossing over is noticeable—as if something dark and heavy peels away from my head, down my shoulders, and drops away. I imagine it lying there, a villain's cloak, in the middle of the road on the Utah side, but I don't so much as glance back in the rearview mirror. Instead, I look straight ahead and consider how untrue the saying is that you can't run from your ghosts. Indeed, I know already that I will never again feel as haunted as I have felt in my homeland.

You can't go back. My friend was right after all. Even the late-period Anasazi—not yet that far from a ten-thousand-year-old, tried-and-true way of life—couldn't find a return route to something more serene and sustainable. In their case, it was too much, too late: at the same time that the drought came into full effect, that agriculture and architecture reached their height of complexity and labor intensity, an extreme amplification of social and religious dogma occurred. The dualities grew to be even more specific, more rigid—and the divisions were no longer just between men and women. Increasingly important were bloodlines—and men now separated themselves accordingly by erecting walls right down the middle of their great circular rooms of ceremony.[1] The result: mass ritual activity and violence came into vogue—indications that desperate measures were needed for any semblance of order. And suddenly the culture was too far gone, its infrastructure too complicated, and everything it held as beloved or necessary was now inaccessible. That the physical world had failed to provide only made it easier to get out of Dodge. And in what has been characterized as a drastic departure, the Anasazi deserted everything.

Ultimately, researchers would summarize the culture's demise from a number of angles:

A spiritual crisis: "[The] religious life of the Anasazi might have grown too extreme, too abstract, too involved in something that had nothing to do with the land. It might have become a system too rigorous to contend with the problems that occur with agriculture in a marginal area."[2]

An ecological crisis: "What may not have been so obvious to them was farming's detrimental effect on their environment . . . In a seventy-five to one-hundred-year period on Cedar Mesa, [the late-Puebloan Anasazi] effectively destroyed the arable lands they created."[3]

A social crisis: "Large communal plazas, tower clusters around springs at the heads of canyons, less carefully crafted building techniques, evidence of decreased trade relations, and introduction of the kachina cult are all indications that Anasazi society was undergoing rapid and stressful change."[4]

A nutritional crisis: "Toward the end of the Pueblo III period and approaching the abandonment [of the region], they began to eat their turkeys. As one archaeologist put it, 'It is like us eating our dogs.' "[5]

An aesthetic crisis: "In Glen Canyon [late-Puebloan rock art] . . . a period of degeneration occurred in which the variety of subject matter declined and designs were poorly executed."[6]

And then there are the Native American theories:

Zuni: The Anasazi went looking for a "center place where they could regain spiritual balance."[7]

In this light, I can't help thinking of my own exodus.

Navajo: The Anasazi were a "brilliant culture which went astray," that "transgressed the laws of the holy beings and of nature as they sought ease through the power which they abused . . . A holy way gone bad."[8]

And this perspective—it begs comparison to life in contemporary southern Utah. Old-time Mormons: mostly ranching families, righteously entitled. The New West: subdivisions of "ranchettes," extreme motorized sports, and tourism—a fate worse than cows. And the tree-huggers: frantically trying to save the desert, but pissing everyone off in the process.

Highly defensive postures. Dualities that get more divided, more rigid, every day. Meanwhile, the landscape that everyone loves—in one form or another—is almost beside the point.

———

OUR CARAVAN RISES UP and over the last foothill on the southern end of the La Sals, then drops down into the twenty-three-mile straightaway of Paradox Valley. This is the very outer edge of the Colorado Plateau—a rough thoroughfare once used by stockmen who bought their cattle from the old Scorup ranch, outside of Monticello, and trailed them to the grasslands surrounding my new home. It was also used by outlaws like Butch Cassidy, who, en route to Utah's canyons after a Telluride bank job, acquired some of his getaway horses from its residents. It is also the location of the last redrock formation I must contend with before ascending onto the mesa woodlands that encircle the San Juan Mountains. It's strange to have this feeling about sandstone. To look on it now is like an encounter with a scorned lover—full of anguish and an unresolved yearning. If my marriage survives, it is the same feeling I imagine having every time I look at my husband.

I pass one car on this isolated stretch, and it's Johnny and Herb, returning to Moab. Faces coated in sawdust, eyes sunken from working straight through three nights and days, they muster a half-wave. I give a curt nod, train my eyes straight ahead. The lonely highway parallels the stone rim that forms the north end of a valley only three miles wide. It looms over my car like a red rogue wave, threatening to engulf me in its mass. I hit the gas pedal hard, as if I can outrun the thing, but must slow again for the cows and calves that are loitering on the road.

Open range. I love the phrase. The wide-open, no-limits kind of feeling it inspires. And as the last of the plateau shrinks away, as the green grandiosity of the San Juans grows in the windshield, it is precisely what I need to feel.

There is also the sensation of forging ahead, the resolve to wait no more. No matter what happens, I want to end the female family tradition. Tamson Egan, the only wife to remain with my great-great-great-grandfather, waited in Salt Lake not only while he accumulated wives, but again while he set up his section of the Overland

Mail Line in the Great Basin. She thought he'd be back when the horse route went obsolete—when the railroad at last connected the continent. Then she waited when he stayed on in the Deep Creeks—leveraging his farmland in order to try his hand at mining—for she thought he'd be back once he discovered the ore to be too low-grade to justify the cost of shipment. She even waited for him when he had at last "exhausted all his resources," when he had nothing to show from that great gray ocean of sand except the fact that he had baptized one hundred Goshute Indians in a single day.[9] She was still waiting in 1875, when he at last returned to Salt Lake to be with what remained of his family. By then, the other two wives had pulled out, and Tamson and Howard would have only three years together before the man who could eat saddle leather suffered an inflammation of the bowels, which put him in the grave at sixty-three years of age.

THE ROAD COMES OFF the end of the Colorado Plateau, snakes along the San Miguel River, then winds up onto Wright's Mesa, which serves as pedestal to a starkly solitary peak called Lone Cone. The green of the landscape is the most welcoming thing I have ever experienced—along with the fact that I am just beyond the boundaries of Deseret. As we cross into the county where I am about to become a resident, Kiley rolls down her window, gives me the thumb's-up. And then we are heading through my new town, passing the saloon where the spurred cowboy first bought shots for Herb and me. Parked in front of the bar is an old pickup, the chin of a red cow dog resting on its tailgate. In the rear window is a round NRA sticker—a reminder that I am not that far from what I know. And there is another sticker, larger, boasting an unfurled American flag and words of promise.

We Will Never Forget.

The phrase has become so ubiquitous that I no longer notice it.

Today, though, the words lunge at me, gnashing wildly. It is a startling moment—to realize that my heart pounds in an agreement both zealous and sentimental.

I will never forget. I am tempted to brandish Herb's betrayal like a sword—to martyr myself on its point. It's in my blood, this shaping of life by the trespasses we suffer. It's Mormon. But it's also American. We are a nation defined in opposition to what we are not, thriving in the face of wrongdoing, and it's been that way since the days that inspired the Boston Tea Party. No wonder Joseph Smith fared so well, so fast, in his spread of Moroni's word. And no wonder the LDS religion has taken root so far and wide.

I HAVEN'T SEEN the house since a month before Ruby was born. Herb kept me posted on the basics—conveying that they were all he had time for. Of course, I had learned to expect this, to see shoot-from-the-hip, MASH-unit kinds of end results—and really, in our current state, there was time for little else. But when I pull up to the house—a small octagon with windows all around—the entire yard has been cleared of construction scraps; not a single nail remains on the ground. The front door has been painted a deep, watery blue; a large red bow is tacked to the jamb above. I take Ruby from her car seat while Kiley goes ahead and turns the knob. Stepping onto a neat little sunporch, I glance at my friend—who is looking almost smug. Every day she hasn't been with me, or in court trying to close the ORV route across her property, she has been here with Johnny and Herb, working on the house. She knows what I am about to see.

I walk across the threshold, and am transported. Between the floor-to-ceiling windows are vibrant bursts of color—not a speck of white to be found. I turn around, taking in the overall effect of light and hue. Then I walk straight to the steel post at the center of the house and look up. The post supports big wooden beams—made not from great old trees but from small farmed ones, pressed together.

They span out to hold up the roof, like the arms of an umbrella. Above them, across the eight-sided ceiling, lie grooved slats of evergreen from the Abajo Mountains in San Juan County. They were salvaged from wildfires and milled by a friend until they radiated gorgeous, smoky hues.

I look down. In the cement that anchors the main post, a mosaic of recycled bits of glass has been laid—Great Basin greens, grays, and blues. Offset among them are two hearts—one the color of real turquoise; the other, the color of blood. And the concrete floor that spans out across the rest of the house is stained in the deep-brown patina that varnishes the canyon walls on Cedar Mesa.

The main room—kitchen, dining, and living areas combined— is painted the tawny orange of Colorado Plateau sandstone. The kitchen counter is tiled deep blue—the desert night sky. Above the stove, a sleek black marble lizard scales the backsplash—a mascot for the landscape I have left behind.

I REMEMBER the last time I saw Ellen Meloy—only weeks after Ruby was born. We had just returned from Salt Lake when Ellen stopped by Pack Creek to meet the baby. She and her husband, Mark, had built their home in Bluff, and we commiserated over the process. I had asked then what she would have done differently if she had to do it again. She had said she would have kept it just the same—she had no desire to build something bigger or more luxurious. But, she said, she would have taken the time to attend to all those exquisite details that make a house a home, that make it a work of art.

"Life is short," she had said. "And you move in, and the days rush by, and you never get to those little intimate gestures."

As she spoke, I was thinking that I had never seen her look more beautiful, more alive. Three days later, at the age of fifty-eight, Ellen died suddenly in her sleep.

I shift the baby to my other hip and walk into the master bedroom. Its walls are a deep, blushing pink—the most passionate and sexy color I have ever seen. My closet—a small, simple recess in one of the west walls—has been carefully customized with wooden cubbyholes to hold my sweaters, scarves, hats, and boots. In the bathroom, surrounding the sunken tub, are silver-green tiles of sagebrush—and more turquoise covers the walls. There is also a marvelous shower lined with stones, each one the opaque coffee-and-cream of silty desert rivers. Interspersed among the stones are tiles from the bathroom of my father's childhood—the same bathroom we grandchildren would use when visiting Lee and Ada. The tiles depicted my father and his brothers at play in the outdoors. Each one had been hand-painted by my grandmother.

The house is soulful and beautiful in an organic sort of way, and imaginative beyond description. And it is a labor of love—every detail completed explicitly on my behalf—for my husband would just as soon live in a trailer or a tepee, or, better yet, a cave.

For he is, in my father's words, a wild-eyed critter.

THERE IS A PICTURE of us on that last trip to Lake Powell. The photograph was taken by our friend Colby—the owner of the Pack Creek house—in black and white. It shows us standing at the mouth of Davis Gulch, a corkscrew canyon that begins just off the Hole-in-the-Rock route outside of Escalante and empties into what was once a free-flowing Escalante River but is now just part of the reservoir. Upper Davis Gulch, which the lake never reached, had always been one of Herb's and my favorite canyoneering adventures. To slither and straddle its corkscrew interior is to see quickly why the Hole-in-the-Rockers chose a blank cliff face instead for their thousand-foot descent to the river.

It was the beginning of Memorial Day weekend, which marked the halfway point in my pregnancy. For the two years leading up to it, tree-ring data verified that the region was drier than it had been at any point in the past three hundred years.[10] Colby and his wife, Holly, had dropped anchor out in the main channel, near a knobbed formation known as The Rincon. It was not an ideal campsite by any means; Lake Powell's soft salmon sand had been hard to come by, not only because of the holiday crowds, but because the water level in the main channel had slipped nearly 150 feet below the bathtub ring. We were moored just beneath several shelves of newly exposed muck, each one covered with dead remnants of aquatic life. What had once been immersed tendrils, gracefully undulating, were now desiccated sticks. From the main stalks, branches jutted straight into the air like raised, frantic arms. The dead plants looked suspended in time—frozen mid-wave, mid-shriek—as if they had been gesturing desperately to the water as it pulled away, as if they had tried to call it back and reclaim the world they once knew.

At the Rincon, Colby and Holly had unhitched from the houseboat a small ski boat. We had climbed in and driven up the Escalante arm, into the mouth of Davis. The boat didn't get far before the bow hit sand, for the water had retreated enough to expose an extra half-mile of canyon. We disembarked to explore the newly revealed stretch, and, walking between colorless walls, alongside a trickle of creek, we craned our necks up at the demarcation line. Above it, where the rock was still red, we could see inscriptions, mostly initials, followed by the numbers "2000." That year—the same year my father did himself in—folks had been able to float right alongside the wall and carve themselves into millennial history.

Back to the photograph: We stand in that new section of Davis, graffiti floating above our heads. Herb, as usual, looks invincible. In this particular instance, it is as if the recessive climactic conditions that threaten the region—combined with the stresses in our life—only strengthened his resolve to flourish.

Now, as I stand in the home he has built, it is the photo that helps me grasp that he is not a lion man at all. He is pure Coyote—

decadent, passionate, and possessing an inherent tendency to thrive in the worst of times.

But there's more. He has his arms around me in a desperate sort of way—as if he's trying to uphold my burgeoning mass. What strikes me now, in thinking about the photo, is how he falls into anything that resembles the work of a savior—that this is how he gets duped into trying to hold the entire world in his hands. Junipers. Tarantulas. Women. It's no wonder he feels so at home in Deseret—where God and biology are in perfect agreement that men and *Canis latrans* should take on as much territory as possible. But, for all his sparkles and grins in that one photographic moment, his eyes are dark and resigned. It is the glimmer of his resentment. The part that blames me for his hind legs' getting caught in the snares of convention and duty. The part that is his in our troubled equation.

And there I am, my body shrinking away from his hungry grasp. The photo reflects just how threatened I grew to be by my husband's animal appetites, by the very maleness of him. I forgot that his natural lusts and longings were bound by an equally natural sense of love and loyalty. But it was inevitable. I had come to fear the corresponding aspects in myself. Accordingly, every sensual and kinetic aspect of me was extinguished. No wonder I couldn't get up and go with my husband. And yet, to judge by the look of my glazed and vacant eyes, I still managed to be missing in action. The photo proves that by the time Herb skipped out on our commitment I was long gone.

His response was that of any trapped creature: to chew his paw off and run.

GOD. DOG. We fail to see the reflexivity of what lives inside us. Henry David Thoreau wrote, "In Wildness is the preservation of the World."[11] He didn't say "wilderness." He knew that no piece of land—no matter how scenic or pristine—would restore what we have lost in ourselves. That's not to say we don't need wilderness—we need it more than ever. For this is the place where Coyote dwells, free of persecution, free of the projection of the abandoned, feared self.

In Coyote is the preservation of the soul. That howl, had I let it rise up into the dark night sky like a prayer, would have grounded me. And at the same time, it would have gotten me out of the house, nose to the ground, loping circles until I found my way. There would have been no map, and I would not have followed any sort of marked route. And it would not have been white tile and gold streets I'd have found. It would have been untrammeled desert—a landscape of faith, desire, and imagination—the landscape of the Other. Scattered across it would be bones, old bones, stained an ancient red. Among them would have been a most original skull, not too large, with a pointed muzzle and sharp teeth. Male or female, it wouldn't have mattered. It would have been the face of God.

Pray or crawl. I never imagined the choice as anything except *either-or*. But really, for thousands of years, they were one and the same.

AFTER POSING FOR the photograph in Davis Gulch, Herb and I had wandered off from our friends, farther up the canyon. In some places we had scrambled over chest-high mounds of mud—remnants of inundation. I was cursing the men who had stopped the river in its tracks, blaming them for the mess, for all that lay buried in that massive tomb of sediment. But Herb was practically dancing with joy, pointing out how, in just a few seasons, flash floods had already scoured out most of what clogged the canyon.

I had stopped. Reclamation is a long and tedious process—but he was right. On the sides of the canyon, already emerging next to the walls, were new sprigs of willow, and moonflower vines in sprawl. There were even cottonwood seedlings.

"And look!" Herb had sucked in his breath and pointed high above our heads, to the bathtub ring.

Bold streaks of red had begun to run from the rock above, down into the bleached section. A canvas washed white and then painted again.

There are contradictions, you know. Stone becomes dust, then stone again. And the dead stand between the grains of sand.

Beauty. Destruction. And now restoration. Some things must be worn away, ground down—to the very bones. Then and only then can we see what might emerge at the edges.

IT WOULD TAKE several years for things to settle, for me to see what there was to work with. Until then, I would go on faith—supplemented by a cocktail of compounded hormones. And I would live off memories and bodily impressions of what once was.

You can't go back. But going forward, that march of progress that accelerates and complicates, was also out of the question. Instead, I would go deep. To the very core of the heart, where a certain neutrality exists. A place that can hold everything, that banishes nothing.

I'm no holy man, but it's a journey not unlike Christ's forty days and nights. It's a venture into the darkness, a place where one must become intimate with all that is not seen, all that is unknown.

Light changes everything.

I am terrified. I still hardly know what will ultimately save my marriage, or the desert wilds. I only know what fails, and that I haven't given up on either. And that I must remain fluid and humble in my devotion, in my positions. For advocacy—of religion, politics, environment, emotions—is a precarious thing.

Now I believe that true lasting change and sustainability—cultural or otherwise—must rely on something more ancient and universal: art—any form that evokes the archetypal imagery that lives deep in the human psyche—can, in words I once heard imparted by the author Terry Tempest Williams, "bypass rhetoric and pierce the heart."

And so I will tell stories. To my daughter. To anyone who will listen. I will string together words that, I hope, will summon from the listener a primordial sound—not simply a dirge, but something lustful, full of grit and soul. For in a chorus of those marvelously complex vocalizations would indeed be the world's salvation.

God help me.

NOTES

I. MIGRATION

1. Online at www.ldschurchtemples.com/facts, April 12, 2007.

2. Howard Egan and Howard R. Egan, *Pioneering the West, 1846 to 1878: Major Howard Egan's Diary*, ed. Wm. M. Egan (Richmond, Utah: Howard R. Egan Estate/Skelton Publishing Company, 1917), p. 9.

3. Wallace Stegner, *The Gathering of Zion* (New York: McGraw-Hill, 1964; reprint Lincoln, Neb.: Bison Books, 1992), p. 65.

4. Ibid., pp. 103–104.

5. Ibid., p. 90.

6. Egan and Egan, *Pioneering the West*, p. 25.

7. Brigham H. Roberts, ed., *History of the Church of Jesus Christ of Latter-Day Saints, Period II. Apostolic Interregnum. From the Manuscript History of Brigham Young and Other Original Documents*, vol. 7 (Salt Lake City: Deseret News, 1932), 7:515–16, quoted in David L. Bigler, *Forgotten Kingdom* (Logan: Utah State University Press, 1998), p. 26.

8. Quoted in Egan and Egan, *Pioneering the West*, p. 107.

9. *Deseret News* 5 (Oct. 31, 1855): 269.

10. Joseph Smith, *Doctrine and Covenants of the Church of Jesus Christ of Latter-Day Saints*, 137:4 (Salt Lake City: Deseret News, 1880); online at http://scriptures.lds.org/en/dc/137.

11. Stegner, *Gathering of Zion*, p. 222.

12. Ibid., p. 225.

13. Quoted in ibid., p. 245.

2. ORIGINS

1. Bernard Shanks, *This Land Is Your Land* (San Francisco: Sierra Club Books, 1984), p. 185.

2. Cornelia Adams Perkins, Marian Gardner Nielson, and Lenora Butt Jones, *The Saga of San Juan* (Utah: San Juan County Daughters of the Utah Pioneers, 1957), p. 24.

3. Scott G. Kenney, ed., *Wilford Woodruff's Journal*, 10 vols. (Midvale, Utah: Signature Books, 1983), vol. 3:241, quoted in David L. Bigler, *Forgotten Kingdom* (Logan: Utah State University Press, 1998), p. 40.

4. George D. Smith, ed., *An Intimate Chronicle: The Journals of William Clayton* (Salt Lake City: Signature Books, 1991), p. 369, quoted in Bigler, *Forgotten Kingdom*, p. 38.

5. Bullock to William, Jan. 4, 1848, in *Latter-Day Saints' Millennial Star*, April 15, 1848, p. 118, quoted in Bigler, *Forgotten Kingdom*, p. 39.

6. Quoted in Dale L. Morgan, *The Great Salt Lake* (Indianapolis: Bobbs-Merrill, 1947), p. 202, quoted in Bigler, *Forgotten Kingdom*, pp. 40–41.

7. Kenney, *Wilfred Woodruff's Journal*, vol. 3:241, quoted in Bigler, *Forgotten Kingdom*, p. 41.

8. Brady, Janeen, "I'm a Mormon" (Draper, Utah: Brite Music, Inc., 1975).

9. Joseph Smith, Junior, *History of the Church of Jesus Christ of Latter-Day Saints. Period I. History of Joseph Smith, the Prophet, by Himself*, 6 vols. (Salt Lake City: Deseret News, 1902–1912) 2: 36–39, and Bruce R. McConkie, *Mormon Doctrine* (Salt Lake City: Bookcraft, Second Edition, 1966), p. 23, both quoted in Bigler, *Forgotten Kingdom*, p. 23.

3. MIRE

1. Paul Shepard, *The Only World We've Got* (San Francisco: Sierra Club Books, 1996), p. 125.

2. Ibid., p. 126.

3. Ibid., pp. 126–27.

4. Ibid., pp. 111–12.

5. Presley, Elvis, "Cool Water" (Alfred Publishing Co., 1988).

6. Ibid.

7. Ibid.

8. Ibid.

4. AMBUSH

1. "Mormonism in a Nutshell," quoting former Church President Lorenzo Snow, online at www.carm.org/lds/nutshell.htm.

2. "Newsroom: Quick Facts: The Missionary Program," online at http://lds.org/newsroom/page/0,15606,4037-1—6-168,00.html (the Church of Jesus Christ of Latter-day Saints' official website).

3. Joseph Smith, Junior, trans., *The Book of Mormon* (Salt Lake City: Church of Jesus Christ of Latter-day Saints, 1920), Introduction, p. i.

4. Ibid., 1 Nephi 14:10.

5. "Newsroom: Quick Facts: Facts and Figures," online at http://lds.org/newsroom/page/0,15606,4034-1—10-168,00.html.

6. Parley Pratt, *Proclamation of the Twelve Apostles of the Church of Jesus Christ of Latter-Day Saints to All the Kings of the World, to the President of the United States of America, to the Governors of the Several States, and to the Rulers and People of All Nations* (New York: Pratt and Brannan, 1845; Liverpool: Wilford Woodruff, 1845), quoted in Will Bagley, *Blood of the Prophets* (Norman: University of Oklahoma Press), p. 27.

7. "Newsroom: Quick Facts: Facts and Figures," online at http://lds.org/newsroom/page/0,15606,4034-1—10-168,00.html.

8. Pratt, *Proclamation of the Twelve Apostles*, quoted in Bagley, *Blood of the Prophets*, p. 27.

9. Smith, *The Book of Mormon*, 3 Nephi 20:15, 16.

10. Robert S. McPherson, *A History of San Juan County* (Salt Lake City: Utah State Historical Society and San Juan County Commission, 1995), p. 286.

5. EXTINCTION

1. "Commission Quote of the Week," *San Juan Record*, vol. 85, no. 19 (Feb. 7, 2001), p. 1.

2. Robert S. McPherson, *Sacred Land, Sacred View* (Provo, Utah: Charles Redd Center for Western Studies, Brigham Young University, distributed by Signature Books, 1995), pp. 35–37.

3. Heidi McIntosh, phone interview, 2001.

4. Todd Wilkinson, *Track of the Coyote* (Minnetonka, Minn.: NorthWord Press, 1995), p. 110.

5. Wayne Grady, *The World of the Coyote* (San Francisco: Sierra Club Books, 1995), p. 91.

6. Wilkinson, *Track of the Coyote*, p. 108–10.

7. Wildlife Services [formerly ADC], *Annual Report* (Washington, D.C.: USDA/APHIS Wildlife Services, 1999), online at www.aphis.usda.gov.ws,

quoted in Brooks Fahy and Cheri Briggs, "A War Against Predators: The Killing of Wildlife Funded by Taxpayers," in *Welfare Ranching*, George Wuerthner and Mollie Matteson, eds. (Washington, D.C.: Foundation for Deep Ecology, distributed by Island Press, 2002), pp. 247–48.

8. Predator Conservation Alliance, *"Wildlife Services"? A Presentation and Analysis of the USDA Wildlife Services Program's Expenditures and Kill Figures for Fiscal Year 1999* (Bozeman, Mont.: PCA, 2001), and Wildlife Services, *Annual Report*, quoted in Fahy and Briggs, "A War Against Predators," p. 248.

9. Jon Krakauer, *Under the Banner of Heaven* (New York: Anchor, 2004), p. 321.

10. *National Vital Statistics Reports*, vol. 54, no. 2 (Sept. 8, 2005), pp. 8–10, online at www.cdc.gov/nchs/data/nvsr/nvsr54.2.pdf.

11. Quoted in Krakauer, *Under the Banner of Heaven*, pp. 120–21.

12. Wilford Woodruff, "Official Declaration—1," also known as "The Woodruff Manifesto," in *The Doctrine and Covenants: Carefully Selected from the Revelations of God, and Given in the Order of their Dates*, online at http://scriptures.lds.org/od/1.

13. Quoted in Krakauer, *Under the Banner of Heaven*, p. 13.

14. William Woodward, "Reminiscences of William Woodward," Church of Jesus Christ of Latter-day Saints' Historian's Office Archives, Box 2, Folder 4, quoted in Marie Irvine, "In Defense of Virtue," 1996, pp. 10–11. Paper presented May 16–19, 1996, Mormon History Association Annual Conference, Snowbird, Utah.

15. Center for Biological Diversity, "Protection and Conservation of Old-Growth Forests in Southwest," online at www.biologicaldiversity.org/swcbd/programs/science/old.html.

16. Wilkinson, *Track of the Coyote*, p. 97.

6. FORAGE

1. Aldo Leopold, "Cheat Grass Takes Over," in *A Sand County Almanac and Sketches Here and There* (New York: Oxford University Press, 1949), p. 155, quoted in Debra L. Donahue, *Western Range Revisited* (Norman: University of Oklahoma Press, 1999), p. 120.

2. Paul Shepard, *The Only World We've Got* (San Francisco: Sierra Club Books, 1996), pp. 110–11.

3. Ibid.

4. Sally Fallon with Mary G. Enig, *Nourishing Traditions* (Washington, D.C.: New Trends Publishing, 1999), pp. 26–27.

5. Shepard, *The Only World We've Got*, pp. 113–14.

6. Defenders of Wildlife, *Amber Waves of Grain* (Washington, D.C.: Defenders of Wildlife, 2000), p. 1.

7. Utah Farm Bureau, *2006–2007 Utah Farm Bureau Policy Book* (Sandy, Utah: Utah Farm Bureau Federation, 2006), sect. 316, p. 25.

8. Ibid., sect. 314, p. 28–29.

9. Ibid., p. 24.

10. Ibid., sect 313, p. 22.

11. *Webster's New International Dictionary*, 3rd ed., s.v. "forage."

7. SHAMAN

1. Howard Egan and Howard R. Egan, *Pioneering the West, 1846 to 1878: Major Howard Egan's Diary*, ed. Wm. M. Egan (Richmond, Utah: Howard R. Egan Estate/Skelton Publishing Company, 1917), p. 189.

2. Public Use Statistics Office, statistics for the National Park Service, online at www2.nature.nps.gov/stats/.

3. Edward Abbey, *Desert Solitaire* (1968; reprint, New York: Touchstone/Simon & Schuster, 1990), p. 152.

4. Richard Manning, *Against the Grain* (New York: North Point Press, a division of Farrar, Straus and Giroux, 2004), p. 18.

5. Polly Schaafsma, *Indian Rock Art of the Southwest* (Santa Fe: School of American Research; Albuquerque: University of New Mexico Press, 1980), p. 77.

6. Mircea Eliade, *Shamanism: Archaic Techniques of Ecstasy*, Bollingen Series No. 76 (Princeton: Princeton University Press, 1964), quoted in Schaafsma, *Indian Rock Art*, p. 71.

7. Schaafsma, *Indian Rock Art*, p. 77.

8. Paul Shepard, *The Only World We've Got* (San Francisco: Sierra Club Books, 1996), p. 129.

9. Ibid., p. 111.

10. Ibid., p. 129.

11. Manning, *Against the Grain*, p. 21.

8. GHOST

1. Mel Bashore, LDS Church historian, e-mail, Feb. 8, 2006.

2. Brigham H. Roberts, *A Comprehensive History of the Church of Jesus Christ of Latter-Day Saints*, vol. 7:515–16 (Salt Lake City: Deseret News, 1932), quoted in David L. Bigler, *Forgotten Kingdom* (Logan: Utah State University Press, 1998), p. 26.

3. Howard Egan and Howard R. Egan, *Pioneering the West, 1846 to 1878: Major Howard Egan's Diary*, ed. Wm. M. Egan (Richmond, Utah: Howard R. Egan Estate/Skelton Publishing Company, 1917), p. 62.

4. Ibid., pp. 62–63.

5. Foundation for Deep Ecology, *Welfare Ranching*, George Wuerthner and Mollie Matteson, eds. (Washington, D.C.: Island Press, 2002), p. 6.

6. Ibid., p. 8.

7. Southern Utah Wilderness Alliance, "Cowboy Welfare Bonanza," *Southern Utah Wilderness Alliance Newsletter*, vol. 13, no. 1 (1996): 18.

8. United States Department of Interior, *Rangeland Reform Environmental Impact Statement* (Washington, D.C.: United States Department of Interior, 1994), quoted in Foundation for Deep Ecology, *Welfare Ranching*, p. 7.

9. Foundation for Deep Ecology, *Welfare Ranching*, p. 10.

10. Forest Guardians, "Wing-Tipped Welfare Cowboys Ride the Range," online at www.fguardians.org/support_docs/factsheet_wing-tip-welfare -cowboys.pdf, p. 1.

11. Pamela A. Bunte and Robert J. Franklin, *The Paiute*, ed. Frank W. Porter III, in Indians of North America series, ed. Liz Sonneborn (New York/Philadelphia: Chelsea House Publishers, 1990), p. 21.

12. Ibid.

13. Gary Topping, *Glen Canyon and the San Juan Country* (Moscow, Idaho: University of Idaho Press), p. 33.

9. MANO

1. Carol Ann Bassett, "The Culture Thieves," *Science*, vol. 249 (July/Aug. 1986): 24, quoted in Robert S. McPherson, *A History of San Juan County* (Salt Lake City: Utah State Historical Society and San Juan County Commission, 1995), p. 45.

2. G. R. Willey and J. A. Sabloff, *A History of American Archaeology*, 2nd ed. (San Francisco: W. H. Freeman, 1980), p. 128; and John C. McGregor, *Southwestern Archaeology*, 2nd ed. (Urbana: University of Illinois Press, 1965), p. 41; both cited in R. G. Matson, *The Origins of Southwest Agriculture* (Tucson: University of Arizona Press, 1991), p. 15.

3. Richard Wetherill to Talbot Hyde, Dec. 17, 1893, quoted in Fred M. Blackburn and Ray A. Williamson, *Cowboys and Cave Dwellers* (Santa Fe: School of American Research Press, 1997), p. 45.

4. R. G. Matson and Brian Chisholm, "Basketmaker II Subsistence: Carbon Isotopes and Other Dietary Indicators from Cedar Mesa, Utah," *American Antiquity*, vol. 56, no. 3 (1991): 444–59.

5. Joseph Smith, *The Doctrine and Covenants of the Church of Jesus Christ of Latter-Day Saints*, 29 (Salt Lake City: Deseret News Company, 1880), p. 8, online at http://scriptures.lds.org/en/dc/29.

6. Howard Egan and Howard R. Egan, *Pioneering the West, 1846 to 1878: Major*

Howard Egan's Diary, ed. Wm. M. Egan (Richmond, Utah: Howard R. Egan Estate/Skelton Publishing Company, 1917), p. 187.

10. BURIAL

1. National Energy Policy Development Group, *Reliable, Affordable, and Environmentally Sound Energy for America's Future: Report of the National Energy Policy Development Group* (Washington, D.C.: Government Printing Office, 2001), pp. 5-7, online at www.whitehouse.gov/energy/Chapter5.pdf.

2. Bureau of Land Management, *Information Bulletin No. UT 2002–008* (Salt Lake City: Utah State Office, Bureau of Land Management, 2002), p. 12.

3. "U.S. Crude Oil, Natural Gas, and Natural Gas Liquids Reserves 2001 Annual Report," Energy Information Administration, U.S. Department of Energy, Nov. 2002, quoted in Mark Lemkin, "An Analysis of Utah Oil and Gas Production, Leasing, and Future Resources," Southern Utah Wilderness Alliance, 2005, online at www.suwa.org/site/PageServer?pagename=library_LemkinReport.

4. Steven A. LeBlanc, *Prehistoric Warfare in the Southwest* (Salt Lake City: University of Utah Press, 1999), pp. 1–41.

5. Ibid., p. 36.

6. Linda S. Cordell, *Ancient Pueblo Peoples*, in Exploring the Ancient World series, ed. Jeremy A. Sabloff (Montreal: St. Remy Press; Washington, D.C.: Smithsonian Books, 1994), p. 41.

7. Letter to the Editor, *San Juan Record*, vol. 85, no. 14 (Jan. 2, 2002): p. 5.

8. Paul Shepard, *The Only World We've Got* (San Francisco: Sierra Club Books, 1996), 136.

9. Ibid., p. 138.

10. Ibid., p. 139.

11. Ibid.

12. Paul Shepard, "A Post-Historic Primitivism," in *The Wilderness Condition*, ed. Max Oelschlager (San Francisco: Sierra Club Books, 1992), p. 46.

11. DWELLING

1. Howard Egan and Howard R. Egan, *Pioneering the West, 1846 to 1878: Major Howard Egan's Diary*, ed. Wm. M. Egan. (Richmond, Utah: Howard R. Egan Estate/Skelton Publishing Company), p. 145.

2. Ibid., pp. 147–48.

3. Marie Irvine, "In Defense of Virtue," p. 8. Paper presented May 16–19, 1996, Mormon History Association Annual Conference, Snowbird, Utah.

4. Southern Utah Wilderness Alliance, "The Facts About Oil and Gas Devel-

opment on Utah's Public Lands," online at www.suwa.org/site/Doc Server/0_GFactSheet_Aug06.pdf?docID=281.

5. Stephen Plog, *Ancient Peoples of the American Southwest* (New York: Thames & Hudson, 1997), pp. 67–68.

6. Carla Hannaford, Ph.D., *Awakening the Child Heart* (Captain Cook, Hawaii: Jamilla Nur Publishing, 2002), p. 4.

7. Ibid.

12. FLIGHT

1. Powder River Basin Resource Council, Introduction, online at www .powderriverbasin.org/cbm/index.htm.

2. Ibid.

3. Powder River Basin Resource Council, "Coalbed Methane Development in Wyoming's Powder River Basin Is Transforming the Landscape: PRBRC and Landowners Respond to Prevent Damage," online at www.powder riverbasin.org/cbm/generalbackgroundcbm.shtml.

4. Paul Shepard, *The Only World We've Got* (San Francisco: Sierra Club Books, 1996), pp. 163–89.

5. Polly Schaafsma, *Indian Rock Art of the Southwest* (Santa Fe: School of American Research; Albuquerque: University of New Mexico Press, 1980), p. 180.

6. Ibid., pp. 180–81.

7. Polly Schaafsma, "Trance and Transformation in the Canyons: Shamanism and Early Rock Art on the Colorado Plateau," in *The Archaeology of Horseshoe Canyon* (Moab, Utah: National Park Service, n.d.); online at www.nps.gov/cany/planyourvisit/upload/HorseshoeBook.pdf. (First published in *Shamanism and Rock Art in North America*, ed. Solveig A. Turpin [San Antonio, Texas: Rock Art Foundation, 1984].)

8. Robert S. McPherson, *A History of San Juan County* (Salt Lake City: Utah State Historical Society and San Juan County Commission, 1995), p. 46.

9. David Roberts, *In Search of the Old Ones* (New York: Touchstone, 1996), pp. 37–42.

13. KIVA

1. Vic Saunders, "Land Grab of the Worst Kind," in Farm Bureau Views archives, Sept. 30, 1996. American Farm Bureau Federation archives online at www.fb.org/index.php?fuseaction=newsroom.focusfocus&year =1996&file=f00930.html.

2. Stephen Plog, *Ancient Peoples of the American Southwest* (New York: Thames & Hudson, 1997), p. 64.

3. Howard Egan and Howard R. Egan, *Pioneering the West, 1846 to 1878: Major*

Howard Egan's Diary, ed. Wm. M. Egan (Richmond, Utah: Howard R. Egan Estate/Skelton Publishing Company, 1917), p. 149.

4. Ibid., pp. 149–50.

5. Ibid., p.150.

14. VESSEL

1. Robert S. McPherson, *A History of San Juan County* (Salt Lake City: Utah State Historical Society and San Juan County Commission, 1995), p. 35.

2. Brigham Young University Museum of Peoples and Cultures, "Anasazi Pottery," 2001, online at http://fhss.byu.edu/anthro/mopc/pages/Exhibitions/Earth/Pottery.html.

3. Polly Schaafsma, *Indian Rock Art of the Southwest* (Santa Fe: School of American Research; Albuquerque: University of New Mexico Press, 1980), p. 135.

4. James M. Aton and Robert S. McPherson, *River Flowing from the Sunrise* (Logan: Utah State University Press, 2000), p. 27.

5. Stephen Plog, *Ancient Peoples of the American Southwest* (New York: Thames & Hudson, 1997), p. 117.

6. Linda P. Wilcox, "The Mormon Concept of a Mother in Heaven," *Sunstone Magazine*, vol. 23 (1980), online at www.sunstoneonline.com/magazine/searchable/mag-text.asp?MagID=23.

7. "Our Mother in Heaven," *Latter-Day Saints' Millennial Star*, vol. 72 (Sept. 29, 1910), p. 619, quoted in ibid.

8. Melvin J. Ballard, in *Journal History*, May 8, 1921, pp. 1–3, quoted in ibid.

9. Spencer W. Kimball, in *Ensign*, vol. 8, no. 3 (May 1978), p. 6, quoted in ibid.

10. Gordon B. Hinckley, "Cornerstones of Responsibility," address, Regional Representative Seminar, Salt Lake City, April 5, 1991, pp. 3–4, quoted in ibid. (copy of address in Wilcox's possession).

11. Gordon B. Hinckley, "Daughters of God," *Ensign*, vol. 21, no. 11 (Nov. 1991), pp. 97–100.

12. Margaret Merrill Toscano, "Is There a Place for Heavenly Mother in Mormon Theology? An Investigation into the Discourses of Power," *Sunstone Magazine*, vol. 133 (2004), p. 15, online at www.sunstoneonline.com/magazine/pdf/133=14=22.pdf.

13. Ibid., pp. 16–17.

14. Gary Topping, *Glen Canyon and the San Juan Country*, (Moscow, Idaho: University of Idaho Press, 1997), p. 28.

15. ABANDONMENT

1. Stephen Plog, *Ancient Peoples of the American Southwest* (New York: Thames & Hudson, 1997), pp. 144–45.

2. James M. Aton and Robert S. McPherson, *River Flowing from the Sunrise* (Logan: Utah State University Press, 2000), p. 25.

3. Ibid., pp. 21–22.

4. Robert S. McPherson, *A History of San Juan County* (Salt Lake City: Utah State Historical Society and San Juan County Commission, 1995), p. 37.

5. Winston B. Hurst, interview with James M. Aton, June 6, 1994, in Aton and McPherson, *River Flowing from the Sunrise*, p. 20.

6. Polly Schaafsma, *Indian Rock Art of the Southwest* (Santa Fe: School of American Research; Albuquerque: University of New Mexico Press, 1980), p. 145.

7. Jerold G. Widdison, ed., *Anasazi: Why Did They Leave? Where Did They Go?* (Albuquerque: Southwest Cultural Heritage Association, 1991), quoted in Aton and McPherson, *River Flowing from the Sunrise*, p. 25.

8. Robert S. McPherson, *Sacred Land, Sacred View* (Provo, Utah: Charles Redd Center for Western Studies, 1998), p. 3.

9. Howard Egan and Howard R. Egan, *Pioneering the West, 1846 to 1878: Major Howard Egan's Diary*, ed. Wm. M. Egan (Richmond, Utah: Howard R. Egan Estate/Skelton Publishing Company, 1917), p. 283.

10. *Citizen's Guide to Colorado Water Law* (Denver: Colorado Foundation for Water Education, 2004), p. 9.

11. Henry David Thoreau, "Walking," in *Excursions and Poems: The Writings of Henry David Thoreau* (Boston: Houghton Mifflin, 1906), pp. 205–48.

SELECTED BIBLIOGRAPHY

Abbey, Edward. *Desert Solitaire: A Season in the Wilderness*. 1968. Reprint, New York: Touchstone/Simon & Schuster, 1990.

Agenbroad, Larry D. "Before the Anasazi: Early Man on the Colorado Plateau," *Plateau*, vol. 61, no. 2 (1990).

Aton, James M., and Robert S. McPherson. *River Flowing from the Sunrise: An Environmental History of the Lower San Juan*. Logan: Utah State University Press, 2000.

Bagley, Will. *Blood of the Prophets: Brigham Young and the Massacre at Mountain Meadows*. Norman: University of Oklahoma Press, 2002.

Bigler, David L. *Forgotten Kingdom: The Mormon Theocracy in the American West, 1847–1896*. Logan: Utah State University Press, 1998.

Birney, Hoffman. *Zealots of Zion*. Philadelphia: Penn Publishing Company, 1931.

Blackburn, Fred M., and Ray A. Williamson. *Cowboys and Cave Dwellers: Basketmaker Archaeology in Utah's Grand Gulch*. Santa Fe: School of American Research Press, 1997.

Bowden, Charles, and Jack Dykinga. *Stone Canyons of the Colorado Plateau*. New York: Harry Abrams, 1996.

Brodie, Fawn M. *No Man Knows My History: The Life of Joseph Smith*. New York: Vintage Books, 1995.

Bunte, Pamela A., and Franklin, Robert J. *The Paiute*. Ed. Frank W. Porter III. In Indians of North America series, ed. Liz Sonneborn. New York/Philadelphia: Chelsea House Publishers, 1990.

Cawley, R. McGregor. *Federal Land, Western Anger: The Sagebrush Rebellion & Environmental Politics.* Lawrence: University Press of Kansas, 1993.

Cordell, Linda S. *Ancient Pueblo Peoples.* In Exploring the Ancient World series, ed. Jeremy A. Sabloff. Montreal: St. Remy Press; Washington, D.C.: Smithsonian Books, 1994.

Donahue, Debra L. *The Western Range Revisited: Removing Livestock from Public Lands to Conserve Native Biodiversity.* Norman: University of Oklahoma Press, 1999.

Egan, Howard, and Egan, Howard R. *Pioneering the West, 1846 to 1878: Major Howard Egan's Diary.* Ed. Wm. M. Egan. Richmond, Utah: Howard R. Egan Estate/Skelton Publishing Company, 1917.

Fallon, Sally, with Mary G. Enig. *Nourishing Traditions.* Washington, D.C.: New Trends Publishing, 1999.

Foundation for Deep Ecology. *Welfare Ranching: The Subsidized Destruction of the American West.* Eds. George Wuerthner and Mollie Matteson. Washington, D.C.: Island Press, 2002.

Grady, Wayne. *The World of the Coyote.* San Francisco: Sierra Club Books, 1995.

Hannaford, Carla. *Awakening the Child Heart: Handbook for Global Parenting.* Captain Cook, Hawaii: Jamilla Nur Publishing, 2002.

Irvine, Marie. "In Defense of Virtue: The Application of Justice in the Cases of Hambleton, Egan and McLean, Men Who Killed Seducers of Their Wives During the 1850s." Presented May 16–19, 1996, at Snowbird, Utah, at the annual conference for the Mormon History Association.

Jennings, Jessie D. *Glen Canyon: An Archaeological Summary.* Salt Lake City: University of Utah Press, 1998.

Krakauer, Jon. *Under the Banner of Heaven: A Story of Violent Faith.* New York: Anchor, 2004.

LeBlanc, Steven A. *Prehistoric Warfare in the Southwest.* Salt Lake City: University of Utah Press, 1999.

Lipe, William D. "The Southwest." In *Ancient North Americans.* Ed. Jesse D. Jennings. New York: W. H. Freeman, 1983.

Lister, Robert H., and Florence C. Lister. *Those Who Came Before.* Globe, Ariz.: Southwest Parks and Monuments Association, 1983.

Lopez, Barry. *Giving Birth to Thunder, Sleeping With His Daughter: Coyote Builds North America.* New York: Avon Books, 1990.

Manning, Richard. *Against the Grain: How Agriculture Has Hijacked Civilization.* New York: North Point Press, a division of Farrar, Straus and Giroux, 2004.

Matson, R. G. *The Origins of Southwestern Agriculture.* Tucson and London: University of Arizona Press, 1991.

Matson, R. G., and Brian Chisholm. "Basketmaker II Subsistence: Carbon Isotopes and Other Dietary Indicators from Cedar Mesa, Utah." *American Antiquity*, vol. 56, no. 3 (1991): 444–59.

McPherson, Robert S. *A History of San Juan County: In the Palm of Time*. Salt Lake City: Utah State Historical Society and San Juan County Commission, 1995.

———. *Sacred Land, Sacred View: Navajo Perceptions of the Four Corners Region*. Provo, Utah: Charles Redd Center for Western Studies, Brigham Young University, distributed by Signature Books, 1995.

Miller, David E. *Hole in the Rock: An Epic in the Colonization of the Great American West*. Salt Lake City: University of Utah Press, 1975.

Perkins, Cornelia Adams, Marian Gardner Nielson, and Lenora Butt Jones. *The Saga of San Juan*. Utah: San Juan County Daughters of the Utah Pioneers, 1957.

Plog, Stephen. *Ancient Peoples of the American Southwest*. New York: Thames & Hudson, 1997.

Roberts, David. *In Search of the Old Ones: Exploring the Anasazi World of the Southwest*. New York: Touchstone, 1996.

Schaafsma, Polly. *Indian Rock Art of the Southwest*. Santa Fe: School of American Research; Albuquerque: University of New Mexico Press, 1980.

———. *The Rock Art of Utah*. Salt Lake City: University of Utah Press, 1971.

Shanks, Bernard. *This Land Is Your Land: The Struggle to Save America's Public Lands*. San Francisco: Sierra Club Books, 1984.

Shepard, Paul. *The Only World We've Got*. San Francisco: Sierra Club Books, 1996.

———. "A Post-Historic Primitivism." In *The Wilderness Condition: Essays on Environment and Civilization*, ed. Max Oelschlaeger. San Francisco: Sierra Club Books, 1992.

Smith, Joseph, trans. *The Book of Mormon: Another Testament of Jesus Christ*. The Church of Jesus Christ of Latter-day Saints, Salt Lake City, Utah, 1830.

Smith, Joseph, trans. *Doctrine and Covenants: Carefully Selected from the Revelations of God, and given in the order of their dates*. Missouri: Herald Publishing House, 1970.

Smith, Joseph. *The Doctrine and Covenants of the Church of Jesus Christ of Latter-Day Saints*. Salt Lake City; Deseret News Company, 1880.

Stegner, Wallace. *The Gathering of Zion: The Story of the Mormon Trail*. New York: McGraw-Hill, 1964; reprint Lincoln, Nebraska: Bison Books, 1992.

———. *Mormon Country*. Lincoln: University of Nebraska Press, 1970.

Topping, Gary. *Glen Canyon and the San Juan Country*. Moscow, Idaho: University of Idaho Press, 1997.

Wilkinson, Todd. *Track of the Coyote*. Minnetonka, Minn.: NorthWord Press, 1995.

Williams, David. *A Naturalist's Guide to Canyon Country*. Helena, Mont.: Falcon Publishing, 2000.

Williams, Terry Tempest. *An Unspoken Hunger: Stories from the Field*. New York: Vintage Books, 1994.

———. "Coyote's Canyon." In *Red: Passion and Patience in the Desert*. New York: Pantheon Books, 2001.

ACKNOWLEDGMENTS

It was writing this book—nine years of my life—that revealed my tribe. Its members are many, and forgive me now for those I neglect to mention. The omissions are strictly a byproduct of sleep deprivation, diapers, and deadlines; indeed, the ways these people surrounded and sustained me are profound and deserve far more honor than I can offer here.

Diane Rickey went above and beyond all mothers-in-law and carried my family through every word—and the book is only in the reader's hands because of her generosity of time and spirit. There is not one shred of hyperbole when I say I owe her everything. Even from a distance, my mother and stepfather, Carlyle and David Cooper, made certain their daughter and granddaughter were in good hands during the dire times—a feat that sometimes required spectacular logistical gymnastics. Elena Stoilova did much of the same, only in Bulgarian. Chuck McAfee created much-needed clarity and delivered the details with devotion; I plan to bestow on him many a fine bottle of tequila for his efforts, and still I will be indebted. Faye Bender has been the agent and beacon that writers dream of—and bless Brooke Williams for directing me her way. Denise Oswald, Jessica Ferri, Laurel Cook, and Brian Gittis—along with the rest of Farrar, Straus and Giroux—made sense of the madness with breathtaking skill; I'll never forget that Denise glimpsed the bones of *Trespass* long before anyone else—and that she knew just how to preserve them. Terry Tempest Williams has been an inspiration all along. It was she who pushed me to get the words out in the first place, and who called me out when I tried to tell too slick and easy a version. It was also Terry who resurrected Coyote. Marie Irvine's research and writings on Howard Egan were indispensable—and the time she took to impart her knowledge served as linchpin for the story. Ruth Ann and John Ritter, along with Marilyn and Jack Willimott, have been there since the beginning, throwing lifelines. Bruce and Rhonda Irvine, along with Bill Bennett, went to heroic lengths to save my father. Nora Gallagher made me first believe—in things both written and unwritten, Mesa Refuge created the space in which to see both. Charles Bowden went above and beyond in every way. Jessica Galbo pointed out the portals; Marc Bregman guided me through them, sometimes kicking and screaming. Colby Smith, Holly Sloan, Kiley Miller, John Rzeczycki, Ginger Harmon, and Jane and Ken Sleight gave the shelter and sustenance that saved our marriage—giving us their very best when we were at our worst. John Bass, Janet Ross, Jim and Wendie Highsmith, Dave and Barb Churchill, Ted Wilson, and Bert and Kookie Tanner provided all the possibilities. Craig Childs, Chip Ward, Andy Nettell, Ginger Harmon, Greer Chesher, Steve Allen, Matt Redd, and Dave Churchill gave sage scrutiny and enduring encouragement. It was the professional expertise and research resources offered by Eve Tallman and the Grand County Library, Diane Kelly, Lindsey Oswald, Red Wolfe, and Cathy Huppe that filled in the crevices in question. Natalie Clausen, Abigail Seaver, McLean Cherry, Jane Simone, Greg Overton, Kory Branham, Todd Mangum, and Rich Merrill provided CPR every time my pulse was weak. The lightning-quick wordsmithing of John Daley gave title to the body of work. The Southern Utah Wilderness Alliance's staff and activists—warriors in the archetypal sense—continue to leave me in awe: of special mention are Brant Calkin, Scott Groene, Heidi McIntosh, Cristy Calvin, Lindsey Oswald, Tom Price, and Liz McCoy. The Buffalo Girls—Kristen Redd, Camilla Baca, Rosemerry Wahtola Trommer, Ellen Marie Metrick, Jessica Galbo, Sage Martin, and Jess Newens—have been the sisterhood. For Brian Mecham, along with his parents, Steve and Donna, there will always be profound fondness and gratitude. Same goes for the Roberts Family on Millstream Drive. Even from the other side, Ellen Meloy and Ada Irvine prompt me to see the beauty, Candace Weed and Rose Reilly remind me to muster courage in the face of apathy and paralysis, and my father still has me wandering in wonder.

Then there is Ruby, who at last let go so I could write, and did so with a grace and understanding far beyond her years—may I make up what it cost her. Finally, at the very heart of things, there is Herb. He is a brave man to have walked through this desert with me—only then to extend beyond everything in his power so that I could put our life, skeletons and all, into words.

Not once did he flinch. And for this I will love him forever.

CPSIA information can be obtained
at www.ICGtesting.com
Printed in the USA
LVHW110823271218
601878LV00002B/84/P

9 780865 477452